They Called Me Doc

They Called Me Doc

Treating Wounded Marines Wasn't Just A Job, It Was A Passion

LARRY C. MILLER

Library of Congress Control Number: 2016905867
CreateSpace Independent Publishing Platform
North Charleston, South Carolina

This book is dedicated:

To all the forgotten Marines and Corpsmen of the Vietnam War who made the ultimate sacrifice for the liberties that we all enjoy today.

To the families of those who made the ultimate sacrifice, I know your Marine or Corpsman will never be forgotten.

To my wife, Carol, who has always supported my ambitions as I romped around the country, attacking yet another windmill.

To my three daughters Denise, Katy, and Kelly; I have taken on this endeavor for you.

Acknowledgments

I want to thank Don Westenhaver (Westy) for tutoring me forty-eight years ago in Vietnam and again during the development of this book. Without you I would have sucked at both.

To Colonel Richard D. Weede, USMC (Ret) for providing the outstanding leadership during so many bad days in Vietnam, for editing this book from the perspective of a Career Marine Officer, and for your friendship that I will cherish for the rest of my life.

To Kay Jongsma a great friend and artist for creating the wonderful painting on the cover of this book, and yes my nose is really that big.

To Bob Evans for taking my old photographs and making them useful.

To GySgt Dave Brennan, you had the unfortunate distinction of being my very first patient and survived anyway. I treated thousands after you but none more memorable.

To Sgt Tim Russell and GySgt Whyte for being a Marine and helping me reconstruct the battles that Delta fought.

To the families of those that I have attempted to honor in this book, I know I can never do them justice but thank you for letting me try.

Contents

The Forgotten Boys of Leatherneck Square

a poem

*There was a location in the Vietnam War; its name was
Leatherneck Square, and many a young boy died in that place, all
with much despair.*

*To die so young, in this faraway place, is just such a shame,
their boyish faces, to many of us, will always remain the same.*

*Their sacrifice and memories we say, will continue to last and last,
but history will show, like so many before, that their lives will fade
to the past.*

*The forgotten boys who gave their lives were all in their primes,
knowing full well that many back home were accusing them of crimes.*

*I was a Doc who treated the Marine to keep him in the fight,
but the forgotten boys continued to die, on both my left and right.*

I treated so many as they struggled for breath,
but for countless boys there was still only death.

As a Marine went over, their families would brag,
praying their boys would not come home draped in a flag.

My year was up, and home I came,
mostly intact, but never the same.

Back in the States, still dressed in greens,
I notify the families of their dead Marines.

I observed many a mother drop to her knees,
screaming at her God, who had ignored her pleas.

Four years of service, and now I was free,
but the boys were there, and only I could see.

I made a pledge to live life the best I could,
to honor those boys who just never would.

What's a Doc do but continue to treat.
I joined the paramedics and served on the street.

I live every day as if it were my last,
in respect for the boys whose lives passed too fast.

Often years later I would awake with dread,
wondering if I had done enough to honor the dead.

Forty years it has been, and I look back on my life,
spending all those years with the same loving wife.

Three wonderful daughters are now fully grown,
with so many delightful children all their own.

Forty-five years in the Fire Service, helping my fellow man,
and now my retirement seems so well in hand.

How many boys would have loved to be me,
instead of their life spent under a tree.

Now sitting on my porch in my rocking chair,
never to forget,
the Forgotten Boys of Leatherneck Square.

Semper Fi

HM2 "Doc" Larry Miller, Senior Corpsman, USMC, 1966–70

The rating of Hospital Corpsman is the most decorated rating in the US Navy, with 22 Medals of Honor, 174 Navy Crosses, 31 Navy Distinguished Service Medals, 946 Silver Stars, and 1,582 Bronze Stars. Twenty naval ships have been named after Hospital Corpsmen.

The Hospital Corps is the only Corps in the Navy that has been singled out and commended by the Secretary of the Navy and the Secretary of Defense.

Preface

So why did I write this book?

My middle daughter, Katy, has such a passion for history that she became a high school history teacher and went on to receive her master's degree in the subject. I, too, have that passion, although as a hobby and not a vocation. Katy's interest is American history, and I am interested in politics and war. Like most people, my interest in politics did not come along until middle age, and like most boys, my interest in war probably started in my backyard with the neighbor kids.

It was always rumored that my great-grandfather on my mother's side was a drummer boy in the Civil War. My daughter Katy, researching on the Internet, found out that my great-grandfather was actually a Union soldier from an Ohio regiment during this significant time in our country's history. We could find little else.

I so wish he had left more information on what his politics were. Was emancipation the reason that he joined, or was he drafted? What was the training like, what was the food like, what were the hardships, and what were the battles like? Yes, I have read many books on the subject, but I wanted to read history from my own flesh and blood. This is what gave me the idea to make a coffee-table book of my military exploits for my girls, my grandkids, and my future generations.

I served one year in the Navy to train as an HM-8404 Field Medical Technician and then spent the next three years with the Marine Corps as a Marine Doc. Earning the privilege to be called "Doc" by the Marines remains at the top of the list of accomplishments in my life. I spent one year as a Doc treating Marines in Vietnam and returned to the States, where I was assigned to independent duty at a Marine reserve unit in Los Angeles. There I made next-of-kin notifications to the families of Marines killed in action in Vietnam.

As I started my research, the project grew and grew. The Internet made the impossible possible and led me to many books, documents, and websites. I have reconnected with several important Marines who were instrumental in shaping my entire life. I have made contact with Marines I had treated on the battlefield and then always wondered about their fate. I have attended the graduation ceremony at Camp Pendleton of the new Docs making the transition from the Navy to the Marines, and if there had been a recruiter present, I would have joined for another four years.

The objective of this book is twofold. It tells my military story to my future generations. However, it also tells a story—from a Doc's perspective—of what it was like to serve with the greatest military organization in the world in the most despised war in American history. It's an observation from an ordinary guy who was surrounded by extraordinary men performing extraordinary acts of heroism.

All the actions are true; however, many of the names have been changed only because I could not remember or find their real names, and in some cases, out of respect for them and their families. I never intended to demean anyone's character or to second-guess anyone's actions; I am just reporting what I actually witnessed while living with these heroes.

I have taken the liberty of telling a few of the stories in first person—as if that person were telling the story—because that is how they relayed the stories to me. Since very few men and women volunteer to serve our country, I want you to feel the "shitstorm" as if you were with us.

In an effort to be historically correct, the language used in this book was the language used by the common Grunt in the trenches. The words shucks, darn, and gosh were never used in Vietnam, and I make no apologies that they are not used in this book, because this was just the way we talked.

This book is not a Marine Corps training manual, so I have taken the liberty of changing some of the military nomenclature into words more easily understood by the average reader. A couple of examples are changing twenty-four-hour time to twelve-hour-time (e.g., using a.m. and p.m. time) and changing distances from meters to yards. I suggest you review the appendices before starting the book to familiarize yourself with military definitions and the Marine Corps Ground Combat Element.

This book is about a time before all the political correctness bullshit that has weakened our society. It depresses me to no end that the Progressive movement is fundamentally weakening the Marine Corps and our nation at the time of this writing.

Additionally, I have taken the liberty of capitalizing the word Marine, and sometimes the words Corpsmen, Captain, Major, Sergeant, Grunt, Hero, etc., regardless of how or where they are used in a sentence, because I choose to honor these words throughout this book regardless of proper English. Also, I was a product of the Los Angeles school system and probably would not know the difference anyway.

This book is written in the first person more as a narrator. The central character who is the hero varies with each of the stories. I had the privilege to be an eyewitness to Giants and Heroes in both the Marines who fought the battles and the Corpsmen who risked their lives to take care of the Heroes when they were wounded.

There were 58,148 men and women who gave their lives for our country during the Vietnam War, and all of them deserve to be remembered and to have their stories told. I have attempted to tell the story of several heroes who touched my life during my service with the Marine Corps. It is my hope that I have honored them correctly.

Whatever success I have achieved, my launchpad was my association with the US Marine Corps.

Semper Fi

Prologue

Time for a Little History

Why Were We in Vietnam?

To better understand my story at ground level we should first look from thirty thousand feet and discuss a little history of Vietnam, why the United States got involved with a war in Vietnam, and where my story takes place in relation to the entire country.

If you are not a history buff, it may be a little boring, but I have attempted to abridge it as much as possible to lessen your pain. If the pain is too great, just move on to chapter 1 and refer back to the maps for clarification.

Here we go

The Vietnamese people have seen little peace in the last two thousand years. The Chinese ruled over them for the first one thousand years, and then came the Mongols in 1284, the Chinese again, followed by the Hindu Empire. Then it was Europe's turn with the Portuguese, Dutch, English, and finally the French in 1860. By 1907, the French controlled all of Indochina.

From 1940 to 1945, the Imperial Japanese Army called the shots in Vietnam. After the war, back came the French to reclaim control over

Indochina. Only this time the French would be haunted by Communist resistance fighters called the Viet Minh and led by Ho Chi Minh.

At first, the Viet Minh were poorly trained and equipped, but with the help of the Soviet Union (Russia) and China, they quickly grew into a well-equipped modern army that, after eight years of fighting, finally defeated the French in 1954 at the final battle site of Dien Bien Phu in North Vietnam.

In Geneva, Switzerland, the Big Four Powers conference was already in session negotiating a settlement in the Korean War. After the fall of Dien Bien Phu, an armistice conference convened with representatives from the United States, France, Britain, the Soviet Union, China, Laos, Cambodia, North Vietnam (Communists), and South Vietnam (the West-backed government).

After much-heated negotiations, it was agreed that Vietnam would be divided into two countries at the seventeenth parallel, which roughly followed the Ben Hai River. A demilitarized zone (DMZ) was established approximately six miles wide to separate the two countries.

The Viet Minh leader, Ho Chi Minh, established the Democratic Republic of Vietnam under Communist rule in North Vietnam, while the strong anti-Communist nationalist Ngo Dinh Diem became the President of the Republic of Vietnam in South Vietnam. The Geneva Accord was not a formal political settlement but rather a cease-fire agreement that lacked the formal signing by most participants on both sides.

THE DOMINO THEORY

These cease-fire agreements for both Korea and Vietnam were a reflection of the main goal of the United States to stop Communism from taking over all of Southeast Asia. Dwight Eisenhower cautioned the western world about the threat of the Soviet Union and China spreading Communism throughout Asia and the domino theory was born. The theory was prominent starting in the 1950s and lasted until the 1980s with the concept that if one country in a region fell to communism, then the surrounding countries would follow in a domino effect.

The domino theory was used by both Democratic and Republican administrations during the Cold War to defend the need for US involvement in halting the spread of Communism throughout the world.

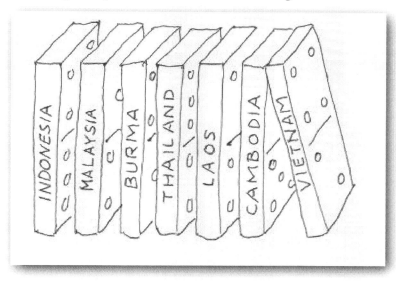

FEARS THAT VIETNAM WOULD BE THE FIRST DOMINO TO FALL

A cease-fire never actually happened in Vietnam. By 1961, guerrilla warfare was widespread in South Vietnam. Communist-led insurgents of the National Liberation Front (NLF) of South Vietnam, commonly referred to as the Vietcong by South Vietnam (not meant as an endearing term), were initiating hundreds of terrorist and small unit attacks per month. Saigon's military, the Army of the Republic of Vietnam (ARVN), was not able to contain the growing insurgency. During the administration of President Eisenhower, a small US Military Assistance Advisory Group (MAAG), who numbered 740 soldiers, had provided training and logistical support to the ARVN. After the Eisenhower administration, President

Kennedy determined that the size and mission of the US advisory effort must change if the South Vietnamese government was to survive. Having just suffered the embarrassment in Cuba (Bay of Pigs Invasion) and Berlin (the Berlin Wall), President Kennedy rejected any compromise and chose to strengthen US support of South Vietnam.

The Vietcong continued to achieve military successes against the South Vietnam Army while at the same time the Buddhist majority protested against claims of religious persecution by President Diem's Catholic-dominated administration. Additionally, there was much dissatisfaction with the Diem regime by the Generals of his Army. The fear of a total collapse of the South Vietnamese government made US officials receptive to a regime change. On November 1, 1963 the ARVN generals mounted a coup that resulted in the killing of Diem and his brother. During this coup the United States was conveniently looking the other way. Only three weeks later, President Kennedy was assassinated.

Within days after his inauguration as President, Lyndon Johnson reaffirmed the United States' goal to assist South Vietnam in its "contest against the externally directed and supported communist conspiracy." But how much US assistance was enough, and what form should it take? By early 1964, aided by North Vietnam, the Vietcong controlled vast areas of South Vietnam. In June, President Johnson appointed Gen. William Westmoreland, then Commandant of West Point, as the Commander in Vietnam.

In the first few days of August 1964, North Vietnamese gunboats fired on two US destroyers located in the Gulf of Tonkin. The Johnson administration used this incident to push Congress for a resolution authorizing the president to use armed forces to protect all US forces currently in South Vietnam and to deter the aggression from North Vietnam. On August 7, 1964, Congress, with almost unanimous support, passed the Gulf of Tonkin Resolution, which gave President Johnson the authority for the needed military buildup. Because of his decisive but restrained response to the escalating war and his promised robust domestic agenda, President Johnson was reelected for his first full term as President.

By June of 1965 there had been five regime changes in the South Vietnamese government with accusations of corruption and infighting plaguing all of them. The Vietcong continued to inflict heavy casualties on the South Vietnam army. US officials were certain that the South would fall if the United States did not escalate involvement from advising to participating in the ground war. President Johnson approved General Westmoreland's request for 150 thousand US troops to enter the ground war. On March 8, 1965, two Battalions of Marines landed at Da Nang that signaled America's commitment to actual combat in South Vietnam. By the end of the year there were over 184 thousand troops on the ground.

To supply the needed troops, the Pentagon wanted to activate the reserves and National Guard, which would have placed the Country on a war footing and give congressional conservatives a stronger footing to negotiate on President Johnson's domestic agenda. To avoid the conflict in Congress, President Johnson used President Franklin Roosevelt's Selective Training and Service Act that created the country's first peacetime draft in 1940. And so it was that the Vietnam War would be fought by the first conscript army since the Korea War.

Conscription in the United States, commonly known as the draft has been used by our government dating back to colonial times. The draft has been implemented every time when volunteers alone were insufficient to raise the needed manpower to augment the professional all volunteer military.

The Vietnam War had a very high percentage of volunteers, mainly because of incentives offered by all four branches of the service. As an example, the Navy and Air Force were almost entirely staffed by volunteers who decided they would rather satisfy their Selective Service requirement on a ship or an Air Force base that was remote from the ground war. That privilege required a four-year commitment.

Draftees who decided to roll the dice and go for the two-year tour went to the induction center not knowing if they were going to be placed with the Army or the Marines and be sent to Vietnam or Germany.

On the day that I went to the induction center, all the draftees were lined up against the wall, and a Marine Sergeant came out and had the inductees count off to twenty-five. Then he shouted, "Congratulations, you lucky bastards, you are now in the Marine Corps." The groans from those selected were quickly drowned out by the sighs of relief from those who were going to the Army. Looking back, I almost feel sorry for the Army guys because they were in for two years and out. A Marine—the proud, the few—are Marines forever!

OK, ON WITH THE STORY.

US warplanes pounded North Vietnam while General Westmoreland directed his ground troops on the Vietcong insurgents in South Vietnam. President Johnson chose a gradual escalation of bombing and troop deployment to limit the warfare in hopes that our direct involvement in the war would not draw in the Soviet Union and China.

General Westmoreland chose a strategy of attrition that would limit US casualties while inflicting heavier losses on the enemy than could be replaced. The strategy was to search and destroy the enemy but not to control the territory. Our ground troops were to be deployed in numerous strongpoint bases scattered along the northwest border with Laos and across the DMZ. They were to engage the enemy where possible, drive them from the field of battle, inflict heavy casualties, and then pull back to their base and look for another battle opportunity. It was a strategy of large-unit operations in the border regions of the country with an all-important "body count" of the enemy.

The Marine Corps Generals disputed General Westmoreland's strategy, contending that we were playing into the enemy strategy of keeping the bulk of our forces tied down in small remote bases along the border regions, near the enemy's logistical support, and away from the major population centers. The Marines preferred to give the borders to the enemy and engage them with heavy air support while conducting small-unit operations, providing security and pacification in and around the major population centers and the surrounding hamlets and villages. If the enemy were to conduct a large-unit operation against an urban center, we would have the available troops to confront them, and it would be on our terms near our logistical support.

General Westmoreland overruled the Marines and continued with his plan of operation. By the end of 1965, Westmoreland touted his strategy as having had some desired effect on the Vietcong insurgents. Whatever the truth was, it provoked North Vietnam to begin the deployment of the regular North Vietnamese Army (NVA) troops into South Vietnam.

Since the United States did not intend to hold the captured territory, the Vietcong and NVA developed the strategy to engage the US military when and where they chose. They would hit a small US force, and when we deployed a superior force, they would simply break off the fight and disappear.

What the good General failed to take into consideration was how well trained, equipped, and committed the enemy was and how experienced the enemy had become from many years of fighting. These tough little bastards were no pushovers, and the one-sided ass-kicking we were going to give them just did not materialize.

Once the United States entered the ground war, reports of American casualties started to make the nightly news in the United States. This was the first war that technology in the media allowed almost real-time pictures of the battles and wounded US solders being carried from the field. I remember coming home from high school and watching the evening news reporting on the current day's killed and wounded American fighting men. It was much different than the later Iraq and Afghanistan wars because of the draft. Volunteers fought those wars; average citizens did not need to be concerned unless they chose to get involved.

The Vietnam War was everyone's problem. Every mother's son, of fighting age, had to go down to the Selective Service office, register on his eighteenth birthday, and wait for that call to duty that would surely come.

Here is where my story starts.

Map Orientation

These maps are designed to give the reader approximate locations of cities, military bases, and military outposts. I would not depend on them to pinpoint an airstrike.

Map One: 1968, Southeast Asia

This map shows that South Vietnam was divided into four Corps, or tactical zones, but they were regional and political entities as well. The areas were labeled with roman numerals I, II, III, and IV Corps. The Marines were assigned to the northernmost portions of I Corps. The Army controlled the southern portion of I Corps and all II, III, and IV Corps. The Gulf of Tonkin is where the US Navy aircraft carriers launched their air strikes into North Vietnam, hitting military and supply targets in and around Hanoi and Hai Phong Harbor, as well as targets in and around the DMZ.

The North Vietnamese moved a lot of troops and supplies across the DMZ, but the major supply route was along the border of Vietnam with Laos and Cambodia where the jungle canopy was triple thick, giving the enemy heavy cover from US warplanes. I am talking Tarzan-type jungle with tigers, elephants, and monkeys. This route was called the Ho Chi Minh Trail. Additionally, the United States had a self-imposed restriction from ever moving our troops across those borders to interrupt this supply route until President Nixon was in office in 1969, and by then it was too little and too late. North Vietnam used the Ho Chi Minh Trail for the entire war to mass troops and supplies and could attack with impunity in all four of the Corps operational areas.

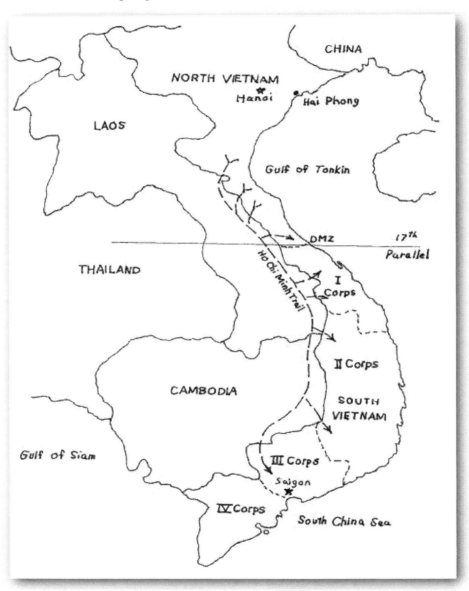

Map Two: 1968, Vietnam, I Corps—Marine Corps Area of Operation

This map illustrates the three most northern provinces of Quang Tri, Thua Thien, and Quang Nam where the Marine Corps was responsible for military operations. I arrived in Da Nang on December 20, 1967, and left Vietnam through Da Nang on December 7, 1968. Da Nang was a city with an important harbor, but it was also home to an enormous US military base that was big and safe enough to land commercial airliners to transport troops in and out of the country. At the time it was the busiest airport in the world.

I took a military C-130 aircraft to Phu Bai on my second day to report for duty with the Third Marine Division and then on to Dong Ha, which looks like a suburb of Quang Tri City now. Back in 1968, the cities and our military bases were separated by several miles of open road.

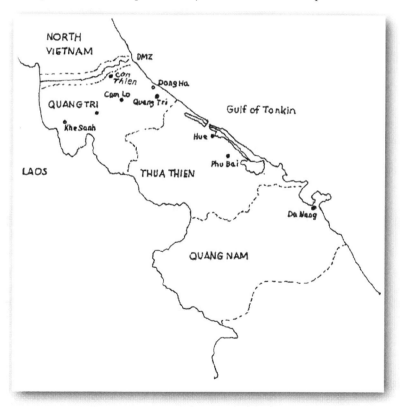

Map Three: 1968, Quang Tri Province, Vietnam (Northern I Corps)

Quang Tri is the most northern province in South Vietnam, extending about forty-five miles north to south from the DMZ and forty miles east to west.

The DMZ was a six-mile-wide buffer zone between North and South Vietnam, similar to the zone between North and South Korea, that neither side was to enter. The North Vietnamese Army (NVA) disregarded this buffer zone and used it to shoot artillery at the American bases in the south and to mass troops to launch attacks on Marine positions in the south. Once again, the United States maintained a self-imposed restriction—for the entire war—to never launch a ground attack into North Vietnam.

The war in the Quang Tri Province was largely the responsibility of the Third Marine Division and since the summer of 1966, the division had stopped several successive North Vietnamese Army thrusts into northern Quang Tri Province. By 1967, the Third Marine Division had grown to over twenty-four thousand men and was now the largest division in Marine Corps history.

Nearly all the Marine Infantry Battalions and support units were stationed at fixed perimeter outposts along the Demilitarized Zone, from Cua Viet in the east to Khe Sanh in the west. On the most western end of Route 9 was the Army Special Forces Camp at Lang Vei, which the North Vietnamese People's Army overran on February 7, 1968.

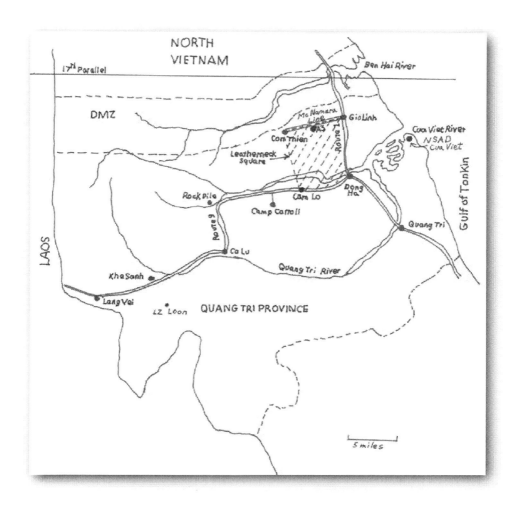

Map Four: 1968, Vietnam, Northern I Corps—Leatherneck Square

To stop or substantially reduce the flow of men and supplies from North to South Vietnam, a barrier was developed by clearing a strip of land, two miles south of the DMZ, supported by strongpoints (Marine outposts). The barrier ran from Con Thien (Outpost A-4) on the west to Gio Linh (Outpost A-2) on the east (eight miles long and six hundred yards wide). Outpost A-3 was a strongpoint in the middle. These outposts provided observation posts and roving patrols to catch the enemy attempting to cross the barrier. The cleared strip of land between the outposts was labeled "The Trace" on military maps but the press quickly labeled it "McNamara's Line" after the Secretary of Defense who championed the barrier plan. The McNamara Line was a major failure and a great example of what happens when civilian college boys with no military experience try their hand at military strategy and tactics.

Fire support bases, located several miles to the south of the Trace, backed the three outposts on the Trace, which received a C designation. The main function of the C fire support bases was to provide artillery support for the A outposts and to shoot artillery shells into North Vietnam.

The four Marine positions at Con Thien, Gio Linh, Dong Ha, and Cam Lo formed a rough square, making it about six to eight miles wide and six to eight miles deep north to south. Thus, the name "Leatherneck Square" would assume a permanent place in Marine Corps history alongside such notable names as Chosin Reservoir, Guadalcanal, Tinian, Wake Island, Iwo Jima, and many other pieces of real estate where Marines would make the ultimate sacrifice in a very big way.

Some of the heaviest fighting of the Vietnam War occurred in this sixty-square mile area. The official figures on losses from March 1967 to February 1969 (twenty-three months) are 1,419 Marines and Navy Corpsman killed and 9,265 Marines and Corpsman wounded in action, or 10,684 casualties.

To put this in perspective, I will give you the following statistic, which is in no way intended to demean anyone who risked it all in the service of our country. It is intended to simply show the shitstorm that the Marines were faced with in Leatherneck Square during this brief period in American and Marine Corps history.

The Chosin Reservoir in Korea, which had a much shorter time of battle, inflicted 836 deaths for the Marines and 2,000 for the Army.

Marines killed at the battle of Guadalcanal—1,202.

In twelve years of combat in Afghanistan the total deaths of all US combat troops is listed as 1,795.

The year of 1968 alone saw over 14,000 US soldiers killed in action in Vietnam compared to 4,486 US soldiers killed in Iraq after nine years of war.

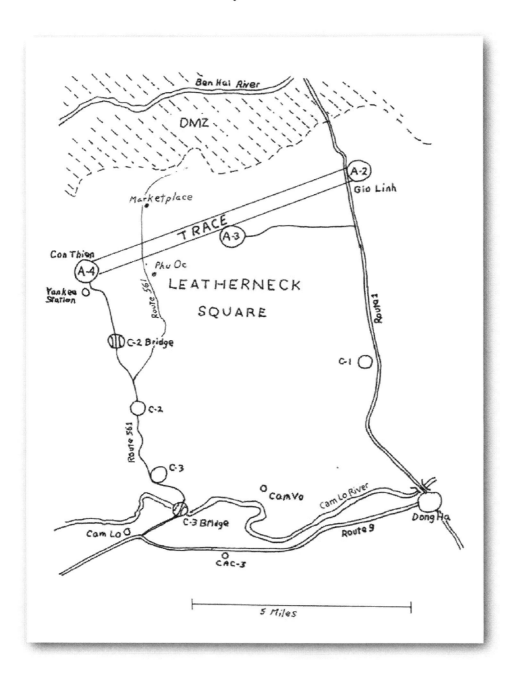

One

No expectations and no boundaries = low performance
—*No author; I lived it*

I grew up in South Los Angeles starting at Sixty-Fourth Street and Vermont Avenue when my family moved from Kansas to LA in the early '50s, and we moved in with my aunt Myrtle. My parents purchased their first house at Ninety-Eighth Street and Vermont Avenue, and I started kindergarten at Ninety-Fifth Street School.

The '50s were a different time. No one thought twice about a five-year-old crossing a four-lane street and walking three blocks to school. I do not ever remember any of the kids being dropped off by their parents, but of course I was only five and may just not have noticed. It was a time when the supermarket was coming of age, but every few blocks there were still small mom-and-pop stores attached to a house where the store owners worked and lived.

There was one such market on Ninety-Fifth Street, across from the school, where I would spend part of my lunch money on Necco Wafers that set me back five cents.

My mom was a waitress, and my dad was a butcher for Vons markets. They both worked six days a week, and my brother and I were latchkey kids with no boundaries, no restrictions, and no expectations placed on us. If my mom ever asked if we had homework, a simple no would quickly satisfy her parental instincts.

On weekends and all summers, my brother and I would walk to Recreation Park at Hoover and Ninetieth Street or over to Sportsman's Park (now Jesse Owens Park) at Century Boulevard and Western Avenue where they had the plunge. The plunge was so crowded with kids that we could not swim—just bounce up and down. The area was a mix of whites, blacks, and Mexicans, and I was smitten with a little black girl in my first grade class. I cannot recall thinking that race was an issue in our relationship, and her mom made the best sandwiches. Of course, I shared my Necco Wafers with her.

When we were sick with measles, mumps, and chicken pox, my mom would have our lunch in the fridge, and we would stay home alone.

For reasons unknown to me, we would move thirteen times before I graduated from high school. For many years, I was the new kid in class. I started the second grade at 135th Street School in Gardena after we moved to Berendo Avenue and 132nd Street. I had to repeat the second grade because of "immature behavior." I often wonder, just how mature do you have to be in the second grade?

In the third grade, now much more mature, I went to Hawthorne Christian School. The fourth grade found me at Trinity Lutheran School, fifth grade at Kit Carson Elementary in Lawndale, and sixth grade at Roosevelt Junior High, where I stayed through the eighth grade.

Roosevelt Junior High was overcrowded so my seventh grade class was on the stage of the cafeteria/auditorium. Being the class clown, I soon found my desk next to Mrs. Pritchard's desk facing the class. This way she could reach me with a ruler.

One day Mrs. Pritchard was absent and in her place came a hulk of a man as a substitute. We all figured that he was going to be a jolly giant, just as easy as Mrs. Pritchard, and that we would continue with the mischief as always. It did not take long to find out that he was not all that jolly. Danny Green, the biggest and toughest kid in the school, was the first to test the water with a small paper airplane that sailed across the room. The giggles were cut short as the Hulk reached Danny's desk in two strides, grabbed him by the neck, and dragged him to the front of the class. The Hulk drew a circle on the chalkboard and drove Danny's nose into it. His baritone voice echoed through the class when he said, "Stay here until I tell you to sit down. Do you understand?" Danny, with tears in his eyes, answered in the affirmative. My God! The Hulk just made the biggest and toughest guy in our school cry. I could only imagine what he would do with me.

The Hulk took his seat at the teacher's desk, and with a move like the monsters out of the *Alien* movie, he turned his massive head, looked at me, and said, "Why is your desk next to mine? I doubt you are here to help me run the class. Are you a troublemaker?"

I quickly responded with a resounding, "NO, I am not a problem!"

"Good," he answered. "Then take an empty seat anywhere but up here."

Mr. Wilson (the Hulk) was with us for two weeks, and I never made a peep. The class was well behaved, and I actually did my homework because that is what he expected.

When Mrs. Pritchard returned, I resumed my position next to her and once again became the class clown.

When I advanced to high school, I decided to take a demanding schedule of one period of auto shop and two periods of vocational art. That left one period each of English, math, life science, and PE, which was the most minimal of schedules that I was allowed to take.

I do not remember having one of my parents ever question my selections.

In those days, the school would send the report card home with you to show your parents, and it did not require a signature or a return from the parents. An F grade was easy to turn into an A; a D, if done right, could look like a B. If not, there was always ink eradicator to save the day.

I maintained this grueling schedule throughout my four years of classes.

One day during my senior year, I came home from school to find that my mom had changed her hair from brown to bleached blond, had given my dad the heave-ho, and launched her pursuit to quench her midlife crises. Within a few days, my mom was introducing me to a revolving door of male barflies who came and went out of our lives.

One fine morning my mom woke me and said, "Come out and meet your new dad." As I walked, with sleepy eyes, out to the dinette, a scrawny alcoholic-looking man introduced himself as Bert. I shook his hand and found that my mom had met him in a bar named the Proud Bird near the Los Angeles airport. They were so smitten with each other that, after a three-hour engagement, they decided to go to Las Vegas and tie the knot. Bert lasted about a week or two and then was gone like all the rest.

My dad was the major casualty in my mom's change in life and he turned to the bottle to find the answers. What he came up with was that my brother and I must have sided with my mom; therefore, we also became the enemy. He cut off all communication from that point on.

I graduated from Leuzinger High School in Lawndale, California, in June 1965, and no, I was not the valedictorian. At eighteen years old, I was an immature young man with no ambition and certainly no plans of what I was going to do with my life. I hated school except for the social aspects that it provided, so I enrolled in only two classes at Harbor Junior College where my lack of effort produced a C and an F.

My pursuit of a higher education ended after that first semester, and I got a job at Northrop Corporation in Hawthorne as a machine parts quality control inspector. The title sounds impressive but in reality I sat at an air gauge that would measure for the correct size of three holes that were drilled into a tiny machine part that went on the F-5 fighter and the T-38 trainer.

I had a fifty-five-gallon drum on my right, full of these tiny parts that I would take one at a time, measure the three holes, and then place the part in an empty fifty-five-gallon drum on my left. When I emptied the drum, they would wheel another drum up to continue the process. The days just dragged.

Why a Corpsman?

The Vietnam War was expanding, and the military draft board was picking off many of my friends. I knew I was not far behind. One of my mom's favorite barflies was a man who went by the nickname of Doc. Doc was a retired Navy Corpsman (Medic) who had served in both World War II and the Korean War with the Marine Corps. Oh sure, Doc was married and had a family in San Diego, but he passed all my mom's high standards for a man.

I liked Doc, and he filled my head with many wonderful and exciting stories about his experiences in combat. As a young man, I ate them up and drank the Kool-Aid. For the first time in my life, I had a plan—to be a Navy Corpsman with the Marine Corps—and if I hurried, I thought I could see battle in Vietnam before the war ended. At the time, I was excited about the thrill of being in battle and not about the responsibilities of being a Corpsman or even what the duties of a Corpsman entailed.

The Marine Corps has only trained killers. The Navy provides those noncombatant positions that the Marines need (doctors, nurses, chaplains, and Corpsman).

I ran to the Navy recruiter and explained my desires to become a Corpsman with the Marines. He guaranteed that I would get my wish to be a Navy Corpsman assigned to the Marine Corps and would surely get to see battle. However, this cushy duty assignment would require a four-year commitment, which I quickly agreed to. Even at this young age I was already quite the negotiator.

Two

Vision plus emphasis = reality

Recruit Training

On July 8, 1966, at 6:00 a.m., my best friend, Keith, dropped me off at the induction center in downtown Los Angeles. I shook his hand, watched him drive off, and entered the building. I fell in line with all the rest of the inductees, and we were quickly separated from all our civilian clothes and personal belongings, including prescription medications. A few had to say good-bye to their teddy bears and blankies, as all our possessions were given to the poor or put in the trash.

We hopped a bus and headed south to the US Navy Recruit Training Center in San Diego, California, for nine weeks of basic training. Windows down, arms hanging out, and yelling and cat calls to the people, and especially the girls we passed. It was great fun, just like a Boy Scout field trip on our way to summer camp. We made a brief stop in Oceanside, grabbed a quick meal, and then got back on the bus for more fun.

As we entered the training center, the bus driver no sooner set his brakes and opened the door when we heard someone yell at the top of his lungs, "OK, ladies, the party is over. Get your asses off the bus and line up in two lines."

One smartass in the front right seat leaned over the rail into the doorway and said, "Excuse me, are you talking to us?" Everyone on the bus just roared with laughter. I am sure he must have been the class clown in high school and was used to the laughter at the expense of the teacher. He had no sooner turned his head in our direction to cast his eyes on his endearing audience when, without hesitation, a sailor reached up and grabbed the funny man by his collar pulling him over the rail and down through the door. The last thing we saw was the bottom of his shoes followed by the sound of a body hitting pavement, a solid meaty punch, and a cry of pain.

The sailor now exploded onto the bus and yelled, "Are there any more fucking clowns"? Hearing only silence, he continued. "I am your Company Commander, and you maggots better get off this fucking bus."

The bus was quiet. Everyone stared with naive disbelief, and as if choreographed, we exploded off the bus as one.

Jumping over the recumbent comic, we were hurried into a rough formation and marched off to the barbershop, where we were given a sixty-second crew cut. Then we were off to supply, where we donated the clothes we were wearing to charity and were issued a seabag of uniforms and bedding.

With seabag in hand, we were marched to our barracks, where we were instructed on how to make our bunks and then lights out, ladies.

My first night in recruit training I could not sleep. As I lay awake in my bunk amid the snoring of my forty-eight or so roommates, outside my open window, I could hear a recruit running followed close behind by MPs, yelling for him to stop. As the recruit reached the chain link fence and started his climb for freedom, he was quickly overtaken by the MPs, and the sounds of a severe beating rang out in the night.

I realized then that I could probably be killed in here and my mom would be informed that I was a victim of a training accident.

I awoke the next morning at 4:00 a.m. to the sound of a thirty-gallon metal trash can being thrown down the center aisle of our bunk room followed by the Company Commander (CC) screaming at the top of his lungs, "Drop your cocks and grab your socks, it's reveille. You maggots have thirty minutes to shit, shave, shower, and get your asses out front in formation."

Most all of us were on time, but several were late, and they paid a price for their tardiness. The CC asked for six bodies over six feet tall to come up front. Now, I had heard that you never volunteer for anything because it would be a trap that would find you pushing a wheelbarrow instead of being a truck driver, or using a shovel instead of operating a forklift. For some reason I raised my hand and was told to come up front and be a squad leader. The CC then told the short shits to move to the back of the ranks. So soon we were in rank by height from tallest to shortest.

As a squad leader, it was the first time in my life that I had been in charge of anything. I was in charge of seven guys in my squad, and all because I raised my hand for being over six feet tall. I got to wear small Second Class Petty Officer (Sergeant) stripes on my sleeve.

It was still dark as we marched to the chow hall for breakfast. Those who were late to fall out for lineup had to run around our formation while we marched to chow, all the time yelling, "I cannot follow orders. I am lower than whale shit."

As we arrived at the chow hall, our CC marched us up and halted us next to another company. We stood at attention with dozens of other companies and waited our turn to enter the food line, which seemed like an eternity. As I finally entered the chow hall, it was not much different from a school cafeteria, except many times larger, and the servers were looking at us with contempt. They were not the wonderful old ladies that I remembered from my school days.

I was introduced to my first meal of "shit on a shingle," which was a runny red sauce and ground beef over a soggy piece of toast (I found it to be quite good). I was moving down the line when we were ordered to attention, given an about-face, and told to take one step away from the serving line. As I stood at attention, I could hear a group of men being marched into the serving line behind us. Our CC came down our line, faced us, and shouted, "Listen up, maggots, these men behind you are in forty/fifty because of crimes committed during their training. If any one of you looks at them, you will join them!"

Most likely the recruit I heard being chased and beaten last night was now in 40/50. They wore a red helmet and were guarded by sailors with clubs called chasers. The rumor was that 40/50 inmates spend their days digging holes and filling buckets, then running with the buckets and burying other holes many yards away that they had dug earlier. These inmates did this day after day until they finally got with the Navy program, and then they were placed back into a new company and started their training again.

Within a few days, we had learned to march in step, wash our own uniforms with a scrub brush on large cement tables, and clean the barracks. We also learned how to fold our clothes to fit into the small lockers that we would later find aboard a ship. Every morning our company would march to a large parade ground and stand at attention with all the other companies in recruit training. The Company Commanders would then hold a uniform inspection on all the companies. Our CC would inspect one of the other companies, and another CC would inspect our company. As you stood at attention, eyes straight ahead, the CC would inspect recruits' uniforms while asking you questions that you had better be able to answer.

The CC would pull the front of your T-shirt down to inspect for dirt inside your collar and shout, "What is your first general order?"

Without hesitation, you would reply, "Sir, my first general order is— to take charge of this post and all government property in view, sir."

God help you if your shirt was not clean or you did not remember your orders. The same guys were always unprepared. The CC would stuff their shirts in their mouths, and they would do push-ups or run around the formation with their 1903 Springfield rifles held high over their heads, while the CC completed the rest of the inspections.

You quickly learned that the best way to survive was not to excel or be a problem child. If at graduation the CC did not know your name, you had played the game right.

About the second week, the recruit to my left had constantly had dirty uniforms and did not know his general orders. In frustration, the CC grabbed him around the throat and began to strangle him, while we were all at attention, eyes straight ahead. I could hear him being strangled, lose consciousness, and then fall against my leg. I did not move.

On our first locker inspection, several CCs from other companies came into our barracks. We were at attention in front of our bunks as they tore our lockers apart. It had taken hours to make sure the uniforms were folded exactly the Navy way and that every piece was as clean as when they were new, and in a matter of seconds it was all undone.

It was a shock to me that several recruits had put their clothes away dirty. One recruit still had skid marks in his boxer shorts. The CC stuffed the dirty boxers in the recruit's mouth and made him suck out the skid marks while crawling around the barracks yelling, "Oink, Oink, I am a pig," while the inspection continued for the rest of the company.

Several recruits never seemed to get the message, and soon the entire company was standing at attention outside the barracks, in the middle of the night, because of these problem children. That was when the blanket party was instituted.

A blanket party comes after lights-out when everyone is supposed to be asleep. Someone pulls the victim's blanket over his head so he cannot identify his attackers, and others hold him down tightly, on both sides, to restrain his arms and legs. Using fists or a bar of soap in a sock or towel, his fellow recruits beat him to impress upon him the importance of squaring his shit away. To emphasize the importance of good hygiene, recruits would drag others into the showers and scrub them with stiff-bristle brushes until raw.

As a squad leader, I received no directions as to my responsibilities, so I resorted to observing other squad leaders in the company. Of the six leaders, five of us would stand around at night, bullshit, and smoke cigarettes while our squads would clean the barracks for the next morning's inspection. When everything was cleaned, we would do a walk-through for inspection. What a great job it was to be a leader. It could not get cushier.

The five of us labeled one squad leader as a Dumb Shit. He actually worked with his men on the cleaning details. He also helped his squad with preparation for the next day's inspections, helped them study for the exams, and even helped them with their locker preparation. Dumb Shit was a great name for such a sucker.

On about the third week of our training, we moved from new recruits to the advanced training side of the base. During the first week of advanced training, all recruit companies assumed the duties of the Grunt work that went on at the base. We were to be assigned to work in the kitchen, washing dishes, loading and unloading trucks, and doing all the menial jobs that are required to keep the base running.

We all stood in line to find out what jobs we would be assigned to during that week. As I came to the desk, they advised me that I was assigned to the scullery, which was the dishwashing crew. I cleared my throat to gain their attention, smugly tapped my fingers on my small Petty Officer stripes, and I gave them a look that surely suggested that they should probably reconsider placing me in a position more befitting of my status.

I could see the smirks come across their faces as they discussed the position change, given my rank. The sailor apologized and changed my work location to the accounting office, which I graciously accepted.

I entered the accounting office, expecting a fairly cushy job. Instead, I was led to a closet where there was a coffeepot and cups hanging on the wall. I was to sit at attention, never speak, then fetch a coffee cup from the wall, and deliver the cup of coffee to whomever called for it. As I served my first customer, I was confident that my good cheer and magnetic personality would soon win these folks over. I carried the coffee on a tray, and as I hovered over the NCO's (Noncommissioned Officer) desk, I grabbed the cup around the rim and set it down on his desk with a smile that would surely garner the response of gratitude that I fully expected. Instead, the NCO looked up over his glasses and said, "Did you just touch the rim of my cup with your dirty dick-skinning hands? YES or NO?"

Knowing that he knew, I answered, "Sir, yes, sir!"

I was immediately moved to stand fire watch in an empty barracks for twelve hours a day. I was to march smartly back and forth across the barracks like the Honor Guards at the Tomb of the Unknown Soldiers. I had plenty of time to reflect on my actions as I marched back and forth across the length of the barracks. I could see that the Navy was attempting to tell me to pull my head out of my ass, and after a very long and boring week, I got the message.

All I could think about was what a turd I had been to my squad and that leadership was more than getting out of work; it was being responsible for the entire squad. Their success was my success and vice versa. That poor bastard was strangled next to me was in my squad, and I could have probably prevented it from happening.

After that realization, two squad leaders were Dumb Shits. Never again did any of my squad fail inspection, get strangled, or fail a test. We cleaned together, prepped for inspections, and studied together.

The day before graduation we were given a Cinderella Liberty—Be back by midnight, or you will be turned into a mouse.

We were to be turned loose on San Diego, and we were now practically old salts in the Navy. No one had ever been as cool as we were. Our company lined up at attention to be inspected by the Duty Company Commander prior to being dismissed to downtown. The enlisted Navy cover (the "Dixie Cup"), the one worn by Donald Duck, is to be evenly, two fingers above both eyebrows. Well, that is what the manual says, but I think I just told you that we were now old salts and almost everyone had his covers cocked to one side, winged out on the sides, or whatever way we thought would look cool—any way but what the manual called for. However, I convinced my squad to wait until we cleared the gate before altering our covers, and they all complied.

The CC stepped out of his office and gave the command to attention, and the company snapped to attention like a well-oiled machine. As he started his inspection of the front line, he only had to come to the first recruit, who had his cover cocked to one side. The CC pulled his arm back and delivered a punch to the recruit's forehead that sent him and his cover sailing back through our ranks. The CC then shouted, "Square those fucking covers away!"

As you can imagine, the covers were quickly squared away. One recruit went on liberty with four lumps on his forehead.

I know some of you might be saying that I took these recruit training scenarios from a very famous movie about Marine boot camp during the 1960s. All I can say is that these events actually happened, and the movie gave a very accurate depiction of recruit training at the time.

Hospital Corps School

On October 20, 1966, I reported to the Naval Medical Center San Diego for fourteen weeks of Hospital Corpsman School. I learned anatomy and physiology, pharmacology, basic diseases and illnesses that can affect men in their twenties and thirties, how to give shots and take blood, and many other subjects that would be the responsibility of a Licensed Vocational Nurse (LVN) in a civilian hospital.

Our introduction to traumatic wound care on the battlefield consisted of placing a battle dressing over a worn-out simulated rubber wound that was strapped to a fellow classmate's limbs or torso. You might find one in a costume shop at Halloween.

At our graduation, the Commanding Officer of the school advised us that many of us were going to be sent to the Marine Corps to receive Field Combat Corpsman training. I was relieved at the news that I was getting what I had asked for. However, this was the first time I realized that most of my classmates did not volunteer to be Corpsmen and were not expecting to go to the Marine Corps. Most felt that they had been tricked or misled by their recruiters and were expecting to be assigned to a ship. Now I started to wonder just who was more naive—me for wanting to go to the Marine Corps or my classmates who were hoodwinked into going? It did not make a difference, we were all going.

Field Medical Training Battalion

On February 13, 1967, I reported to the Marine Corps Field Medical Training Battalion at Camp Del Mar, one of many camps inside massive Camp Pendleton, California. This is where a Navy Corpsman bound for service with the USMC earns the rating of HM-8404, Field Medical Service Technician. Only after successful completion of the training do you receive the privilege of being called "Doc" by the Marines.

A Marine Corps Drill Sergeant was assigned as our Company Commander. He had the formidable task of taking the sailor out of us and replacing it with the heart and soul of a Marine, and he had only four short weeks to get it done. Sgt. Darrell Smith was a black Marine, a three striper with one tour in Vietnam, and only a few months away from his second. Raised in South LA, Sergeant Smith was no one to screw with.

On the first day that he lined us up at attention, he shouted, "I want you to look at the man to your left. Now look at the man to your right. One of you motherfuckers is not coming back. I know you ain't shocked because you know you are going to war, and in war men die. Don't worry though. It doesn't have to be you. It is probably the dumb ass to your right or left because they won't take this training serious. They will just grab-ass their way through just like they have for their entire pitiful life. You, on the other hand, are going to listen to everything that I and the other instructors tell you, because we intend to teach you those things that will save your life and the lives of your fellow Marines. Do I make myself clear?"

With a weak, uncoordinated response, the company shouted back, "Sir, yes, sir"!

Sergeant Smith came back, "What the fuck was that? You do not call me sir! I work for a living. I want to hear, 'Yes, Sergeant,' followed by an Ooh-Rah as loud as you can scream it. Do you understand?"

We responded, "Yes, Sergeant, Ooh-Rah!"

Field Med training provided us with specialized training in advanced emergency medicine and the fundamentals of how to act like the Marines. We qualified with the M-14 rifle and the Model 1911 .45-caliber pistol. We made long marches back into the hills where we would walk through simulated Vietnamese hamlets looking for booby traps, conducted night patrols, sitting ambushes, and learned basic battlefield tactics. One night just prior to graduation we set up in a defensive perimeter where the Marines would probe our lines at night and call our mothers bad names.

This made several of my classmates angry enough to charge down the hill—at the Marines—to defend their mothers' honor.

I am not sure if they were mad about the name-calling or thought they would fail training for going crazy—and therefore get out of going to Vietnam. All that they did get was an ass kicking by a squad of Marines waiting at the bottom of the hill. It was hard for me to get into the realism of battle when we were sitting in premade fighting holes, on a hilltop overlooking the town of Oceanside, and watching the movie *Bonnie and Clyde* on the drive-in theater screen about a mile away.

Naval Medical Center San Diego

On March 15, 1967, after completion of my USMC Field Medical Training, I was assigned to the Naval Medical Center San Diego, where I first worked on an ear, nose, and throat surgical ward. The Corpsman took the place of the LVN you see in the civilian hospitals today. There was a charge nurse (an officer) on duty for each shift, and the Corpsman did most of the hands-on Grunt work.

After several months, I applied and was accepted to work in the ear, nose, and throat clinic, where I assisted the doctors with patient treatment. I then advanced into the surgical unit where I learned to be a surgical technician and ran the surgical suite for operations such as tonsillectomies on dependent children, middle-ear bone replacements, and major radical neck cancer operations on older veterans.

I loved the work in the operating room so much that I almost never went home on the weekends. Instead, I would stand extra duty so I could catch emergency tracheotomy operations on a crash cart throughout the hospital. In surgery, it was just you and the surgeon, and there was never a nurse present. Anticipating the doctor's next move and having the correct instrument ready for his use was so rewarding.

On November 9, 1967, my original dream was realized. I received my orders for reassignment to the Third Marine Division in Vietnam. I was given thirty days' leave and ordered to report to Norton Air Force Base in San Bernardino, California, on December 16, 1967, for my flight to Vietnam.

Toward the end of my leave, my mom suggested that I contact my dad and advise him that I was going off to war. I had not had any contact with my dad for quite some time, and I was hoping his anger about their divorce would have dissipated by now and enabled him to see me as a casualty and not as a collaborator.

When my dad answered the phone I said, "Dad, this is Larry, I wanted to call and tell you that I am leaving for Vietnam in a few days with the Marines."

My dad answered back quickly, "Not to worry—Marines don't die from bullets; they die from syphilis." With that he abruptly hung up.

Ah, that emotional talk between a father and son prior to going off to war. The father holding back tears, the hugs, and reassurance masking the deep-down fear that I might never return. Yes, I was hurt, but I was also disappointed that he hung up before I could advise him that gonorrhea is much more common than syphilis, and that neither is fatal nowadays.

The last time to wear Navy blue.

Three

I TURNED GREEN

The Marines have given you a new first name. The day you
check into your new unit no one will care what your first name
was; it's now Doc and it will be Doc for the rest of your life. The
Marines all have first names of Joe, Fred, or John. Yours will
forever be Doc and with that, the expectations are almost unfair.

—MAJ. GEN. LAWRENCE D. NICHOLSON,
FIRST MARINE DIVISION, USMC

The Hop over to Vietnam

On December 16, 1967 I boarded a Tiger Airlines jet that flew to Anchorage, Alaska, for refueling and then on to Okinawa, Japan, for the final stop before Vietnam.

In Okinawa, we finished paperwork for my transfer to Vietnam, received Marine green utilities (work uniforms), and stood around waiting for our names to be called for our flight out.

The chow line took forever and was full of Marines and Corpsmen who were just going over and those who had survived and were just going home. One reason for the slow lines was because E-5 Sergeants and above were allowed to go to the front of the line. What a great perk. I thought just maybe, when I come back in a year, I will be an E-5 (Hospital Corpsman Second Class) instead of the lowly E-3 I was now. I could visualize strutting to the front of the line as a veteran of combat and looking through my battle-hardened eyes at the FNGs (fucking new guys), who were waiting for their flight to the war, and without a word, I would just step in front of them.

Three days later, our paperwork finished, Navy blues traded for Marine green, all the Corpsmen boarded a commercial aircraft that took us to Da Nang, Vietnam.

ARRIVAL IN VIETNAM

I arrived in Da Nang on December 20, 1967. Some in our group went with the First Marine Division, which had the operational area around Da Nang, and the rest of us were loaded on a military aircraft and sent to Phu Bai, which was the Headquarters for the Third Marine Division.

In Phu Bai, our group was outfitted with combat gear that consisted of a helmet, flak jacket, jungle utilities, gas mask, field pack, and a Colt Model 1911 .45-caliber pistol. We also received our assignments to fill Corpsman vacancies in Battalions throughout the Third Marine Division operational area, which was mostly concentrated north of the city of Quang Tri.

MY FIRST ASSIGNMENT WITH THE GRUNTS

Several of us were assigned to the First Battalion, Fourth Marine Regiment (1/4),* whose rear area was at Dong Ha about ten miles south

---

* *A Regiment consists of three Battalions, led by a Colonel (2,700 to 3,600 from the Marines and Navy). The Regiments are numbered First, Second, Third, and Fourth Marine Regiment and so on. The Battalions are numbered First, Second, and Third Battalion.*

A Marine Battalion consists of four Rifle Companies, a Weapons Company, and one Headquarters and Service Company (H&S Company), commanded by a Lieutenant Colonel (900 to 1,200 from the Marines and Navy).

The Rifle Companies are identified by the NATO phonetic alphabet. Four rifle companies with the letter designations of Alpha for A, Bravo for B, Charlie for C, and Delta for D made up 14. The 2/4 Companies were Echo for E, Foxtrot for F, Golf for G, and Hotel for H. The 3/4 Companies of the Demilitarized Zone (DMZ), the buffer zone between North and South Vietnam.

The Marine clerk looked up at us and said, "Congratulations, gentlemen, you are on your way to rocket city. You better learn to keep your ass down."

The others were assigned to the Second Battalion, Twenty-Sixth Marines (2/26), stationed right here in Phu Bai. The clerk looked at them and said, "You lucky bastards are home free. There ain't shit that happens around this garden spot." Luck would change for 2/26 in the very near future when they would be moved to Khe Sanh.

By the time we were through with the check-in process, it was too late to report to our next duty assignment, so we dumped our gear on our overnight bunks and hit the closest EM Club. A club might be an exaggeration for the plywood hooch,** where enlisted men could get a beer, sit outside, and bullshit.

Six or eight of us had gone through the Navy Basic Training, Hospital Corps School, and the Marine Corps Field Med School together, and now here we were in Vietnam, sipping a beer, with the sound of outgoing artillery fire as our background mood music, toasting our final night together. No one said it, but we all thought it—which one of us would not be going home?

REPORTING FOR DUTY

I arrived in Dong Ha on December 21, 1967, and reported to the First Battalion, Fourth Marines, rear area. The rear area at Dong Ha

---

were India for I, Juliett for J was not used because it is a feminine name, Kilo for K, Lima for L, and Mike for M. The Rifle Companies for the other Regiments were labeled the same.

Each company is staffed with approximately two hundred Marines, Corpsmen and their officers. The H&S Company comprises the Battalion Commander and his staff, and it provides all of the logistical support for the rifle companies.

See appendices for more details of staffing.

** *Hooch—A slang term for the typical military one-room huts that were made up of half-inch plywood siding with a corrugated tin roof.*

comprised the supply, motor pool, office clerks, rehab for injured Marines, and everything else that supported the thousand or so Marines of the Battalion's actual fighting units that were assigned to smaller bases farther north. Dong Ha was a large base that served as the main forward supply base for the Third Marine Division and had the nickname of Rocket City because of the constant threat of enemy rocket fire.

After I checked in, I was assigned a cot in a tent along with six or eight other Corpsmen who had just arrived as replacements. Around ten o'clock at night I was outside talking with a First Class Corpsman who was the X-ray technician assigned to the 1/4 rear area Battalion Aid Station. Just then, sirens started going off, and we could hear explosions off in the distance. The Petty Officer told me to quickly get my helmet and flak jacket and meet him in the trench just outside our tent. He had been in country for eight months, and I quickly submitted to his rank and experience. Within seconds, I was in the trench, armed and ready for action.

The Chief Corpsman of the Battalion just happened to be walking by and saw us standing in a chest-high trench. He asked me to come out and talk to him, which I did. He put his arm around me, walked me away from the trench, and said, "The Corpsman in the trench is afraid of his own shadow, and you need to look around and see what everyone else is doing and act accordingly. You will never hear the round with your name on it, and if the rounds you hear are far off, then you are probably going to be OK. It's a very large base, and the rounds are most likely aimed at the airfield a quarter of a mile away. Now put your gear away and get some sleep." The Chief slapped me on the back, welcomed me to the Battalion, and walked off saying, "You will get used to it."

I looked around the camp and saw no one else in the trench line except the one Corpsman. Sounds of laughter over a card game and music echoed in the night along with the sound of rocket impacts in the distance. Embarrassed, I walked back to my tent, talking under my breath, "Christ, how was I supposed to know what to do and who to trust?"

OFF TO THE FRONT

After January 1, all the new Corpsmen were loaded in the back of a deuce and a half*** and sent to the 1/4 forward Battalion Aid Station at C-2. Fire Base C-2 was a new installation that was developed to provide artillery support for the bases farther north along the DMZ. Alpha and Bravo Companies with the Battalion Command Group defended C-2, while Charlie and Delta Companies occupied the C-2 Bridge position a few miles farther north.

The big guns at C-2 were the M110 eight-inch Howitzers that could shoot a two-hundred-pound projectile up to eighteen miles and reach North Vietnam. The tent we were assigned was placed one hundred feet or so in front of the muzzle of these big guns. When they fired, the shock wave would blow out our candles in the tent, and the muzzle blast left your ears ringing. A fire mission from these guns came without warning all through the day and night, so a good beauty rest was out of the question. In addition to the big guns at C-2, 81 mm and four-deuce mortars were used for close-in fire support for the base, the Marine patrols, and ambushes out in the surrounding area. The mortars were in constant use, shooting at small groups of NVA (North Vietnamese regular army) who were sighted outside the perimeter or returning fire on enemy mortar and rocket positions who were shooting at us.

Almost every day, our compound would receive a few incoming rounds and we were constantly reminded to "Spread out—one round will get you all!" To a new guy, a few rounds exploding in the perimeter and causing a casualty now and then seemed like what it must have felt like in London during the Blitz of World War II. But the more experienced Marines said that this January was a day at the beach compared to the constant pounding and large-unit contacts that they had experienced all through 1967. It seemed to be the lull before the big storm.

*** *Deuce and a half—The standard two-and-a-half-ton military truck used for carrying troops and supplies.*

During my training at Camp Pendleton, we were told about the high humidity and searing temperatures that we would endure in Vietnam. But no one ever said a thing about the cold monsoon rains and storms during the winter. The rain seemed to never stop, and the red dirt turned to a thick, sticky mud that attempted to pull your boots off with every step. Temperatures dropped to the low fifties, and everyone was soaked to the bone. The dirt floors in our tents soon joined the fun and made it impossible to take off the water-soaked mud-caked boots.

NAPOLEON SAID, "AN ARMY MARCHES ON ITS STOMACH." WELL, HE NEVER MET A MARINE.

Chow was served outside in the rain. As you went through the serving line with your metal mess kit, you would dump the rain out one last time just prior to the hot food hitting your cold tin pan. The food would be floating and cold before you could find a place to sit down. The meal usually consisted of some kind of roasted beef that was so tough that you would chew the bite until the flavor was gone and your jaw muscles gave up. You then attempted to swallow the chunk and hoped not to choke.

The side dishes were either canned corn, peas, or green beans. Over forty-five years later, I cannot get near a restaurant roast beef carving station.

One Marine sitting near me made a comment about how bad the food was, and a Gunny Sergeant, overhearing the complaint, shouted back, "The Marine Corps never promised that the food would be tasty, only that it would produce a turd the next morning. If any of you ladies can't shit tomorrow, come see me; it may just be stuck, and I will beat it out of you." There was dead silence, and then laughter broke out and everyone started eating again as if it was five stars. Now you tell me—how do you not laugh at that?

At the completion of your dining experience you would pass four thirty-gallon metal trash cans. The first was the garbage can to dump any delicious cuisine you just could not find room to finish. The second was a prewash with a toilet brush to remove any leftovers. The third had a diesel-fuel-fired immersion heater that brought the soapy water to slightly above room temp, and you dunked your mess kit in. Then you moved to the fourth trash can, which held the lukewarm final rinse that contained floating food particles and a mild film of soap scum.

A GIFT FROM VIETNAM

Almost everyone new in country received a special gift from the welcome wagon. It was called dysentery, the poop chills, Montezuma's revenge, green apple quickstep, or just simply "the shits." Whatever your preference, it just added to your new-guy experience. To add the finishing touch to your misery, you had to walk briskly, with your butt cheeks squeezed tightly, to the six-man outhouse a dozen or so times during the day and night. On your arrival you were greeted with standing room only by your fellow Marines, who exhibited the same symptoms. One learned very quickly that upon the first urge, you had better start moving in that direction.

If modesty was an issue, then dysentery was the cure. The six-man outhouse was fitted with six holes on two wooden benches that opposed each other, three holes on each side. You would sit knee to knee with the Marine across from you and a Marine on each side that made airline coach seating seem luxurious. The only conversation was "pass the paper." If you just needed to take a piss that was easy. Scattered around the compound were "piss tubes" whereby an empty powder canister from an artillery shell was stuck in the ground, out in the open. The soil was mostly clay and did not provide much drainage so the tubes were usually filled to overflowing.

On January 7, I was doing the quickstep over to the outhouse when I heard a terrible screech go over my head, followed a second later by two huge explosions that dropped me to my knees. Someone yelled, "Incoming," and I was faced with the dilemma of running for safety and possibly soiling my pants or continuing on with my mission at hand.

I can assure you that I was not the only man in the bunker giving off an odor. Later, fragments from the ordnance and a crater analysis identified them as US radar suppression missiles that were probably shot from a fighter jet escorting B-52 bombers on their way to North Vietnam.

We were lucky that no one was injured from these missiles that our own forces shot. The term "friendly fire" described the event. This was my first experience with friendly fire, but it would not be my last.

It took several weeks for your body to get used to the new germs and contaminants that you were now playing host to, and slowly the dysentery started to abate. Many Marines needed weeks in the rear area to overcome dehydration and rid their system of parasitic protozoa, bacteria, bugs, and whatever was causing the shits.

After a few days, we were moved out of the tents and into one of the freshly built "Dyemarker Bunkers," Dyemarker was the code name for the strongpoint defensive line of outposts strung out along the DMZ. At C-2, eighty-one of these new bunkers were designed to take a direct hit from a Russian 130 mm artillery shell.

The bunkers still needed many layers of sandbags applied to the roof, so during the day we would fill sandbags with this red sticky mud trying to improve the protection of the Aid Station bunker and our dorm bunker. At night, we would sit around and listen to war stories from some of the Corpsman who were rotating out of the Marine Rifle Companies, and one by one, we new guys started replacing them in the field.

ONE NIGHT WITH A HERO

One night a Corpsman (Doc Hal Jones) arrived in our bunker. He was twenty-three years old and very mature for his age. He had spent six months in a Rifle Company, and he was on his way to Hawaii to meet his wife for nine days of R & R (rest and recreation). Doc Jones was one of those individuals who controlled a room by just his presence. He was not arrogant but very confident. You could tell that the old salts respected him; when he talked, even they listened.

He was like a celebrity—bigger than life and a great storyteller. We new guys were glued to his every word like children around a campfire hearing their first ghost story. We stayed up late that night as he attempted to quench our thirst for knowledge of what we could expect in our very near future.

The next morning, January 8, 1968, Doc Jones boarded a helicopter for the first leg of his journey that would take him to Hawaii to see his wife and mark the end of his Rifle Company assignment. We went back to filling sandbags. Later that afternoon we received word that the helicopter that Doc Jones was on went down, and all aboard were killed.

Halcott Pride Jones Jr. is honored on the Vietnam Veterans Memorial, Panel 33E, Row 87.

A DREAM ASSIGNMENT

I had just taken the exam for HM-3 (Corporal) just prior to shipping to Vietnam. However, the Navy waived the time requirement between ranks when in a war zone. I must have scored well, because on January 16, 1968, I was promoted to HM-3 and assigned to Delta Company, First Battalion, Fourth Marine Regiment (D/1/4) as their Senior Corpsman. A Senior Corpsman was an E-5 (Sergeant) position, and I guess they must have been shorthanded on E-4s and E-5s because I got the job as a new E-4.

Four

The Washout

*You guys are the Marines' doctors; there's none
better in the business than a Navy Corpsman.*

—Lt. Gen. Lewis "Chesty" Puller, USMC

**A story about the history of the "Washout" and the previous
tenants**

The C-2 Bridge position was halfway between C-2 and Con Thien.
The objective of the units assigned there was to protect the bridge,
which was the main supply route to Con Thien; protect the water source,
which was the main water supply for C-2 and Con Thien; and to conduct
patrols to intercept the North Vietnamese Army attempting to infiltrate
the south.

To the Marines, the bridge site was known as "the Washout" because
Marine engineers had originally installed large culverts in the creek bed
and built the road over them. As the monsoon season came in, the creek
quickly became a raging river and washed the culverts and the road
downstream. To ensure year-around road access to Con Thien, a steel
girder bridge, capable of supporting a tank, had been installed in early
October of 1967.

On September 21, 1967, the Second Battalion/Fourth Marines were conducting a sweep mission east of Con Thien near the abandoned village of Phu Oc (you will hear this name later) and walked into the kill zone of an NVA Battalion-size bunker complex. As they broke contact with the enemy, they had to leave fifteen dead Marines behind.

On October 6, the Third Marine Division Commander ordered a two-Battalion assault on the NVA position at Phu Oc to recover the dead Marines. The action started with day and night bombardment from artillery, and air strikes followed on October 10 with a ground assault from 2/4 and Battalion Landing Team 2/3 (about fifteen hundred to two thousand Marines). The assault found the bunker complex had been abandoned, most likely because of the constant bombing from the previous four days.

The Marines of 2/4 not only had to endure the task of collecting the decomposing bodies of their dead friends, the NVA had also mutilated them. It was reported that one of the men had a Marine Corps tattoo skinned from his chest and tacked to a tree.

On October 12, 1967, 2/4 was moved into the new bridge site to provide security and to recover from a month in the field and devastating battle losses that decreased their Battalion strength from just under one thousand Marines down to fewer than five hundred.

The stream at C-2 Bridge intersected the road to Con Thien at a right angle and usually ran, chest high, from west to east. The ground sloped upward from the stream and created a flat area on both sides. The site looked like a figure eight with the bridge in the middle of the eight. The road ran straight through the middle of the compound north to south. I would guess that the perimeter was about one hundred and fifty yards wide and three hundred yards long.

On October 13, a Hotel Company patrol from 2/4 discovered a mortar-aiming stake near a church at the abandoned village of Nha Tho Bai An. It was aimed directly at a tank emplacement inside the bridge perimeter. Needless to say, the tank was moved that night.

That evening, 2/4 received eleven new Officers and dozens of new Grunts to replenish their previous month's losses. Things were looking up for 2/4.

On October 14, 1967, at 1:25 a.m., the bridge site came under intense artillery, rocket, and mortar fire. A Marine-squad-size ambush outside Hotel Company's wire reported NVA movement toward their position and opened fire. They had taken several serious casualties and requested permission to reenter the perimeter (permission is not always granted). The Hotel Company Commander approved the request and, once the squad was in the wire, called in the prearranged artillery and mortar coordinates that denied the enemy the approaches to the perimeter wire.

A Marine sniper team using Starlight Scopes* spotted a large NVA force preparing to launch an attack only forty-five yards from the wire. The Company held their fire until they could see the whites of their eyes (kind of like Bunker Hill in the Revolutionary War). As the enemy charged, the Company opened fire, supported by two tanks firing their 90 mm canister rounds (a hugh shotgun shell filled with 1,200 steel pellets). The NVA Company was cut down, and it dissolved prior to reaching the wire.

As the assault on the Hotel Company lines withdrew, Golf Company lines came alive with pinpoint mortar fire followed by a ground attack from a very large NVA force. The enemy had scouted the Marines' two machine gun positions and adjacent fighting holes and within minutes had taken them out with RPGs (rocket-propelled grenades), which opened a clear lane into the compound. The advance from the enemy was accompanied by the use of tear gas, which caused the Marines to lose precious time on targets while they donned their gas masks. This

---

* A Starlight Scope is an optoelectronic device that allows images to be produced in levels of light approaching total darkness. The images seen through the eyepiece have a green tone because green creates more shades than any other color. This passive device uses available light and amplifies it by twenty thousand times, turning night into day for the observer using the device.

delay was all the enemy needed to fully breach the wire and overrun the Marine positions.

Explosive satchel charges and automatic weapon fire followed, finding their mark on the Golf Company Command Post, killing the new Company Commander and the Foreword Artillery Observer Officer. What followed was everyone's worst fear—the dreaded hand-to-hand combat, a no-rules fight for your life using rifles, pistols, knives, fists, kicks, bites, and whatever weapon you can get your hands on. Many new enlisted Grunts along with two new Lieutenants and a Captain lost their lives on their first full day in country.

The Battalion Commander, Lt. Colonel Hammond, directed Foxtrot and Echo Companies to mount a counterattack into Golf Company's portion of the perimeter and drive the NVA from the compound. Supported by artillery, "Puff the Magic Dragon"** raked the retreating NVA.

At first light, a company from 3/4, stationed at C-2, arrived as reinforcements and found the compound littered with dead NVA and Marines. The official enemy killed was listed as twenty-four but drag marks from the dead and wounded would suggest the number to be more than one hundred twenty. The casualties from 2/4 were twenty-one Marines killed and twenty-three wounded.

Following the ground attack on the bridge, 2/4 was moved to Dong Ha for much-needed rest and rehabilitation. Elements of 3/3 relieved 2/4 at the bridge until Charlie and Delta 1/4 moved in on December 27, 1967.

The perimeter protecting the bridge was originally designed for a Battalion-size operation (four companies, or about one thousand Marines). Charlie and Delta Company 1/4 were slightly more than four hundred men, so the defensive lines needed some work.

** *"Puff the Magic Dragon," or "Spooky," an AC-47, was an old World War II propeller-driven cargo plane armed with the new miniguns that could shoot at a variable speed from two thousand to six thousand rounds per minute. Puff would circle the battlefield overhead and rain down a hellish storm of bullets on the enemy below.*

A little over two months earlier, four companies of 2/4 were almost overrun by the NVA, and now 1/4 was there with only two companies, which did not leave anyone with a great feeling of security.

I guess it is kind of like why there are laws that require the seller of a house to disclose to the new buyer when someone has died in the house. In our case, there were twenty-one people murdered and twenty-three others wounded in the house just six weeks prior, and they still had not repainted or changed the carpets.

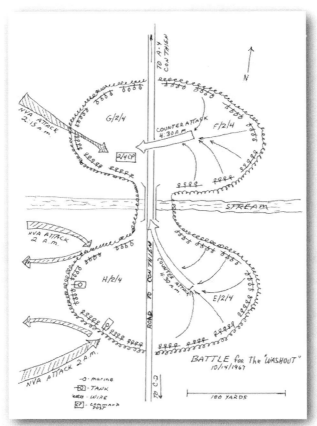

The Battle for the "Washout"
Second Battalion/Fourth Marine Regiment
October 14, 1967

Five

I Am Now a Devil Doc

The Marines have their few good men…they are called Doc!

—*Probably a Corpsman*

Introduction to my new unit

I hitched a ride from C-2 to the C-2 Bridge site, located the Delta Company Command bunker, and reported in. The Company Commander, Captain Richard Weede, was in the bunker along with his Command Group, which was comprised of the Company Gunnery Sergeant, Carl Sponenberg; the Company Radioman, Don Westenhaver; the Battalion Radioman, Bill Chastain; Radioman Russ Whiteleather; and a Marine interpreter. The Senior Corpsman I was to replace was already gone.

I did not ask—because I did not want to know—if I was replacing Doc Hal Jones.

Captain Weede's demeanor was professional but relaxed, not a hint of arrogance, and he instantly made you feel welcome and part of something special. As I was introduced around the room, I received a similar welcome from the rest of his staff.

Most every successful person can point to someone who helped him or her along the way, and I have been fortunate to have had quite a few mentors over the years. Usually the most important mentor is the one who affects your life when you are still young, impressionable, and searching for who you are and what you want to be. Captain Richard Weede was that guy for me. He was not the big brother; he was more like the star captain of the high school football team when you were just a pimple-faced freshman. He was thoughtful, inclusive, brilliant, and courageous. My worst fear was that I would disappoint him.

Captain Weede suggested that I get settled into my bunker and be back for the company meeting to discuss the night operations. I took up residence in a two-man bunker, next to the Company Command bunker, with another Radioman who was also assigned to the Company Command Group. My new bunker mate was Cpl. Jimmy Howe.

Our two-man bunker was a hole in the ground with a two-foot-wide dirt walkway in the center and a dirt shelf carved out on either side where we placed an air mattress for our beds. You could sit up in bed but not stand up in the walkway. The roof of the bunker was covered with steel runway matting that supported three or four layers of sandbags. The opening to the bunker was covered with a plastic poncho. I introduced myself to my new bunker mate, stowed my gear, and went back to the Command Post for the evening meeting.

As a member of the Company Command, I would be sitting in on all the company briefings along with the Platoon Commanders. Because of this privilege, I would have more knowledge than the average Grunt about what was happening in and around the Battalion and beyond.

On my first-night briefing, Captain Weede advised the group that a Platoon-size patrol from Charlie Company found a U-shaped trench, approximately 60' x 1½' x 3' deep, a few hundred meters from our perimeter. In the trench, they found four NVA bodies that had been steverything except their tennis shoes. Artillery was the apparent cause of death, as four craters were found within a few yards of their position. Additionally, a squad from Charlie Company was providing security for a bulldozer, and they spotted two NVA in heavy brush approximately fifty yards east of the perimeter. The squad fired one hundred rounds of small arms and gave chase. While checking the area, they spotted another NVA moving in an easterly direction and fired an additional thirty rounds of small arms at the enemy. A search of the area produced negative results.

Captain Weede advised his officers to have the LPs (listening posts) and ambushes be extra alert because of the numerous sightings of enemy soldiers around our perimeter. The NVA appeared to be aggressively reconning all the bases, and intelligence suggested a possible ground attack was in the works for one of the bases in the area.

The locations of the ambushes were discussed and marked on the maps. The Captain went on to stress the need for additional care and cleaning of the M-16 rifle because of numerous reports of malfunctions during combat operations. Each Lieutenant reported out on the continuing improvements to his respective portion of the perimeter defenses; adding more German concertina wire, tangle foot, and trip flares. A little more information was exchanged and the Platoons' Lieutenants were dismissed to hold their own Platoon meetings and prepare for the night LPs and ambushes.

I was advised that I would stand the 10:00 p.m. to midnight watch with the company Radioman Don Westenhaver, and he would instruct me on my duties as a night radio operator. I was then dismissed to be back for my watch.

As I walked the fifteen yards back to my bunker with my new bunker mate, Jim advised me to expect some unwanted visitors during the night, because at night, the rat was king. We crawled into our bunker, each lit a cigarette, and we sat on our bunks knee to knee. Then he went on, "The fucking rats will crawl all around inside the bunkers looking for food and will piss all over your gear. Don't swat at them because the little fuckers will bite the shit out of you. Most every day, we are sending a Marine to the rear for a week of rabies shots from the prior night's rat bites." With that, he ground his cigarette out on the dirt floor, laid back on his bunk, rolled away from me, and said, "Sweet dreams, Doc," and within seconds he was snoring.

At 10:00 p.m. I was back at the Command Post (CP) and met with Cpl. Don Westenhaver to be instructed on the procedures for standing radio watch. Corporal Westenhaver told me to just call him Westy, and then he went on to explain our job. Three radiomen, a Marine interpreter, and I stood two-hour shifts every night. We had to monitor the radios to check in with our listening posts and ambushes that we had out in front of our lines.

Westy explained that a Listening Post (LP) is comprised of two to four Marines with a radio set out in front of our lines to provide an early warning against an enemy attack. We would have four or five LPs spread out along our lines. Should they hear any enemy movement, they were to call back and warn us. One of the drawbacks of this assignment was the knowledge that they were expendable. Should the enemy launch an attack from near their position, there was no way for the LPs to get back into the protection of our line except to make a run for it and risk being shot by the Marines inside the wire. Otherwise, they could hunker down where they were and risk being discovered by the enemy or killed by our own artillery.

I know what you are thinking. How can you get that cushy job? Well, just join the Marines and ask to be a Grunt.

The LPs never talked on the radio unless it was an emergency. My job was to call them every fifteen minutes for a situation report, and ask them if they were "cooling off" (meaning were they OK). If they were OK, they would key their handsets twice, which would make a squelch sound on my receiver. If I did not receive the two squelch sounds, I was to ask them if they were "NOT cooling off" to key their handset one time. Depending on their answer or if there was no answer, I was to wake Gunny Sponenberg and Captain Weede for further orders.

An ambush was usually a Squad of thirteen Marines and a Corpsman or a Platoon of forty-five Marines and two Corpsmen that would be much farther out from the lines and positioned along a known trail that was used by the enemy in hopes of catching them in an ambush. The radio contact was handled in pretty much the same way as the LP's.

After Westy ran through the procedure, he handed me the handset of the PRC-25 radio and said, "Go ahead, Doc, give it a try." I took the handset, looked at the list of LPs and the call signs that they had selected for themselves, cleared my throat, keyed the mic, and said, "Wet Dream, Wet Dream, this is Smitty Delta. If you are Cooling Off, key your handset twice." I held my breath, my heart pounding…back came the two squelch sounds through the speaker in the handset. I relaxed my shoulders and went on to the next LP, "Sitting Duck, Sitting Duck, this is Smitty Delta. If you are cooling off, key your handset twice." Again my pulse raced… and again, back came the two squelch sounds. Now I relaxed, but I was very excited about my new job and knowing I was finally doing something constructive. I went through the rest of the list without a hitch. Before I knew it, my shift was up. I woke my relief, gave him a quick briefing, thanked Westy for his help, and I was off to my bunker.

HOME SWEET HOME

Almost as soon as I crawled into my bed, I heard digging and scratching noises on the small shelf just above my head. I thought to myself, "Those fucking rats are here," and with that, I gave a quick strike to the bottom of the shelf to scare the little bastards. There was a little squeal and then a thump on my chest. I rose quickly, striking my head on the ceiling, as the rat ran down my leg and jumped to the floor.

I sat there in the pitch black for a moment and thought, "*Did I just let out a small scream and did my bunker mate hear it?*" A second later, both of my questions were answered. From out of the dark came a voice, "Damn, Doc, you scream like a little bitch. I told you not to swat at the little fuckers." And within a second, he was snoring again.

The next morning I set up a mosquito net around my bed and tucked it under my air mattress. I could give a shit less about the mosquitoes but I was hoping that it would keep the rats off my chest.

Cpl. Jimmy Howe and I hit it off immediately, and within a few days, we became good friends. He was not a tall man, but what he lacked in stature he made up in courage, heart, and he was all Marine. He had these steely eyes and a smirk that signaled he was very confident, and you probably should not fuck with him.

It took only a few shifts to settle in to my new radio duty, and I found it to be exciting and an honor to be trusted with the responsibility for the watch over all the activity that was going on in our company. I was always surprised at how often the Marines on the LP would fall asleep, which left the Captain not knowing if they were dead and an enemy attack was imminent.

Supposedly, you could be shot for falling asleep on guard duty, but it never happened here. However, when morning came, and the Marines on the LP were coming back through the perimeter wire, Gunny Sponenberg was there to welcome them with a good old-fashioned Marine Gunny ass-chewing. One night, he got so mad that he went outside the wire to the LP's position and found them sleeping. He delivered a slight beating to the two Marines. As word spread through the company and on through the entire Battalion, so grew the rumor of injuries from the beating. It started with cuts and bruises and grew to near-death injuries. Truth be damned, but the result was the sleeping issue was solved. It seemed that the threat of having your throat cut by an enemy solder was not as much of a deterrent as worrying about an ass-stomping from Gunny Sponenberg.

The radio work and attending the command meetings quickly became routine but what haunted me was my real job of Senior Corpsman. Two weeks after my twentieth birthday, I found myself responsible for all the medical needs of one hundred eighty to two hundred Marines (it varied depending on casualties), and I had six Corpsman as my subordinates. I was clearly in over my head. I did not yet understand what the basic duties of a Platoon Corpsman were, much less what the Company's Senior Corpsman responsibilities were. I did not get to have a briefing from the Senior Corpsman I was replacing, and there was no job description for the position. If there was, I did not think to look for one. Looking back, I could have walked across the bridge, introduced myself to the Charlie Company Senior Corpsman, and asked him for advice, but it never crossed my mind.

IN OVER MY HEAD

I had about the same medical training as a current-day EMT 1, but the Marines treated me with great respect—as if I was their doctor. Even in the nightly command meetings, if there were any medical issues, the Captain and Lieutenants would turn to me like students to a teacher. The first time they did it I turned to look behind me to see just who they were talking to then blushed when I realized it was me.

The stress of my responsibilities drove me to take a trip back to the Battalion Aid Station at C-2 to discuss my medical shortcomings with our Battalion surgeon. He reminded me that most of the medical needs of the Marines would be trauma, and that my corpsman and I DID have adequate trauma training to stop the bleeding, maintain airways, prevent shock, and medevac the Marine to a field hospital. Additionally, Marines are among the healthiest segment of our society and sick call should be dealing with dysentery, colds, and minor illnesses. Should you suspect something more serious, just put them in a jeep and get them to the Aid Station for the Battalion doctor to assess them further. Our big job is to keep them healthy—promote good hygiene, make them take care of their feet, insist they take their malaria pills, and emphasize sanitation. If you don't know the answer, don't bullshit anyone; find the answer. Most of this is just plain common sense.

After the pep talk from the Battalion doctor, I felt so relieved. Breaking down my job description to the basics put it into prospective. I felt more comfortable going around the Company and getting better acquainted with my Platoon Docs. My first visit was to the First Platoon, where I met Doc Ted Schindeler. Ted was the son of a Dutch oil executive and grew in the Dutch Caribbean island of Aruba, just off the coast of Venezuela. He spoke Dutch and flawless American English. Why he was here, I did not know. Maybe, like me, he was here for the excitement.

Ted was outgoing, very competent, and loved by his Marines. The other Corpsman for the First Platoon had just rotated out, and we were waiting for his replacement. Doc Mike Pinckney arrived the first week in February as the replacement and was quickly accepted by his Marines. Doc Pinckney was a quick study, good looking, blond, stout compared to the rest of us, and he was quickly dubbed "Doc Pinky."

The Second Platoon Corpsmen were Doc Mike Ferguson and Doc Harley Cowan. Doc Ferguson was also very outgoing, easy to like, respected by the Marines, and would volunteer for anything. Mike was an average size man, skinny like the rest of us but courageous beyond belief. Doc Harley Cowan was quiet, unassuming, got along with everyone, and was a peach of a guy whom his Marines respected very much. Harley seemed very cerebral, and if I were to guess, he would probably wind up as an educated professional after he returned to the world.

The Third Platoon Docs were Ken Walker and Anton Livingston, two of the nicest men you could ever meet. Ken was from North Carolina, played the guitar, and composed his own songs. Doc Livingston was like the others—easygoing, conscientious, passionate, and willing to do whatever it took. All six of the guys were amazing, and I could not have handpicked a better bunch of Docs.

During the research for this book, I came across the daily activity logs for the Battalion, the "Command Chronology." Each Chronology covered a month of activity for the Battalion and spanned the entire Vietnam War. In addition to the daily activity, the Chronology also listed the number of Battalion KIAs, WIAs, enemy killed, and other routine information. One of the sections was labeled "training," and it listed the Battalion- and Company-level training that was conducted for the month. As an example, in May 1968, the training topics listed were M-16 care and cleaning, map and compass reading, ambush techniques, radio procedures, and first aid/buddy aid. The first aid/buddy aid caught my attention. As I looked through the logs for every month I was with 1/4, I saw medical subjects that were supposedly covered by the company and Platoon Docs. I do not remember anyone in my medical chain of command ever advising me of what topics to cover or checking to validate if a topic had been covered.

This is not an indictment of the Marines, but it certainly pointed to a failure on the part of the medical corps that I was a part of. Back at our Battalion rear area at Dong Ha, there were at least five Navy Chief Corpsmen and five First Class Corpsmen who were assigned to the Battalion during my time with Delta. These senior Noncommissioned Officers (NCOs) were all career Navy Medical Corps. Surely one of them was responsible for making out a training schedule and checking up on us Docs in the field to ensure we completed them. I never saw a single senior Navy NCO the entire time I was with Delta.

Captain Weede held a meeting every night with his officers and senior NCOs to make sure his Marines knew their jobs. Then he walked the lines to ensure they complied.

I will shoulder part of the blame for not taking the initiative to teaching subjects that might have helped a Marine save his buddy or even himself, but at nineteen or twenty years old, you do not know what you do not know unless someone with experience tells you.

WHAT TO DO WITH YOUR TIME OFF

If you were not on some kind of watch or out on an ambush, many Marines played poker and watched their paychecks change hands. Poker not being my thing, I found myself helping out up in the OP (Observation Post), which was an elevated platform to better scan the area, looking for any signs of the enemy. The tower was equipped with a large Starlight Scope, also called a NOD (Night Observation Device), and this new technology turned night into day when you looked through the eyepiece.

Gooks* would sneak around our perimeter thinking they were invisible in the dark but the NOD could watch them picking their nose two

---

* *Gook is a derogatory term for Asians and is considered to be highly offensive. It was predominantly used by the US military during the Korean and Vietnam wars when referring to Communist soldiers.*

hundred yards away. You could see the confusion and terror in their face when a 60mm mortar would drop in their lap or when their buddy's head would explode as a result of a Marine sniper equipped with a similar NOD mounted scope.

I did not actually signup for a watch assignment at the OP but I would join whoever was on watch, shoot the shit, or keep watch while they got some chow and used the head. I especially enjoyed talking with the Foreword Artillery Observer (FO), Lieutenant Carolyn, and watching him call in mortars and artillery assignments when NVA** troops were spotted. He and I struck up a very nice friendship.

Hygiene

In any one of the numerous forward bases it was not unusual to go a month or longer between a shower or a bath.

At the "Washout" we were lucky to have a stream that ran straight through the middle of our compound. The stream provided a real perk for the Marines to wash cloths, bathe, and swim.

Gunny Sponenberg was always the wet blanket and warned us that the NVA were very good at what they did; a swim in the stream was always likely to bring in pinpoint artillery or mortar fire on our position. So to prevent a multicasualty incident, he made sure that only a few Marines could use the stream at any one time. No matter how much we bitched, he would just shout, "I don't give a fuck how bad you stink or how long it's been since you washed your balls. One round could get you all."

I can tell you from experience that after a month without a bath, it was worth the risk.

** *NVA refers to the North Vietnamese Army, which was the main enemy soldier that the Marines fought against in the Leatherneck Square and all of I Corps. The NVA were well trained, well equipped, and would fight to the death. Many Marines referred to them as Mr. Charles.*

Other names for the bad guys:

Vietcong or VC referred to the Communist-led insurgents and was not meant as an endearing term.

Charlie was another common name for the Communist-led insurgents.

A NEW ASSIGNMENT

On January 22, Delta Company chopped OPCON to the Ninth Marine Regiment (that's Marine talk for us being loaned to the Ninth Marines because they were short on manpower). We were loaded on trucks and headed off to Dong Ha.

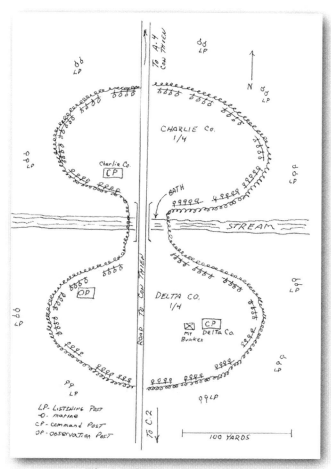

The Washout or C-2 Bridge
Charlie and Delta Companies
First Battalion/Fourth Marine Regiment
January 1968

C-2 Bridge site looking north, Charlie Company north of the bridge, Delta on this side, four-man shitter in the foreground (pardon my French). Bathing area just to the right of the bridge.

Delta Company Command Post at C-2 Bridge, left to right,
Lt. Muir, Captain Weede, and Cpl. Westenhaver

Radioman Bill Chastain on radio watch in the Delta Command
bunker at the C-2 Bridge. If this was the Command Bunker
can you imagine what the Grunts' bunkers looked like.

Six

THE TET OFFENSIVE

It is too late to whet the sword when the trumpet sounds.

—*AESOP'S FABLES, 1881*

A NEW MISSION

Our new mission working with the Ninth Marines was to conduct small-unit operations, including security for road sweeps going north up Route 1 from Dong Ha to Gio Linh and going west on Route 9 from Dong Ha to Cam Lo. The objective of a road sweep was to clear the roads of mines and foil any possible ambush so the roads could be opened for troop and supply trucks.

This operation took the better part of the morning because Marine engineers had to walk behind their metal detectors, similar to those used by hobbyists looking for coins at the beach, almost the entire nine miles. If the detector pinged on anything metallic, the engineer would have to probe the spot with a knife or other tool. I never got close enough to see exactly how he probed. If a mine were discovered, the engineer would have to uncover it, attach explosives, and then blow it up in place.

Delta Marines were not just standing around watching the engineers. They fanned out on both sides of the road in a V pattern where the arms of the V projected forward, out both sides of the road in front of the engineers. This formation was called "flankers" and would take the Marines behind any enemy lying along the roadside prior to the engineers ever reaching the kill zone of an ambush. For added protection, the sweeps were accompanied by two quad 50s or two M-42 Dusters. A quad 50 was a deuce-and-a-half truck with an antiaircraft turret in the bed. The turret was outfitted with four .50-caliber machine guns. A duster was a light-armored track vehicle that was mounted with two 40 mm cannons. The quad 50 and Duster were both designed for an antiaircraft role but had proved highly successful against ground forces.

The road sweep did not require the strength of the entire company, so the company was divided up to provide the security for the sweep of both Route 1 and Route 9 at the same time.

There was much more local traffic on Route 1, and the road was busy with people going about their lives. Men on scooters went in many directions, and women with six-foot poles on their shoulders carried large woven rice baskets at each end as they trotted to and from local markets. Many times a mama-san would approach us with her sick or injured child, and I would hold a quick sick call on the side of the road. I started carrying extra medical gear and medicines to meet their needs. On several occasions, I used the interpreter to advise the mother to meet our sweep the next day, and I would have the medicine that she needed. That evening I would discuss the case with our Battalion surgeon and return the next day with the treatment. In the big scheme of things, it was insignificant. But for me, it was pure satisfaction.

Near the end of January, Delta Company had been on the road sweep assignment for about a week. One of the big advantages of this mission was spending our nights at the base at Dong Ha, where we got hot showers, hot food, fresh new jungle utilities, and best of all, a full night's sleep with no LPs, no ambushes, and no guard duty for the Marines or radio watch for me.

HEAVEN CUT SHORT

Intelligence reports warned of large concentrations of enemy troops sighted around Khe Sanh, Camp Carroll, and along Route 9. January 1968 had been a relatively quiet month. Those with more time in country were saying that it was too quiet—something was coming. The Tet lunar New Year holiday, traditionally a time for celebration for the Vietnamese population, was January 31. Both North and South agreed to a thirty-six-hour cease-fire starting on the twenty-ninth. The cease-fire did not include the Marines in I Corps because of the recent intelligence and low expectations that the truce would even hold.

Delta Company 1/4 would continue to provide road sweeps but would end the day providing nighttime protection for the Combined Action Companies (CAC) on Route 9. A CAC unit was a small thirteen-member Marine rifle squad with one Navy Corpsman placed in a village or hamlet. Together with the local residents, they would form a village defense Platoon to deny the enemy a safe sanctuary at the local level and protect the villagers from Viet Cong terrorists. With the buildup of enemy troops in the area, it was feared these units would be easy targets for the enemy to overrun and claim a propaganda victory over the Marines. We were there to prevent that from happening.

The Delta Company Command Group with the First and Third Platoons took up residence at CAC-3 about two miles east of Cam Lo, while the Second Platoon would continue to work out of Dong Ha and provide road sweep security up Route 1.

The CAC-3 outpost was designed for thirteen Marines and a Corpsman and was now playing host to an additional two rifle Platoons and the Company Command Group. The hot meals, showers, and cots were now gone, replaced by C Rations,* the clothes on your back, and sleeping in the dirt.

---

* *C Rations—The Meal, Combat, Individual (MCI) was the Vietnam version of the World War II C-Ration and we continued to refer to them as "C-Rats." The meal came in a cardboard carton that contained one canned meat item; a canned bread item composed of crackers and a small flat can containing a cheese or peanut butter spread; one canned fruit or dessert item. An accessory*

The compound was so small that the Marines literally stood shoulder to shoulder around the perimeter. Captain Weede lost no time in getting his Marines busy improving the fortifications.

Several more rows of concertina barbed wire were added around the entire perimeter. It was so thick it appeared as a brown haze when you attempted to peer through. Command-detonated claymore mines, tangle foot, and rolls of barbed wire packed with blocks of C-4 explosives graced all the approaches. The Artillery Officer plotted prearranged artillery strikes that would provide a wall of exploding metal fragments at least a hundred yards wide before the enemy even got close to our first strand of wire.

It came as no surprise that on the night of January 29, the Tet truce was broken in I Corps by a massive attack on the city of Da Nang followed the next day by attacks on the ancient capital city of Hue and Quang Tri City. Large enemy unit battles raged throughout most of the major population centers across all of South Vietnam.

We now braced for the enemy to attack us, but Captain Weede had done such a great job at preparing our defensive position that the Delta Marines bristled with confidence.

At his regular evening briefing, Captain Weede introduced an idea to his staff, saying that he was contemplating having leaflets dropped into the nearby villages and countryside challenging the enemy to try attacking us. His logic was if they did not attack us, the NVA and VC would look like cowards to the local population. If they chose to attack us, we would kick their asses, and the enemy would "lose face" with the locals. In the Captain's mind it was a win for us either way the enemy chose. As I looked around the bunker, all I could see were the smiling faces of the officers and staff NCOs nodding in total agreement.

---

pack came with each meal and included salt, pepper, sugar, instant coffee, nondairy creamer, two pieces of Chiclets chewing gum, toilet paper, four cigarettes (Camel, Chesterfield, Kent, Kool, Lucky Strike, Marlboro, Paul Mall, Salem, or Winston), and a book of moisture-proof matches. A small can opener called a "John Wayne" or a "P-38" was used to open all the cans and was usually carried around your neck on your "dog tag" chain.

I sat there in shock and thought, "*Have you all lost your fucking minds? Do you know there IS a third possible outcome to this scenario?*" But then I remembered I was the only Navy puke in the room.

Trouble in Paradise

All around Leatherneck Square signs and sightings began to grow. At 3:25 p.m. on February 1, Charlie Company 1/4 received only one round from a Russian 82 mm mortar that landed right in the bathing point at the C-2 Bridge site and wounded fifteen Marines. I could not help thinking about Gunny Sponenberg limiting the number of Delta Marines who could swim and bathe at any one time. I guess he was not as big a hard ass as we thought. All boys need some adult supervision, and the Gunny was ours.

On that same afternoon, the CAC units reported observing that the locals did not return to the fields after their midday break, and the usual civilian traffic in and around the villages was nonexistent. Whatever the enemy was planning, it was going to happen soon.

Captain Weede was called to a meeting back at Dong Ha where the Army Major, who was the senior officer at the Cam Lo District Headquarters, expressed his concerns about an impending attack on the District Headquarters that very night. He was requesting assistance from the Marines.

At the conclusion of the meeting, it was decided that Delta Company would be tasked to provide reinforcements for the protection of the District Headquarters. Upon the Captain's return, we loaded up two squads from the First Platoon and a machine gun squad along with the two quad 50s and engineers from the road sweep and sent them off west on Route 9 to bolster the defenses at the Cam Lo District Headquarters.

Just prior to dusk, the artillery officer completed his night defensive firing around our perimeter at CAC-3. I crawled into my bunker, choked down a can of C-rations, and attempted to get some sleep before my 4:00 a.m. radio watch. At about 2:30 a.m. on February 2, I awoke quickly to the sound of rifle and machine gun fire, mortar fire, and artillery bursts outside my bunker. I just knew the enemy was in the process of redeeming our hides for the leaflets that Captain Weede must have dropped. I donned my flack jacket and pistol, grabbed my Unit One (medical bag), and crawled out. As soon as I stood up, I realized that the sounds of battle were coming from somewhere else.

Westy, who was already up and ready, looked over to me and said, "Cam Lo is under a ground attack from a large NVA force."

Holy shit! I thought, *"That is Doc Schindeler and the First Platoon."* All the Marines in our compound were at their posts and ready. Our 60 mm mortar crew was firing illumination rounds to light up the outside of our perimeter in anticipation of an imminent attack on our location.

THE BATTLE OF CAM LO

Two squads from First Platoon Delta 1/4 defended the Cam Lo compound. They included a Delta machine gun squad, a squad from Echo 2/9, the two Army quad 50s, the Marine engineers from the road sweep team, a CAC Squad of Marines, a few US Army Advisers, and some Popular Force and ARVN soldiers of South Vietnam (slightly less than fifty US Forces).

At around 1:30 a.m., the First Platoon Squad Leader, Cpl. Tim Russell, caught a faint smell of marijuana in the air and figured that it just might be the enemy smoking a little courage prior to an attack. Tim quickly woke his entire squad and got them ready for what he thought was about to happen. Tim and his Marines did not have to wait long to confirm his hunch.

The Cam Lo District Headquarters started receiving heavy incoming rounds from rockets, mortars, and recoilless rifles at 2:15 a.m. During the opening moments of the attack, the Command Post (CP) was struck by a recoilless rifle round, killing the senior US adviser, Army Major James C. Payne, as he was attempting to call for artillery support. The explosion also disabled the main communications with the outside world. The two

Army quad 50s guarding the east and west gates into the compound were also knocked out without getting off a single shot.

At 2:30 a.m., the enemy launched an initial ground attack against the southern perimeter near the motor pool. Protecting this area was the road sweep crew consisting of the Marine engineers and transport drivers, Army security, and the ARVN Regional Forces. The gooks initially penetrated the perimeter but were successfully driven back. These Army Soldiers and Marine Grunts were able to hold off the bad guys while dealing with the burning vehicles in the motor pool and the exploding ammo from the two destroyed quad 50s on both of their flanks. And they could still hear the screams of one of their own as he burned to death in the quad 50 wreckage after a failed rescue attempt.

LEADERSHIP HAS NOTHING TO DO WITH RANK

At 3:00 a.m., the main enemy attack was launched against the north and west perimeters. Corporal Russell, the First Squad leader responsible for protecting the western perimeter, had been temporarily knocked unconscious and suffered fragmentation wounds to his arms and legs from an enemy rocket during the initial moments of the attack. Within seconds, Corporal Russell was back on his feet, refusing treatment for his wounds so he could control and direct the fire of his Marines against the assaulting enemy forces. Tim was constantly moving throughout the fire-swept area, directing the fire of his squad and encouraging his men. At one point, the enemy penetrated a portion of the western perimeter, which threatened the Marine defenses, Tim directed his squad to not only hold the line but mounted a counterattack that forced the enemy to withdraw while taking thirty-eight prisoners.

THE ONLY EYE IN THE SKY

An observation tower was located directly behind the western perimeter and had a commanding view of the battlefield. Delta First Platoon Lt.

Michael Stick, a Marine armed with an M-79 grenade launcher, and a Radioman fearlessly exposed themselves to the intense enemy fire. They climbed to the top of the forty-foot tower so Stick could more effectively observe the enemy's movements and direct his men in the defense of the compound. Although suffering from fragmentation wounds to his hip, he remained in this precarious position and continued to shout instructions to his Grunts holding the line, all while the grenadier launched over eight hundred small bombs from his M-79.

As if he had nothing better to do, Corporal Russell further exposed himself by climbing the tower several times to provide ammo resupply to Lieutenant Stick and his men.

THE ULTIMATE SACRIFICE WAS MADE

Cpl. Larry Maxam, a Fire Team Leader from the Third Squad, First Platoon, observed the enemy massing for an assault into the compound through a gap in the northeast defensive line created by the retreating South Vietnamese Popular Forces. Corporal Maxam unhesitatingly proceeded to the open section of the perimeter, sustaining multiple fragmentation wounds from exploding grenades. Reaching an abandoned machine gun position, he commenced to deliver murderous fire upon the advancing enemy.

Corporal Maxam's position received a direct hit from a rocket-propelled grenade (RPG), knocking him backward, and inflicting severe fragmentation wounds to his face and right eye. Although momentarily stunned, he continued to deliver withering machine gun fire, causing the enemy to retreat back through the defensive wire. In a desperate attempt to silence his weapon, the enemy deployed a recoilless rifle against his position, wounding him two additional times. Too weak to reload his machine gun, Corporal Maxam fell to a prone position and continued to deliver effective fire with his rifle. After one and a half hours, during which he was wounded numerous times from grenades, rocket fragments, and rifle fire, he succumbed to his wounds, but not before he had successfully defended nearly half the perimeter single-handedly.

A Doc making house calls

Doc Ted Schindeler was keeping himself busy, moving from one wounded Marine to the next. Treating wounded Marines was every Doc's passion, but these Marines were also Ted's friends. At one point, Ted removed his own flak jacket and helmet to cover a Marine in order to provide better protection from flying fragments while he treated his wounds. At another location, Ted was attempting to drag a wounded defender to safety. Once again, Corporal Russell showed up to lend a hand, and both of them were wounded by an exploding ordinance (it was the second wounding for Corporal Russell).

Ted was seen constantly running back and forth across the perimeter, through a hail of small-arms fire and exploding grenades and mortars. He was able to quickly treat and bandage many wounded Marines, allowing them to remain in their fighting positions and continue to deliver a heavy volume of fire against the assaulting enemy force.

Artillery finally enters the battle

Using a secondary radio, contact was finally established with a counter-mortar radar unit located just a few miles away at Camp Carroll. The radio operator at Camp Carroll could hear all the commotion coming from Cam Lo and was searching different channels in an attempt to listen in on all the action. Switching through the different radio frequencies, he got lucky and came across the frantic calls for help from the Cam Lo Army adviser. He offered his assistance. For the rest of the night, Lieutenant Stick, in the tower, provided targeting information to Army soldiers in the CP who then relayed the information to the radio operator at Camp Carroll, who then passed the information on to the anxiously waiting artillery batteries. Finally, after what seemed like an eternity, artillery rounds exploded across the battlefield, inflicting devastating losses to the enemy and turning the tide on the attackers.

After a five-hour slugfest, the enemy attempted to break off contact but the Marines were just getting their second wind. They advanced beyond their defensive perimeter and started taking prisoners. Even Doc Schindeler, wounded and armed with his World War II vintage M-1 carbine, joined his Marines and took prisoners of his own. The capture of these enemy soldiers would later prove to be of enormous value to the intelligence community.

THE REST OF DELTA CAME RUNNING

Before first light, Delta Company, at CAC-3, was up and ready to march on the Cam Lo District Headquarters and help our First Platoon Marines finish the fight. As soon and it was light enough to see, we took off, following minesweeping engineers and several tanks west on Route 9 toward Cam Lo. We closed the distance very quickly, and as we entered the area, I think we were all shocked to see enemy bodies still hanging on the barbed wire, lying inside the compound, and out across the fields as far as the eye could see. We were only on the ground for a few minutes when Captain Weede advised his officers that Delta Company, along with a reaction force from 2/9, planned to pursue the retreating enemy. They hoped to reengage and push them into a blocking force from C-3 that was waiting for the enemy to attempt to cross the Cam Lo River.

Delta Marines spread out in a single line, like you would if on a large quail hunt, and started a sweep, looking to flush out stragglers, weapons, and dead or wounded enemy soldiers. We had not gone very far when we came upon the first NVA soldier, who was hiding in a small clump of bushes. He was bent over in the fetal position and would not come out. Captain Weede called for the Vietnamese scout to try to get him to "Chieu Hoi" ("open arms"), a program of the South Vietnamese government that granted amnesty to NVA and VC defectors. Suddenly the enemy soldier stood up and threw a hand grenade, which struck the Captain in the side of the face and then fell to the ground. We all dove for cover, but it failed to go off. Gunny Sponenberg responded with buckshot at five yards from his Mossberg shotgun, which brought a rapid end to the confrontation.

At another clump of bushes, we discovered one more NVA soldier and he, too, refused to surrender. This time the Captain was not taking any chances. After several attempts to coax him out, a forty-five ton M-48 tank was ordered up, and it drove over the mound, which flatly put an end to the negotiations. This now very thin bad guy joined his compatriot on the back of the tank.

There were sporadic exchanges of rifle fire as we kept bumping into their rear guard. As we came to a tree line that opened into a clearing one hundred yards across, we were confronted with the possibility of a sniper who would fire on our position when we attempted to leave cover. Captain Weede gave the order that on his command we would all step out in the clear and start the march across the clearing. We were to watch for the muzzle flash of the sniper's rifle and then quickly return fire. Hopefully, we would lose only one of us in the exchange. Forty-five years later, I can still remember feeling the sniper's crosshairs burning into my chest as we marched across that clearing, just waiting for the impact of the bullet—but it never came.

As we moved on, we came across one wounded soldier hiding in a bush. He would not come out until one of our Marines hit him hard with the butt of his rifle and dragged him out. The enemy soldier pointed to a bullet wound in his leg, and my natural Corpsman instinct took over. I moved forward, swinging my Unit One around to access the battle dressings, when a Marine put his arm across my chest and said, "Doc, don't even think about treating this bastard." Seeing a dull rage in the Marine's eyes, you bet your ass I complied with his wishes. With that, the enemy was hogtied and thrown on the back of a tank with other enemy soldiers.

Delta Company continued to push the enemy into the waiting arms of the reaction units from C-3, on the south side of the Cam Lo River, where the Marines routed the retreating enemy. Additionally, the reaction force of Alpha 1/4, responding from C-2, engaged the remaining

NVA who had managed to get across the river in their exodus north, and they completed wiping out and mopping up the rest.

Toward midafternoon, we were ordered to break off the pursuit, and we returned to Cam Lo with several prisoners in tow. While we were out hunting bad guys, the Marine engineers had been busy digging a mass grave for the enemy. The grave was the size of a large swimming pool and the bodies had filled it to overflowing. They had to drive the dozers over the bodies to compact them enough to fit into the hole. I guess I am not surprised that the pictures I took of the event did not make it back from being developed.

Delta Company was loaded on several deuce and a halfs in a convoy heading east on Route 9 toward Dong Ha. As the convoy was pulling out, the Cam Lo Headquarters and village started receiving a barrage of mixed rocket and artillery fire (about seventy rounds in total). The initial rounds hit about 250 yards north of our position and started walking in toward us. Thank God the drivers did not wait to receive additional orders to move their asses a little faster because the entire convoy moved out quite briskly. I looked back and could see that the Cam Lo Headquarters and village were taking a beating. Old men, women, and children poured out from the village into the surrounding fields as the enemy shells pounded their homes. I sat back in the truck and thought, *"It must suck to be a peasant in a war zone."*

At about that same time, Alpha Company 1/4 at C-2 received sixty rounds of mixed ordinance, including 152 mm artillery (that is some big scary shit). It seems the NVA were poor losers, kind of like crosstown high school football rivals, where the home team got its ass kicked so bad the only thing they could do was throw shit at the visitors' busses as they were leaving the stadium.

AFTER ACTION

The NVA attacked the Cam Lo District Headquarters with two Battalions of NVA plus a sapper company (Combat Engineers), one thousand to fourteen hundred soldiers in all.

The US forces totaled fewer than fifty defenders.

Unlike our compound at CAC-3, the officers at the Cam Lo were not allowed to prepare their compound for the possible ground attack by programming night defensive artillery fire because of the proximity of the Cam Lo village and Civilian Relocation Camp. The communication failure further hampered the effectiveness of artillery until later in the battle.

Then there was the problem of a low cloud ceiling that night that prohibited the use of aerial assets such as "Puff the Magic Dragon."

There was some talk that the NVA might have infiltrated the local Popular Forces (PFs) and ARVNs that were located inside the compound, and they might have sabotaged the early efforts of the defenders. That could help explain why the NVA never attacked the eastern perimeter of the compound where the PFs were supposed to defend prior to their defection.

The final figures for the battle of Cam Lo vary from source to source, but the enemy losses were estimated to be as high as two hundred forty-four dead and fifty-three prisoners captured, I don't believe that counted the NVA killed near the Cam Lo River during their retreat.

The US forces sustained casualties of seven KIA and fourteen WIA.

Captain Weede stated later that he never dropped any leaflets. He did not need to because the battle of Cam Lo became one of the most lopsided ass-kickings of the Vietnam War. The local population saw it, and the North Vietnamese Army felt what it was like to fuck with the US Marine Corps. Pardon my French.

A TRIBUTE TO A FEW HEROES
Cpl. Larry L. Maxam, USMC, received the Purple Heart and the MEDAL OF HONOR posthumously for his actions that night. **Larry is honored on the Vietnam Veterans Memorial, Panel 36E, Row 78.**

Cpl. Timothy Russell, USMC, received the Purple Heart and the Navy Cross (the nation's second-highest combat award). After his service with the USMC, Corporal Russell went on to serve the City of Cleveland, Ohio, as a police officer. You will read more about this Hero later.

Lt. Michael O. Stick, USMC, received the Purple Heart and the Silver Star. I was advised during my research that Lieutenant Stick became Michael O. Stick, MD, after his service with the Marines. God Bless Lieutenant Stick for his superior leadership during the Battle of Cam Lo.

Theodore K. Schindeler, Corpsman, US Navy, received a Purple Heart and the Silver Star. When you read the official phrasing of Ted's Silver Star Award, it talks about Ted advancing beyond the defensive perimeter to treat and capture injured enemy soldiers. What I know is that Ted was almost more Marine than he was a Doc. He may have in fact patched up some of their wounded but he was there to capture them along with his fellow Marines. Ted was one of the bravest and most competent Corpsman I ever had the pleasure to work with. Just his presence on the battlefield made you want to push yourself a little harder.

You will not find Ted Schindeler's name on the Vietnam Veterans Memorial, but the war did finally claim his life. Ted took his own life on December 19, 1998.

TED'S DAUGHTER LEFT A MESSAGE FOR HER DAD ON AN INTERNET WEB PAGE.

Ted Schindeler left behind his mother, father, sisters, and brothers (a twin brother). He was a husband and a father of four children. He did not live to see his first grandchild—born twenty-seven days after his death. He lost his battle with his flashbacks of Vietnam. Memories that made him an insomniac for over thirty years. Unable to handle relationships, responsibility…fatherhood.

I am not angry with him. I miss him, although I did not know him. He left when I was eight. Fatherhood carried with it too much stress. I wish I knew more about him. I wish he knew more about me. I wish he met his first grandchild. I know he is finally at peace. Rest in Peace, Dad. I love you, your daughter."

My heart sank when I read this. I have prayed for Ted and his family many times. I hope you will also. For some things in life, there just are not any words.

There were many more Heroes in the Battle of Cam Lo, including another Navy Cross, two more Silver Stars, and many Bronze Stars. Almost everyone there was wounded and received purple hearts, but the four I mentioned above are personal to me.

THE ENEMY OFFENSIVE CONTINUED

Even after their staggering losses on February 2, the enemy did not hold back. All the bases in Leatherneck Square continued to observe enemy movement and absorb constant incoming rounds. Both C-2 and the bridge were constantly receiving rocket fire as well as mixed caliber artillery impacting inside the perimeters.

On February 4, C-2 received seventy rounds in seven minutes. These artillery rounds included air bursts meant for troops in the open as well as delayed fuses meant for troops in the bunkers.

When you are in a fixed position like C-2 and receiving incoming artillery, a Marine rifleman is just about useless. The only thing that will stop the enemy from firing artillery on your position is to launch counter-artillery fire that drives the enemy into their bunkers. I have been in a bunker, praying for the artillery to stop, and the only thing to stop them was the Marine artillery that was returning fire. Watching a Marine artillery battery return fire was like watching a well-trained NASCAR pit crew at Daytona. The biggest difference was that no one shoots at the pit crew while they change tires. These glorious and Heroic Marines could identify the location of the enemy artillery, set a fire mission, and return fire in three to five minutes. Not sure what it is today, but back in 1968, that was amazing. It is worth mentioning again that this was done all while receiving incoming rounds on their position. Talk about Heroes!

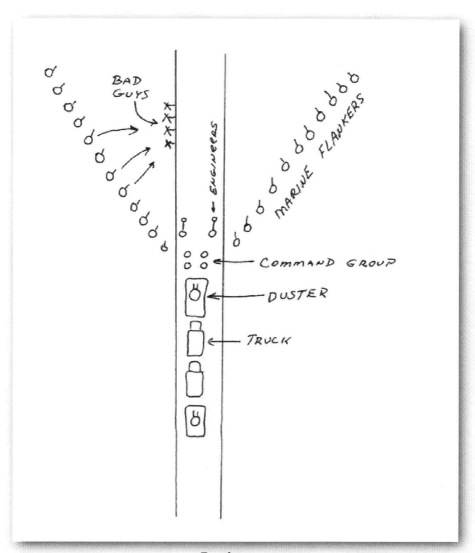

Road sweep
protecting the flanks with the
deployment of flankers

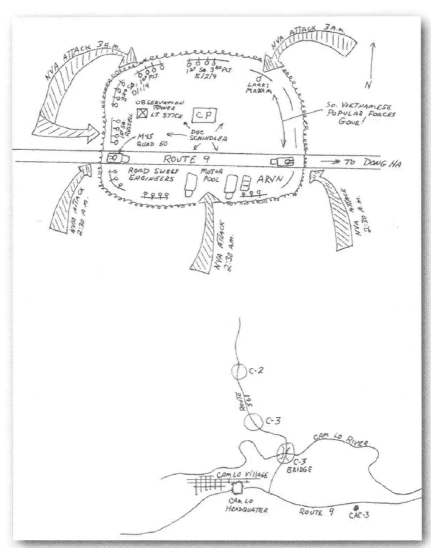

The battle of Cam Lo District Headquarters
February 2, 1968, at 2:15 a.m.

Seven

A Sleepover with Strangers

Failure is not falling down but refusing to get up.
—*Robert A. Schuller*

My First Ambush

On February 4, a Platoon from the Ninth Marines came into CAC-3 just prior to dusk. One of their Docs had a bad chest cold and a cough; he could not go on their ambush that night. The Platoon Lieutenant asked Captain Weede if they could exchange one of our Docs for theirs. I had been with Delta Company for two weeks and had not had a chance to be with a small-unit ambush or patrol. I asked Captain Weede if I could take the ambush and give my Corpsman the night off. He seemed delighted that I wanted to volunteer and granted my request. Don't think for a minute it was gallant of me; I really hoped to see some action.

I quickly applied camo paint to my face, grabbed my Unit One bag, and reported to the Lieutenant. He explained that he, the Radioman, and I would position ourselves in the middle of the Platoon as we walked single file west on Route 9. This way, depending on the need, we could move easily in either direction along the line of Marines to coordinate the action or treat the wounded. After about a half mile, we left the road and quietly followed the point man on a trail that went for another quarter mile. Then we went on to a third trail, where we stopped and moved into the thick ground cover about fifteen yards to the side of the trail. Several Marines placed claymore mines[*] along the trail, led the control wire back to our position, and settled in.

I was so excited that I never slept that entire night. My hearing was hypersensitive to every little noise that the jungle made. I was lying next to the Radioman and could hear the Command Post ask if we were "cooling off." I chuckled to myself with satisfaction knowing now what it was like to be on both ends of the radio communications. I was not an old salt by any means, but I felt like my learning curve was straight vertical. Soon all I could hear was the constant buzz of mosquitoes in my ears, very small creatures invading my trousers looking for a new homestead, and the snoring of the Marines all along the line. I thought, *For Christ's sakes, the gooks will hear the snoring a hundred yards away.* Those on watch kept nudging the others to quiet them down, and I joined in with the Marines I could reach.

Soon the first light from a new day was upon us. It was time to collect our weapons and head back to CAC-3. All we had to show for the night's work were dozens of mosquito bites plus a few larger welts in places where the mosquitoes did not have access. God only knows what other critters were lurking in the dark.

Even though we did not make contact with the enemy, I felt very good about making another baby step toward the understanding of my new normal.

DOCS COWAN AND FERGUSON EARN THEIR KEEP

I had just gotten back to CAC-3 when we heard our Second Platoon on the radio reporting that their road sweep was under heavy small arms, automatic weapons, RPGs, and mortar fires. The Platoon Commander

---

* *Claymore Mine—A command-detonated antipersonnel mine filled with seven hundred steel balls pressed into C-4 plastic explosive. When detonated, the devise shot out the steel balls like a giant shotgun blast. The claymore was used when setting up an ambush or as a defensive weapon around a night perimeter.*

reported that he had several Marines down, one deuce and a half was destroyed, and both Dusters had been damaged. He was requesting a medevac for the wounded and additional reinforcements.

Moments later, a relief force from the Ninth Marines with Dusters and one tank responded, and a second relief force was mounted from the 3/4 rear area at Dong Ha. As the Ninth Marines reached the road sweep, they also came under heavy fire as they attempted to move up on the bad guys. Then several Huey Gunships came on station, providing aerial reconnaissance, machine gun, and rocket fire on enemy positions. The elements from 3/4 also arrived and commenced their engagement with the enemy. After a four-hour firefight, outgunned and being outmaneuvered, the enemy broke contact and retreated into the jungle, dragging their dead and wounded with them. Docs Cowan and Ferguson treated and stabilized four wounded Delta Company Marines and medevaced them out, the two damaged Dusters were retrieved, and the one destroyed deuce and a half was left at the scene.

MORE FRIENDLY FIRE

Later in the afternoon, an air-to-surface missile impacted Alpha 1/4 at C-2, killing one Marine and destroying the radar instillation. Fragments collected made a positive ID that the missile was shot from a US jet fighter thinking that our radar was a Russian antiaircraft missile site.

AN ENCOUNTER WITH BAD GUYS

Also on the morning of February 5, Doc Livingston and Doc Walker from the Third Platoon hitched a ride to Dong Ha to take the HM-3 exam (Navy term for Corporal) and wouldn't return until the next morning. The entire Third Platoon was scheduled to go on an ambush that evening, and they were even taking a 60 mm mortar squad with them.

Well now, being somewhat of an expert regarding an ambush and wanting to make a good impression on the Grunts in my own company,

I approached Captain Weede and volunteered my services for a second night in the bush, which he enthusiastically approved.

Toward dusk, I started my preparations. Having only a medical bag and a pistol to carry, I thought it would be very smart to ask the Marines if I could help lighten their burden. I first went to the machine gunners and requested to carry one two-hundred-round ammo can, which they gladly agreed to. Receiving such a warm reception, I thought it best to also ask the 60 mm mortar squad if I could help them. Again, receiving their gratitude, I took two mortar rounds from their cache. The machine gun ammo can and the two mortar tubes all came with slings attached, so I could easily carry them over my shoulder and keep my arms free. I returned to my bunker, applied my camo paint, and checked my medical bag to ensure I had enough battle dressings. I did not need to check my pistol because I had come up with a foolproof system that eliminated the pesky need for constant cleaning.

Back at the C-2 Bridge, I had watched my bunker mate Jimmy Howe meticulously clean his weapons every night. I, on the other hand, was way too busy to be bothered with such a mundane task. After much thought, I came up with an amazing solution. I would give my pistol one very thorough cleaning, and then I wrapped it in an oil-soaked sandbag and covered it all with a plastic bag. Now, I would never need to clean my gun again.

I know what you are thinking. *"A pretty clever boy!"*

The one drawback to this amazing invention was the bulk that it created. The pistol would not fit into my holster without a great amount of force required to get the cover snapped. When I finished, I looked over at Jimmy, fully expecting to see an expression of amazement. Instead, he took one look, shook his head in disbelief, and went back to cleaning his rifle. I thought to myself, *"After a little more field testing, he will certainly see the benefits."*

OK, BACK TO MY STORY.
Now that all systems were a go, I slung my Unit One medical bag over my shoulder, along with the extra ammo, and I was instantly surprised at the

weight and bulk of all this equipment. It was too late to change my mind now; I would just have to live with it.

As dusk turned to darkness, the Third Platoon of Delta Company formed up and prepared to leave the compound. I was looking for Lieutenant Berkery and his Radioman, Cpl. Dave Brennan, toward the middle of the line of Marines, when I heard the Lieutenant shout, "Hey, Doc, come up front with me." I moved to the Lieutenant's position, where he informed me that he liked to walk point and wanted me just behind his Radioman in the third position. With only one ambush under my belt, who am I to argue with a Lieutenant on where I should position myself?

As we entered Route 9, walking toward Cam Lo, the Platoon was divided with equal numbers of Marines walking on both sides of the roads. As a new arrival, with no experience, I was amazed at how much noise we made as we scuffed along on the gravel road. The moon was not full, but it was bright enough to see the Marines on the right side of the road peel off, and they were gone. A few minutes later they reappeared. Having a quick mind, I quickly surmised that they left and were back in an effort to throw off the enemy as to where we were going to insert the ambush. A few minutes later, my theory was confirmed as my side also left the road, went down a small foot trail for a hundred yards, and then reappeared back on Route 9 next to the other column of Marines. I was overjoyed with just how enlightened I had been with my observations, and I was just living the dream of a Marine Doc.

We continued this leaving and coming back diversion for another quarter mile or so, and then the entire platoon moved off Route 9, to the left, went down a small trail for about twenty-five yards, and stopped. At this time, Staff Sargent Youmans took one squad with mortars and positioned themselves along the trail. Lieutenant Berkery and the rest of us continued down this moonlit trail to establish the major ambush site for the night.

Lieutenant Berkery was on point; the Radioman, Dave Brennan, was second; I was third in line; and the rest of the Marines followed. We had gone only about fifty yards when I heard someone speak Vietnamese off to my left. Dave Brennan turned to me, his eyes wide, and asked, "Did you hear that?" As I shook my head in agreement, the Lieutenant stepped back and asked why we had stopped. Brennan advised the Lieutenant of what we heard, but he quickly overruled our concerns with an order to move forward.

We moved on across the moonlit field to where hedgerows lined both sides of the trail about eight feet high and six feet apart. As we started down through the hedgerow, I could see the figure of a man crouched down at the other end, only fifteen yards ahead. The Lieutenant turned to Dave and me, and with his finger over his lips, gave us the sign that your mother gave when she wanted you to be still just prior to a surprise.

I quickly surmised that this must be a meeting between us and ARVNs (South Vietnamese Army) where we were going to sit in and slaughter the enemy; otherwise, why would the Lieutenant be so relaxed and unconcerned with his actions? I could not wait to move forward with the Lieutenant and be involved with the discussion on just how our ambush would be laid out. I thought, "*If my friends back home could see me now.*"

Lieutenant Berkery, now hovering over the sleeping soldier, again gave us the mother's quiet sign. Dave Brennan moved close to the Lieutenant, and I moved close to Dave, not wanting to miss any of the dialogue. My smile of anticipation quickly turned to shock as the Lieutenant gave a hardy downward thrust of his M79 grenade launcher onto the soldier's helmet. The immediate reaction was a shower of bullets from the startled man's AK-47. The arc of the bullets sent Lieutenant Berkery and the Radioman, Brennan, flying backward into the hedgerow. As I felt the flash and heat from the bullets move ever so close over and across my head, I also fell backward against the hedge.

Now it was silent. Not a single Marine made a move or a sound. I checked myself for injuries and found none. I laid there for what seemed like an eternity as I contemplated my final moments prior to the enemy taking my life. I thought to draw my pistol to at least defend myself in my final moments, but I could not pull the snap loose on the holster because of the bulky plastic bag and sandbag that I had wrapped my gun in. I had a quick flashback to Jimmy Howe shaking his head in disbelief at my new invention and then thought, "*OK, I get it now!*"

Every time I made the slightest move, the machine gun ammo can rattled to announce my current position. I was absolutely overwhelmed and useless, and then I heard the familiar yell of a Drill Instructor's voice that shocked me back into the reality of the moment. Staff Sergeant Youmans had come forward with his squad, which was positioned near Route 9. The Sergeant gave the order to return fire in the assumed direction of the enemy and ordered four Marines forward to carry the Lieutenant back to the rice paddy, on the other side of Route 9, to regroup.

As the Marines opened fire, I started my assessment of the Radioman's injuries. I looked under his blood-soaked shirt and discovered that a large portion of his shoulder was missing. Seeing my first battle wound, which looked nothing like the fake rubber wounds I practiced on, I let out an uncontrolled "Holy fuck!" Dave looked up at me and asked, "Is it bad, Doc?" Getting control of myself, I answered, "Nah, it's not too bad" (as if I knew what I was talking about). Dave also had a massive gut wound with his intestines trying to escape through the opening. Sergeant Youmans yelled at me to pull back, and I advised him that I would just as soon as I finished applying the bandages.

The Sergeant responded with a shorter version of his first order and yelled, "I said NOW!" He followed this with a quick but firm kick to my ass, which raised me to my feet. Complying with his order, I ran next to Dave, trying to assist him while holding his intestines in.

The entire Platoon pulled back across Route 9 into the rice paddy, where the standing water was about a foot deep and full of cow manure and God only knows what else. I helped Dave lie down and attempted to hold his intestines behind a large battle dressing, which I secured around his waist. I administered an injection of morphine to dull his pain. At that time, the machine gunner came over to us and said, "Dave, you got your ticket home. Doc, you are wanted over there to check out the Lieutenant."

I quickly moved to Lieutenant Berkery and knelt next to his head to assess his vital signs. Finding none, I advised the Marine positioned at the Lieutenant's chest to start CPR. As I started to ventilate, the first compression came at the same time and forced the Lieutenant's blood back up through my mouth and out my nose. I sat up quickly and moved my head to the side in an effort to clear my mouth and nose, and I to quell the nausea that had overtaken me. I do not ever remember them mentioning this experience during the Resuscitation Anne classes in training. Several more attempts at compressions confirmed that the large hole in the Lieutenant's chest went clear through his heart, and he had died instantly.

Our Lieutenant was dead, and the Radioman was seriously injured. It would now take twelve Marines to carry the two bodies back down Route 9 to the relative safety of CAC-3. Sergeant Youmans again took charge and started the Platoon moving east.

Sergeant Youmans had the twelve Marines with the two bodies in the middle of the road and spread the rest of the Platoon out as flankers on both sides of the road to about fifty yards. The machine gunner took the point position on the road and started walking while spraying both sides of the road ahead with bullets in an effort to provoke an early reaction from the enemy, should they be lying in wait to ambush us. This tactic was called "recon by fire."

I positioned myself on the road next to Sergeant Youmans. No longer hampered by the weight of the extra ammo, I was able to exert enough pressure on my holster snap to force it open. I withdrew my pistol, removed the plastic bag and oil-soaked sandbag, and I gave them a disgusted heave to the side of the road. Holding the pistol in my hand, I thought to myself, "*What a dumb shit. If the enemy saw me, they would realize I was probably worth more to them alive than dead.*"

The walk back to the CAC-3 compound seemed to take forever; we were sure the enemy would reengage us now that we were so vulnerable to an attack. Luck was on our side, as we reached CAC-3 without further incident.

Captain Weede had already called for a medevac, and the chopper was sitting on Route 9 when we arrived. The Marines placed the wounded Radioman (Dave Brennan) and Lieutenant Berkery in the chopper and then stood back as the chopper lifted off. Lieutenant Berkery's Marines then snapped to attention, gave a hand salute, and said, "Good-bye, sir."

MICHAEL WAYNE BERKERY IS HONORED ON THE VIETNAM VETERANS MEMORIAL, PANEL 37E, ROW 31. SEMPER FI, LIEUTENANT!

I attempted to brief the Captain as to what I saw, but I could hardly talk given the excitement of the evening. Captain Weede put his hand on my shoulder and said, "Doc, try to get some sleep, and we will talk in the morning." I squeaked out a "Yes, sir" and crawled into my bunker completely exhausted.

Gone forever was the boyish vision and anticipated excitement of war. It was not at all like playing army in our front yards as kids, where we broke contact with the enemy to go eat dinner with the family. Nor was it as romantic and exciting as the stories my mom's boyfriend, Doc, told regarding the one-way ass-kicking of an ill-trained enemy in Korea. I lay on the ground, staring at the ceiling of my bunker, my uniform soaked in the dried blood of two Marines, and the taste of the Lieutenant's blood still lingering in my mouth. I could not stop seeing the muzzle flash from the enemy rifle and feeling the heat from the bullets just barely missing my head. I thought, *"I have eleven more months of this shit, if I am lucky."*

AFTER ACTION

The next morning, Captain Weede sent out a Platoon to the ambush site and found that the trail that we had taken made a Y split, where one trail went east, and one trail wandered in a westerly direction. As luck would have it, we had taken the westerly trail that led us behind the NVA ambush; we encountered only the rear guard.

Had we taken the east trail, it would have led us into the kill zone of a Platoon-size ambush, which would have forever changed my entire family's history, along with the histories of forty Marines.

I only had one night with these two Heroes, and then they were gone—but never forgotten. I contacted Radioman Dave Brennan while researching this book and found that he survived his wounds and went on to a full career with the Marine Corps, including a second tour in Vietnam.

I think of Lieutenant Berkery often. In my research, I discovered that the Headquarters brass had sent word out that they needed human intelligence and that every effort should be made to try to capture an enemy soldier alive for interrogation purposes. Given that order, it was most likely that Lieutenant Berkery was attempting to take the NVA soldier as a prisoner when he struck him on the head with his weapon. Whatever he was attempting to do, this brave and heroic Marine risked and ultimately gave his life for this country.

IT'S GREAT TO BE US

On February 9, we were moving west on Route 9, conducting our routine road sweep duties with one Platoon and Delta command. At around 8:30 a.m., the Marine flankers sprang an NVA ambush on the left side of the road. Small-arms fire was exchanged, and we started receiving enemy 60 mm mortar rounds.

Captain Weede closed the right flank of the V and started moving on the enemy, which forced the NVA to break from their position and retreat into the bush. The Captain formed the Platoon on line, and we gave chase. A few more shots were fired at the retreating enemy that resulted in several NVA killed. When we reached the bullet-riddled body, a debate ensued over just who actually shot him and which shot actually killed him. It was like watching hunters on opening day of dove season— they all wanted to claim the kill.

As we returned to the road sweep, Doc Schindeler had treated and medevaced one wounded Marine. The engineers had found two command-detonated mines and destroyed them in place.

OOPS, MISSED ONE

Over a three-day period, from February 13 to February 15, Charlie Company 1/4 relieved Delta on the road sweep mission. On the fifteenth, at the completion of our road sweep duties, Charlie Company arrived at CAC-3. While the brass were doing what they do, we Grunts hopped in the back of a deuce and a half for the leisurely ride back to the C-2 Bridge.

We instantly started a grab-ass session. I was listening to the Marines bust one another's balls. They were concentrating on one lanky, red-headed, freckle-faced Marine. Apparently, he came from a very rich family and the other Marines were kidding him as to his dumb-ass choice of winding up as a Grunt. It was the first time that I had ever heard of, or had ever seen, a Rolex watch like the one that Red was wearing. I could tell by the tone that everyone liked this Marine very much.

A loud BOOM interrupted the grab-ass session, and the front end of the truck was thrown up in the air. The truck was quickly emptied, and the Marines were spread out along the road and ready for action in a matter of seconds.

As the dust and smoke cleared, we could see that the right front tire was mangled from the explosion. A call went out for another deuce and a half and an engineer to find out what we had hit. A tow truck arrived and pulled our wounded truck back so the engineers could examine the site. A little probing revealed an undetonated antitank mine was still in the ground. Apparently, the detonator went off but failed to activate the main explosion that would surely have caused major casualties.

In just a few days I had experienced two very lucky near misses. We all hopped in the back of a new truck and picked up the grab-ass where we had left off.

JUST ANOTHER DAY AT THE OFFICE

At about 6:45 p.m. on February 16, a Huey Gunship was shot down, east of the C-2 Bridge, while attempting to extract a Marine Recon team. The Second Platoon/Bravo, from C-2, got the call to Sparrow Hawk (rapid deployment) to the crash site. As the Platoon approached the site, they came under heavy fire from small arms, machine guns, and grenades from three sides including from the vicinity of the gunship. The Platoon received one killed and four wounded and withdrew to a position 150 yards southeast of the downed helicopter and called for a flare ship to provide elimination for the entire night and 81mm mortars and artillery for defensive fire.

At 8:30 a.m. the next day, the Second Platoon advanced again and retrieved the body of their dead Radioman. By 9:10, they had reached the crash site. Upon arrival, they found four dead but miraculously found one crew member still alive. The area was secured, and a medevac chopper was called in to extract the five dead and five wounded Marines from the Platoon and downed gunship.

Two helicopter crewmen were still missing, and all of Bravo Company responded to join the search. The Second Platoon search party found another dead Marine from the gunship, which left only one more to find. Bravo Company now on scene with the Second Platoon, the search continued for the last missing Marine. Shortly after the search began again, Bravo Company made contact with an unknown-size enemy force receiving small-arms fire, machine gun, grenades, and mortar fire. Bravo returned fire and called in 81 mm mortars and artillery on the enemy positions, which caused the enemy to break contact.

The search continued, resulting in finding the last crash site victim alive. A medevac was called in and transported one happy rescued Marine and one more Bravo Company wounded. At 3:30 p.m., Bravo Company burned the helicopter wreckage and headed for home.

THE KILLER TEAM

Someone came up with the idea of a "Killer Team" patrol. These patrols were a specially tasked unit of volunteers (ten to fifteen Marines) led by an officer or an NCO. The mission was to search out the enemy on his own turf, utilizing observation positions and ambushes. They would stay out for several days and patrol day and night in hopes of finding the enemy.

Captain Weede asked for volunteers for the Killer Team deployment, and my bunker mate Jim Howe gladly volunteered. Lt. James Muir volunteered to lead the team, and all who were involved were glad that he did. Lieutenant Muir was from Tucson, Arizona, with a graduate degree from the University of Hawaii. He was the Delta Company XO (executive officer or second in command), and he was well liked, trusted by all the Marines, extremely intelligent, and had a lot of common sense. Lieutenant Muir chose the Killer Team call sign of "Kamehameha" in honor of the Hawaiian king who consolidated all of the islands into the Kingdom of Hawaii.

In the last week of February, just prior to first light, Lieutenant Muir led these brave Marines out of the wire and deep into never-never land.

The Killer Team patrolled all the first day with no enemy contact and then set up an ambush position for the night. During this time, I was in the Command bunker, helping man the radios. My bunker mate Jim was the Radioman on the Killer Team, and when I would call, "Kamehameha, Kamehameha, this is Smitty Delta. If you are cooling off, key your handset twice." The pause was only a second or two but agonizing until I heard the squelch sound twice. It was as if I could almost tell that it was Jim on the other end.

No contact was made during the first night, so Lieutenant Muir saddled up his Marines and started to patrol deep in enemy territory. At around 10:45 a.m., the team was moving southeast when the point man heard NVA voices and sounds of digging and chopping through the thick jungle foliage just ahead on the trail. The point man heard movement coming toward him. He motioned for the team to withdraw back to a bomb crater where they set up a hasty ambush. As the NVA soldiers broke through into the small clearing, ten yards to their front, the ambush was sprung. Noise indicated approximately fifteen NVA soldiers were caught in the ambush. The left flank of the ambush killed two NVA, the center killed two more, and large pools of blood and drag marks indicated at least two more kills. Cries and moans could be heard in the undergrowth in the kill zone.

Lieutenant Muir, realizing that the enemy now knew exactly where they were, had his Marines break contact and called in artillery to cover their withdrawal. The team moved as quickly as possible toward home, but always vigilant of a possible counterattack. It seemed like their trek took forever, and there was a lot of hand-wringing at the Command bunker, until I heard Jim announce on the radio that they were coming in.

Hell, that was fun, let's do it again!

Again, on February 28, a new Killer Team was assembled and would be led by S. Sgt. Dan Whyte. At the team briefing, Captain Weede cautioned Staff Sergeant Whyte to validate his target before opening fire because there might be a Marine Recon Tem in the area.

The team was gone for several days while I helped man the radios at the Company Command. Around 10:30 a.m. on March 2, the point man of the Killer Team observed one NVA twenty yards to his front in a fighting hole and motioned back to the team that he saw something up ahead. Staff Sergeant Whyte, wanting to make sure that it was not the Recon Team, moved up and whispered to the point man, asking if he had seen a Marine or a gook. The young Marine was so frightened that he could not speak. Frustrated, Staff Sergeant Whyte slapped the Marine on the side of his helmet and asked again. This time the point man took his fingers and pulled on the side of his eyes so he looked like an Asian.

That is all Staff Sergeant Whyte needed to see. He quickly put the team on line and gave the order to move forward. They broke through the foliage into the clearing with guns blazing. They caught men still in their hammocks strung between trees; others were shot down as they ran in all directions. Within moments, it was all over. It was not until the shooting stopped that they discovered that it was a makeshift hospital. Ten NVA medical personnel were killed. The team quickly picked up what intelligence they could carry and withdrew before reinforcements could arrive. Artillery was called in to cover their withdrawal, and the team headed for home without further contact.

CAN WAR BE MONOTONOUS?

From the end of February to the first week in March, the activity became the same old thing. Killer Teams from the other Companies were having similar successes as Delta, the usual incoming rounds causing the usual wounded, some kind of roasted beef, many of the FNGs with the shits, LPs, ambushes, etc.

SOME BAD NEWS

Rumors had been floating around Delta and the rest of the Battalion, that 1/4 would be the next Battalion to rotate into Con Thien. During the first week in March, the rumors turned to truth, and we were ordered to pack our shit because we were moving to the "Place of Angels." Many of the senior Delta Marines had spent time there before, only now they were short timers (time in Vietnam was almost up), and they were not looking forward to this being their last assignment.

Stories abounded of NVA ground attacks, being overrun, hand-to-hand combat, and constant artillery bombardments to which the veterans all confirmed. Con Thien was one of those places that songs and books would be written about, but you were not sure you wanted to be part of the lyrics.

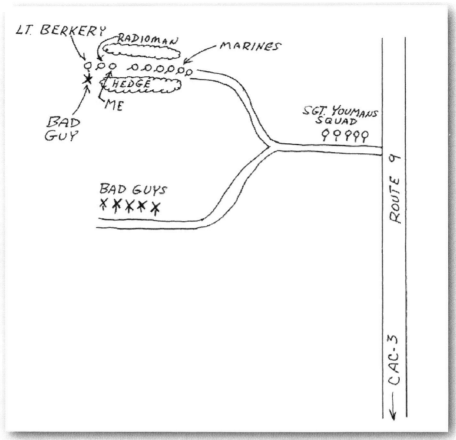

The encounter with bad guys

Me in front of my home at CAC-3. This was the aid station in the event of an attack. OK, I borrowed the hand grenade to look tough for the picture.

Eight

THE HISTORY OF CON THIEN BEFORE MY ARRIVAL

*Be quick in occupying the raised and sunny spots before
the enemy, and carefully guard your line of supplies.
Then you will be able to fight with advantage.*

—*SUN TZU*

THE MARINES ARRIVE AT THE "PLACE OF ANGELS"

When you look directly north from the C-2 Bridge, about a mile and a half, you could see the relative flat landscape gently give way to the rise of a small prominence labeled on military maps as Nui Con Thien. This little hill had been the center of many bloody battles, dating back to when the famed French Foreign Legionnaires built the first concrete fort to exploit the high ground and keep watch over the once lush French colonial plantations. The rich red soil, tropical weather, and cheap labor were perfect for growing rubber trees, pineapples, rice, coffee, tea, bananas, and spices.

When the fighting became untenable, the French colonialists returned to the safety of France, with their riches in tow, leaving the Vietnamese people to the village life that they had known for many generations. French trained Vietnamese Catholic priests and nuns remained behind to tend the churches, missions, schools, and hamlets of the predominately Catholic flock that surrounded Nui Con Thien.

After the French, the South Vietnamese Army (Army of the Republic of Vietnam, ARVN) took command of Con Thien and installed land mines to protect their perimeter. In February 1967, the US Army Special Forces took possession and improved the protection by adding more barbed wire, bunkers, and fighting holes with connecting trenches. Big Army guns were moved in to shell the NVA positions in North Vietnam. They were quickly answered by two months of constant mixed artillery, mortar, and rocket fire by the bad guys, causing the Army to withdraw their guns. Apparently, the Army experiment did not go as planned; in April 1967, the decision was made to turn the hill over to the Marine Corps.

The name Nui Con Thien has no exact translation into English, and most books use the translation of the tiny hill as "The Hill of Angels," which is probably the most correct. There are actually three hills in the complex, and it is not clear how they got the name or why. There is some thought that the locals named the elevation "The Hill or Place of Angels" because of all the deaths that have occurred there over the years. Maybe it was because there were so many calls for forgiveness and mercy from the occupants who stood watch over the hills.

The Marines had several other names—the Meat Grinder, Camp Hell, the Alamo, etc. However, most Grunts prefer the name posted on the front door, "The Place of Angels."

As hills go, Con Thien was certainly not impressive. Rising only about 150 feet above the surrounding landscape, you could not appreciate its military significance until you were on top, and then it became obvious. From the observation post on the crest of the Angels, you could see fifteen miles in all directions. With magnification you could see well into North Vietnam. Looking east, you could see to the ocean, west to the mountains, and south all of Leatherneck Square and the large Marine base at Dong Ha. It was apparent to anyone who stood there that the Place of Angels would need to be held if the Marines were going to have any presence in northern I Corps, and that presence would cost the Marines dearly.

In April 1967, the Marines were ordered to start construction on the first phase of the controversial "Trace" or "McNamara's Line" (code named Dyemarker) that was to be a bare swath of land six hundred yards wide and six miles long, extending from Strong Point A-4 (Con Thien) in the west to Strong Point A-2 (Gio Linh) in the east. This bare strip would allow the observation post at Con Thien to see all the way to Gio Linh and spot the NVA if they attempted to cross the Trace. As part of this strategy, thousands of Vietnamese peasants were moved out of their villages and hamlets that surrounded Con Thien. They were moved into a Vietnamese government refugee camp at Cam Lo to create a free fire zone north of the Cam Lo River (we could shoot anything that moved).

Another part of the Dyemarker strategy was to improve the protection of Con Thien. This called for new bunkers that could withstand a direct hit from large-caliber enemy artillery and creation of a three-hundred-yard clear field of fire completely around the entire perimeter. It would be filled with antipersonnel and antitank mines, and topped it off with miles and miles of barbed wire and razor concertina wire obstacles to cover the entire three-hundred-yard kill zone.

Alpha and Delta Companies from the First Battalion, Fourth Marine Regiment (1/4) with the Battalion Command were the first Marines to be selected to take over the defense of Con Thien. The Battalion motto was and still is "Whatever It Takes," and it was going to take a lot. Their orders were to provide protection for the Engineers and Seabees[*] who were clearing the Trace, improve the defenses at Con Thien, and provide interdiction patrols in the operational area that surrounded Con Thien, a tall order for some four hundred Grunts (common-ass rifle company Marines).

---

[*] *Seabees—Members of the Navy Construction Forces. The word "Seabees" comes from the initials "CB," which mean "Construction Battalion." The Seabees build bases, roadways, airstrips, and a myriad of other construction projects.*

During the days, the Grunts of 1/4 would provide defensive patrols to help suppress enemy ambushes and snipers. They strung miles of barbed wire and filled thousands of sandbags for the new bunkers. Incoming mortar rounds and sniper fire were a constant threat and "Corpsman Up" was the call of the day as another Marine would fall victim to a bullet or the shrapnel from a mortar or artillery fire. The Docs would stabilize the wounded, litter bearers would whisk them off to the Aid Station, and the medevac chopper would carry them to the rear.

To add to the engineering and logistical problems, expanding the perimeter brought the old minefields, which protected the smaller perimeters of the French and ARVN, inside the new perimeter. The mines were now in the way of where some of the new Dyemarker bunkers were to be placed.

To compound the problem, the old minefields were covered with waist-high grass, which made locating the mines almost impossible. Several attempts were made to clear these old minefields, which resulted in the deaths of several Marine Engineers. The solution was to put a barbed wire fence around the old minefields with a few warning signs to keep the Marines out as they stumbled around in the dark inside their own perimeter.

If I sound critical, I am not! I was there and still have no better solution. This is yet another reason to say, "War is Hell!"

At night, the Marine Engineers and Navy Seabees would bring their bulldozers and graders inside the wire and join the 1/4 Grunts. Additionally, Army Special Forces still shared the compound on the southeast side of the perimeter. As part of their mission, they always seemed to hang around with a bad crowd.

Con Thien was no exception because their guests were the Montagnards, a group of Chinese descendants who were mercenaries from the remote mountain areas of Vietnam. The Marines had little trust of anyone called mercenaries and strung concertina wire to separate them from the rest of the compound. As darkness fell over the Place of Angels, the residents would relax somewhat because the snipers could no longer find a target, and the NVA forward artillery observers could no longer call in mortars or artillery fire.

THE BAD GUYS TEST THE MARINES OF 1/4

At around 2:45 a.m. on the morning of May 8, 1967, the Grunts at Con Thien witnessed a green flare shoot skyward from a tree line in the distance. Moments later, they heard the thumps from dozens of 60 mm and 82 mm mortar tubes, followed by the unmistakable boom and flash of the mixed caliber ordinance now impacting all over their small perimeter. The thump, thump, thumps and boom, boom, booms grew to a rapid pace, like popcorn popping in a microwave. The sounds vibrated the air like thunder rapidly rolling across the prairie, and then came the sound of automatic weapons fire and the familiar red line of tracer bullets going outbound from the Marines' machine guns on the front lines. At the same time, green tracer bullets were coming inbound from the NVA machine guns near the tree line.

The Marines hunkered down in their bunkers, trenches, and fighting holes. Most were praying that the next round would not find them, but their biggest fear had to have been the knowledge that this much incoming could possibly signal that an all-out ground attack was likely to follow.

Their worst fears were confirmed when NVA Sapper units[*] hit the Marine lines at several points on the northeast and southeast perimeters. Bangalore Torpedoes[**] breached the wire in several locations. Quickly, small enemy units moved inside the perimeter, heavily armed with satchel charges (a pack full of explosives). They began to blow up bunkers and trenches filled with young and inexperienced Marines still hiding their heads from the incoming artillery.

---

[*] *NVA Sapper units—Enemy explosive engineers who were used to sneak up and blow open US Military fixed defenses, such as barbed wire, just prior to an attack.*

[**] *Bangalore Torpedoes—Explosives packed into a 1 ½" to 2" diameter tube about 5' long or several tubes connected together. Used by combat engineers to slide under barbed wire and other defenses to clear an opening prior to an attack.*

As the Sapper units moved through the breach in the wire, they had placed small pennants on bamboo spikes to mark the way for the main attacking force. Around 4:00 a.m., two reinforced Battalions of NVA soldiers (approximately 1,500 strong), armed with flame throwers, RPG rocket launchers, explosives, and automatic weapons, joined the assault through the breach made by the Sappers.

The right flank of the Delta Company line tied into the Special Forces Sector on the southeast perimeter where the Montagnards gave way to the advancing enemy. Delta Marines were now engaged in hand-to-hand combat, and the Marines were struggling for their very lives against the masses of NVA streaming through the gap in the wire. To complicate matters, the battlefield went dark when the 81 mm mortars ran out of illumination rounds and it took some time before a flare ship (an aircraft that drops illumination flares) arrived on scene and provided illumination through the rest of the night.

Delta Marines on the northern perimeter supported by the one surviving tank firing Bee Hive rounds and machine gun fire inflicted heavy casualties on the enemy and stalled the attacking force on the northeast. A Platoon of Marine Engineers was moved to support Delta's right flank on the southeast, where the gap in the wire and the action was most intense.

Alpha Company was protecting the south and west portions of the perimeter and was directed to send the First Platoon as a reaction force to support Delta's right flank as well as to escort two amtracs (tracked armored personnel carriers used for amphibious landings) and two M-42 Dusters with ammo resupply for the Delta Marines.

En route to Delta's right flank, they were engaged by NVA units who had broken through the perimeter and were overrunning the base. The NVA took the vehicles under fire, using RPGs (antitank rocket propelled grenades). Both M-42 Dusters were hit and burst into flames, and one of the amtracs was damaged by a satchel charge and had to be abandoned by the crew.

While attempting to maneuver, the remaining amtrac got entangled in barbed wire and became stuck. An RPG struck it, and it immediately exploded, trapping the crew and a squad of Marines inside.

Alpha Marines could hear the screams from their friends as they were quickly consumed by the fire and the exploding ammunition. The vehicle fires and ammo explosions continued until long after daybreak.

The remaining Alpha Marines advanced on the NVA units and pushed them back. Assisted by the Marine engineers they were able to close the breach in the Delta line just prior to daylight. The NVA escape route was now cut off. A large number of bad guys found themselves trapped inside the perimeter. They needed to either surrender or die fighting, and the Marines were most happy to accommodate their second choice. The Marines continued to hunt down and kill the trapped NVA until past 11:00 a.m., and only eight bad guys either decided to surrender or survived the retribution.

The enemy troops who escaped back through the breach were not all that lucky because when they attempted to cross the recently cleared Trace on their retreat north, they were caught in the open and provided an excellent target for direct fire weapons from Con Thien, artillery, and air strikes.

At first light, a Platoon from Bravo 1/4 set out from Gio Linh, heading west on the Trace to assist Alpha and Delta 1/4 at Con Thien. They had been subjected to a vicious bombardment of mixed caliber artillery all through the night but, without the ground attack. Whatever they had suffered was not as bad as their brothers at the Place of Angels. A little less than a mile from Con Thien, NVA solders from the south side of the Trace, were flushed out and taken under fire. The Marines pressed the attack and overran a bunker complex, resulting in twenty-six enemy KIAs.

Back inside Con Thien, the perimeter had now been cleared of enemy stragglers, and helicopters were able to land and start the evacuation of the friendly casualties. The bodies of the wounded and dead Americans were lined up outside the Aid Station bunker, and there were many. The walking wounded and litter bearers continued to increase the patient load as the morning wore on.

Many Marines knew that their friends and comrades were wounded, possibly dying or dead at the aid station, but it was the Corpsman who actually touched them all. The Doc treated everyone's friends, even his own. Those with minor wounds were quickly patched and sent back into the action. He triaged, treated, and transported the severely wounded to the rear and most times never knew their final fate.

Those friends who were less fortunate, the Docs could only sit with for a moment—maybe say a prayer and think of the good times that they had together and the shitstorms they endured. Then they said their good-byes and went back to work.

When it was all said and done, forty-four Americans were dead, and a hundred ten were wounded. The bad guys had to leave two hundred twenty-six of their dead behind. It was estimated that another two hundred were killed by direct fire, artillery, and air strikes during their retreat, and only God and the NVA know how many of their boys were wounded.

FOLLOWING THE ATTACK OF MAY 7, 1967

NVA General Giap, the mastermind of the May 7, 1954, French defeat at the battle of Dien Bien Phu, had planned the assault on Con Thien on its anniversary date to be the Americans' Dien Bien Phu. What the good general failed to realize was that he was no longer fighting the French, ARVN, or even the US Army. Instead, he was now facing the United Stated Marines who did not eat croissants or listen to violin music. Marines only need one meal a day just to make a turd, only need one hour of sleep a night, and shit better fighting men than the North Vietnamese could produce. At least that is what Gunny Sponenberg told us and he would finish with, "May I have an Ooh-Rah from you ladies!"

THE MISERY NEVER STOPPED

The threat of another ground attack was always a possibility, and hundreds of mixed-caliber artillery impacted the compound every day and into the night. On one day, the count reached 1,200 rounds of incoming artillery, mortars, and rocket fire. The term "shell-shocked" had not been heard of since the First World War, but the constant earthshaking booms and cries from the wounded rattled even the toughest Marines. If that was not bad enough, during the monsoon season the hill turned to calf-high mud, and the fighting holes and trenches that lined the perimeter would fill with water and collapse bunkers. Can you imagine the misery of enduring the fear of incoming artillery while crouched in a trench or fighting hole in neck-high fifty-degree water?

The constant beating that the Marines endured month after month was a result of yet another self-imposed limited war with rules of engagement where the enemy was allowed to invade South Vietnam but the United States could not send troops into North Vietnam to silence their big guns. If only I had graduated from Harvard, was a liberal trust-fund baby, never actually fought for my country, and now I was a politician, I could probably explain why this was a good strategy.

To reduce the mental fatigue at Con Thien, a thirty-day rotation policy was initiated for the Battalions—thus, the name "Hotel Hell." You would check in for thirty days and hope that YOU did not check out early. The most common term was "your turn in the barrel."

During the fall of 1967, Con Thien was the poster child for what the war looked like and was constantly on the evening news back home.

Time magazine featured the story on the cover of its October 6, 1967, issue, which was instrumental in bringing the reality of Vietnam combat to American readers.

David Douglas Duncan's photos of "*Life at Con Thien*" were featured in the October 27, 1967, issue of *Life Magazine* and in his book *War without Heroes.*

CBS News aired a special report on October 1, 1967, "The Ordeal of Con Thien," hosted by Mike Wallace, that featured interviews from the Grunts and film from the Place of Angels. You can access this special report in the appendices.

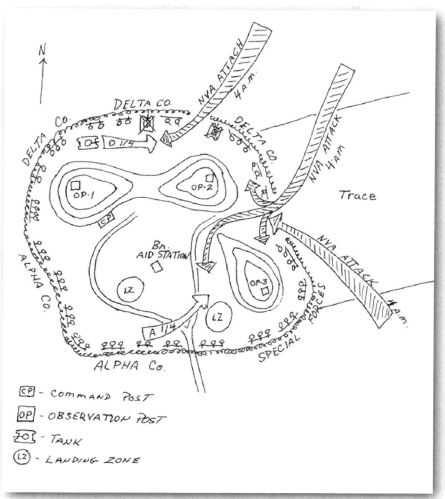

Con Thien on the night of May 7, 1967, or early morning
May 8, 1967, whichever you prefer.
The NVA started a mixed-caliber artillery and mortar attack at 2:45
a.m., followed by Sappers that blew holes in the perimeter wire. At
around 4:00 a.m., the main NVA force struck in several locations and
got into the compound. The bold white arrows show the counterattack
by a portion of Delta Company, the one remaining tank on the
north, a Platoon from Alpha, and Combat Engineers on the south
who pushed the bad guys back and closed the holes in the line.

Nine

*We are swatting flies in the South when we should
be going after the manure pile in Hanoi.*

— GEN. CURTIS LEMAY

A BEDTIME STORY ABOUT CON THIEN

The night before we were to move to Con Thien, the Delta Command Group was sitting around in the Command bunker and bullshitting about our move the next morning. Captain Weede spoke up. "Westy, weren't you with Delta on the night of May 7, when Con Thien was attacked?"

Westy answered back, "Yes, I had just gotten to Delta a few weeks before."

Captain Weede came back again, asking, "Can you tell us what it was like that night?

Westy told us his story. "I was first selected to go to sniper school, where I spent only one day in training, then I went on liberty and ended up in the brig for drunkenness. I was kicked out of the sniper school, but somehow I ended up in the Vietnamese language school. The language school was an intense, two-month, language immersion program to become an interpreter where we spoke nothing but Vietnamese, day and night, in the class and after class. If you wanted or needed anything, it had to be requested in Vietnamese.

"Upon graduation, I was sent to Vietnam and assigned to Delta 1/4. I reported to the company just after they had moved to Con Thien. When I reported to the Second Platoon, I proudly informed the Lieutenant that I was there as his new interpreter, to which the Lieutenant replied, 'Up here we don't talk to them. We kill them.' And that was the end of my interpreting career."

We all sat there stunned for a second and then broke out in laughter until our eyes watered (you can't make this shit up. You have got to admire the flexibility of the Marine Corps).

Westy continued, "On the evening of May 7, now back to a basic rifleman, I set out with the Second Platoon to set up a night ambush outside the wire of Con Thien. I had only been in country for thirteen days, and I was confused and too naïve to be afraid. We set up our ambush in a ditch, just to the side of a road. It was so dark that I could not tell if my eyes were open or closed. The only sound was the buzzing of mosquitoes in your ears.

We were all wide-awake, no two hours on and two hours off, no talking, and no cigarettes. I was in a state of suspended animation. About four in the morning there was a rustle on the road that kept getting louder. Then I thought I saw movement. Someone to my left opened fire followed quickly by the entire Platoon. Red tracers from the M-60 machine guns lanced out toward the trail. A flare burst overhead, and suddenly it was bright as day. After the hours of pitch darkness, the light hurt my eyes. There on the trail, about twenty enemy soldiers were diving for cover, yelling, and firing back at us. The noise was deafening as everyone blasted away, firing from the hip with rifles, blazing with machine guns, tossing hand grenades here and there. After about fifteen minutes, a thousand dollars' worth of ammunition had been used, twenty enemy soldiers were dead, and every bush in the vicinity had been shredded.

We had a couple wounded, but they weren't in bad shape. The Corpsman patched them up, and the Platoon radioman called in to home base. 'Delta, Delta, this is Delta 2….ambush successful…. twenty Charlies KIA, nothing serious on our side.'

"The report was broken off by the heavy thump of distant artillery. Several miles away at Con Thien, the sky was all lit up by parachute flares. The radio came alive: 'Delta 2, Delta 2, Delta…we are getting hit hard! Come a'runnin'!

"Lieutenant Stover got us up on the trail, and we double-timed it toward the camp. We were spaced wide apart to avoid too many of us getting hit by an enemy grenade or mortars, and we kept our eyes open as we loped along the winding trail, rifles at the ready. The noise increased rapidly. Now we could hear the rapid fire of the .50-calibers and the M-60 machine guns coming from Con Thien.

"About a half mile from camp we heard the light flicker of rifle fire coming our way. Then a couple of grenades exploded off to our left. I dove off the trail into a ditch on my right. I couldn't fire because the first squad was between me and the gooks. Evidently, we had hit only a small force, and soon they disappeared.

"By the time we had worked our way back into the perimeter of Con Thien, the main battle was over. In the dim light of predawn, I was shocked at the sight of the camp. Bodies laid everywhere. Shelter-halves, ponchos, and other gear were shredded and strewn here and there. Some of the bunkers had been blown apart. The iron support beams were twisted crazily and dirt poured out of torn sandbags. Cries of 'corpsman-up!' and the smell of gunpowder filled the air. I ran into my buddy Hayworth, from First Platoon. Hayworth had come over to Nam in October '66 and had seen a lot of action. His face was drawn and pale, ten years older than it had been just yesterday.

"'Westy,' he said, 'you wouldn't have believed it! There must've been a thousand of them, and they weren't Viet Cong. They were hard-core NVA regulars. The bastards got in through the wire and they were running all over the camp, screaming like animals, and throwing satchel charges. Finally, the word was passed to get in our holes and stay there. Then anyone not in a hole must be an enemy. They were so close we couldn't use the mortars or artillery. Even using a rifle was dangerous because you might miss and hit a Marine.'

"From others I got much the same story. The Marines had heard those awful words for the first time since boot camp training: 'Fix bayonets!' I didn't know about everyone else, but being shot at was nothing compared to hand-to-hand combat. Getting hit with a bullet seemed much nicer than being cut or stabbed with a blade; a rifle battle was much less personal. The enemy wasn't trying to kill you personally; he was just doing his job. But with close-in fighting it was one-on-one; you could see his eyes. The prospect had always frightened me and I had managed to miss out on this ugly scene by sheer good fortune.

"The captain of Delta Company had been shot in both legs and medevaced to a Navy hospital ship off the coast. The NVA had strapped loops of wire to their ankles before the attack; in case they got hit, they could be dragged off. This cold-blooded kind of thinking told me something about the kind of people we were up against.

"It took most of the morning to clean up the camp. I was assigned to the meat wagon, a little flatbed truck with sand-dune tires, called a mule because of its strength and durability. Five or six of us drove the mules around and picked up the bodies of the NVA soldiers.

"I was in a state of shock. There was too much blood and too many mangled bodies for it to hit me emotionally. The others had varying degrees of combat experience (one adjusts quickly) and were sort of euphoric, some kicking the dead bodies and shouting, 'Reveille, reveille, wake up, you maggot!' A bulldozer was enlarging a bomb crater. We dropped the stiffs into this mass grave and drove off in the mule to get some more.

"Helicopters came and went in a steady parade, carrying off our dead and wounded. Finally, the rest of us were taken in trucks and tanks back to Dong Ha. Bravo Company took our place guarding the hill. We should have been ecstatic about getting back to civilization, but we were all pretty quiet now, even the veterans. I had been in Vietnam thirteen days and already I was a changed person. Gone completely were my visions of glory. War was exciting, but not in the way I had pictured it. I had seen enough dead and wounded to last a lifetime. I was beyond a feeling of fear—a sickness filled my heart, a sadness for the parents, girl-friends, and brothers and sisters who would receive the news that their worst fears were realized."

After Westy finished his story, we all sat there for a moment until Captain Weede broke the silence and told us to get some sleep because tomorrow we would get to experience the Place of Angels firsthand. I can assure you, that there were no sugarplum fairies dancing in our heads that night.

MOVING TO OUR NEW HOME IN A VERY BAD NEIGHBORHOOD

Shortly after first light, on March 8, 1968, the first elements of Delta Company moved out from the C-2 Bridge and started the one-and-a-half-mile-walk to Con Thien. The Marines are trained to do a Force March with full gear and full packs at a rate of about one mile every fifteen min-utes. The word was passed and pounded into us to not bunch up, keep ten yards between you and the man in front of you, keep your eyes open to the tree lines, and expect enemy contact and incoming mortar and artillery rounds at any time. I thought to myself, *"Can it be that bad up there? Or are they just trying to scare the shit out of us?"* Either way, it was working.

The reason we had to walk rather than ride in trucks was NVA Artillery Forward Observers were always watching and would call in an artillery strike on any vehicle carrying troops or important equipment. Every eye in our long column was in constant motion—from scanning the tree lines, to scanning ahead for a possible roadside ambush, to the constant search for a hole or depression that you could dive to in the event of an attack. Every ear was tuned to the possible thump of a mortar tube, the screech of an incoming rocket or artillery round, or the pop of a rifle round as it whizzes past your head.

It took less than an hour to cover the distance, but it was the longest hour of my life (not counting Mr. Wolf's geometry class in the tenth grade). The first portion of Delta, including Captain Weede and the Company Command Group, reached Con Thien without incident and relieved Golf Company 2/1, who then departed for the C-2 Bridge to replace us. Once they arrived at the C-2 Bridge, they relieved the rest of Delta, who then joined us at Con Thien. By late afternoon, all of Delta Company was inside the wire at the Place of Angels, and the Marines wasted no time setting up the perimeter defenses while they still had some daylight.

This changing of the guard took some three weeks, as the Third Marine Division Command continued to use the OPCON strategy that saw Charlie 1/4 move from the C-2 Bridge to the Ninth Marines at A-2 (Gio Linh), and Hotel Company 2/1 was assigned to 1/4 to occupy Yankee Station. Two weeks later, Charlie 1/4 moved back to C-2 Bridge, and Hotel Company 2/1 moved back to their parent Battalion 2/1. Bravo 1/4, who was assigned to A-4, now moved to Yankee Station, while Alpha 1/4, who was OPCON to 2/1 at C-2, was now moved to A-4 (Con Thien).

If you are confused, can you imagine how challenging it had to be for the Battalion and Company Commanders who had to try to make it all work smoothly?

Finally, Alpha and Delta Companies occupied strong point A-4 (Con Thien or the Place of Angels), Bravo Company occupied Yankee Station, and Charlie Company continued to occupy the C-2 Bridge with the help from the Third Platoon from Lima 3/1. Even though 1/4 was still OPCON to the Ninth Marine Regiment, at least all four of our companies were back working together.

OUR NEW DIGS WERE NOT ALL THAT BAD

The Delta Company Command Group moved into a Dyemarker bunker next door to the Battalion Commander's bunker. Captain Weede, the second in command Lt. James Muir, Gunny Sponenberg, Westy, Battalion Radiomen Chastain and Whiteleather, a Marine interpreter, my old roommate Jimmy Howe, and I were all now in the same bunker.

Being in the high-rent district, we even had electric lights that worked most of the time. We did not have showers or hot food, but Captain Weede got a small ice chest delivered to him on occasion with his two-beer ration. The Captain allowed his new bunker mates to put our two beers in the ice with his. We did not get beer all that often, but when we did, the atmosphere became almost festive. Tilting that cold frosty can up and taking that first large gulp that made your eyes water was pure heaven. The first beer went fast but the second beer we all savored. Just sitting around bullshitting with a beer made you almost feel you were somewhere else and safe.

As for the rest of Delta Company, each of the three Platoons had a Dyemarker bunker that housed the Platoon Lieutenant, the Staff Sergeant, the Radioman, and the two Corpsmen. The Platoon Grunts were dispersed along the western perimeter in smaller bunkers and fighting holes directly on the line. As usual, the living conditions for the Grunts did not change when they moved from the C-2 Bridge to the Place of Angels, except that they lost the one hot dinner meal and the swimming hole. Oh, and they still drank their two-beer ration at room temperature (up to 120 degrees with 90 percent humidity), and of course, no electricity.

THE FIRST NIGHT IN OUR NEW HOME

The first evening in our new home did not go well, when around 8:00 p.m., the "Four-Deuce" mortar crew accidentally struck a primer that set off a propellant charge in the ammo bunker, which started a fire that ignited other ordinance, and a deadly fireworks show ensued. When it was over, four Marines were badly burned and sent to the Battalion Aid Station. Corpsman from all over the hill ran to the aid station to help the over-worked Battalion surgeon. The four Marines were stabilized and medevaced to the rear. As was always the case, we never heard of their outcome.

TIME TO EXPLORE

Within a few days, I was settled in at my new home and went off exploring the Place of Angels, visiting my Platoon corpsman, shooting the shit with the Grunts on the line, and visiting OP-1 (Observation Post-One) where my favorite FO (Forward Artillery Observer), Lieutenant Carolyn, was stationed. OP-1 was the most northern observation post in South Vietnam, and the view was amazing. Looking through the telescope, to the east down the Trace, you could see past Gio Linh to the ships at sea some fifteen miles away. Looking south toward the Marine Base at Dong Ha, you could see structures and large vehicle movement. North you could see across the Ben Hai River well into North Vietnam.

Looking with just your eyes around the local landscape, one could imagine the lush farmland carpeted green with crops of coffee, pineapples, rice, and tobacco. Large stands of rubber and banana trees provided texture and a canopy for as far as one could see. Now, after a few years of war, this once beautiful setting had been reduced to a moonscape—pockmarked by bomb craters and defoliated by bulldozers, napalm, and Agent Orange. Where farmers once planted crops, going back dozens of generations, now explosive engineers—from both sides—planted mines that would plague farmers for generations to come.

YANKEE STATION

Sometime after the May 1967 ground attack, a small perimeter, protected by one Marine Company, was added about five hundred yards southwest of the main gate of Con Thien. The little outpost was about seventy-five yards wide and one hundred yards long. It had none of the Dyemarker bunkers or help from the Marine Engineers or Navy Seabees to help dig the fighting holes. The individual Grunt and Corpsman who occupied the space made it and improved it. History is very vague as to the reason for its existence. It may have been there to help protect the main gate of Con Thien, which is always the weakest point of a hardened perimeter, or it may have been there to protect a blind spot on the southern approach to Con Thien. Whatever the reason, it was there because of Con Thien. This little shit hole was called Yankee Station, not to be confused with the more well-known position in the Gulf of Tonkin where the US Navy launched carrier-based air strikes into North Vietnam.

Thus Con Thien and the lesser known stepchild, Yankee Station, were a set piece—no running water, no showers, no hot meals, but plenty of bad guys who did not want us there.

GETTING TO KNOW OUR NEW NEIGHBORS

Unlike the activity level we experienced at C-2 and the C-2 Bridge, where we would get excited if we saw a few enemy soldiers every few days, up here on the edge of the DMZ, contact with the enemy was constant. The Marines on daylight patrols and night ambushes were in shootouts with small units of NVA on a daily basis. There were constant sightings and contact with small units (four or five soldiers) carrying large heavy packs full of supplies intended for enemy units farther south. Our daylight patrols discovered and destroyed numerous enemy bunker complexes that ringed Con Thien, only to return later to find them rebuilt.

On one occasion, an Alpha Company patrol found what looked like a battalion-size bunker complex, about 1,200 yards south and west of Con Thien. The facility served approximately four hundred enemy soldiers. There were sixty bunkers, six feet by four feet, with two to four layers of four-inch logs covered with dirt with connecting trenches, and four mortar pits. One tunnel, two and a half feet wide, extended forty feet deep, at a 70 percent angle, and opened into a room ten feet wide and eighteen feet long, with a ten-foot ceiling. The tunnel appeared to have been dug by a dud bomb and improved by the enemy. There was an Observation Post in a tall tree with an excellent view of C-2, C-2 Bridge, and Con Thien. Thirty-three graves were found, and half of them had wooden head markers (possibly Catholic, or at least they were religious). I had often wondered—if we were both Christian and both praying, how would God work that out?

The Observation Posts on the crests of the three hills that made up the Place of Angels were a target-rich environment. All day, every day, and all night, every night, there were constant sightings of troop movements, muzzle flashes from enemy artillery, and lights from enemy vehicle convoys. The FOs who manned OP-1, OP-2, and OP-3 were constantly on the radio, calling in fire missions on the enemy positions. I spent many a night in OP-1 with Lieutenant Carolyn looking through the Starlight Scope, spotting targets, and watching him call in artillery strikes.

The target-rich environment comment worked both ways. If you can see them, then they can see you, and the enemy sniper was a constant threat. Everyone knew not to walk on the crest of the hills where the deep blue sky would silhouette your body for the ever-vigilant sharpshooter.

THERE ARE NO ATHEISTS IN A FOXHOLE

Never have truer words been spoken. When you are scared to death and your survival is in question, almost everyone eventually turns to divine intervention, and I was no exception. I did not come from a religious background, and my family never attended church. My dog tags listed me as Methodist, but I am not sure why I picked it as my religion.

Catholic Father Evan Greco was assigned to 1/4 in mid-March, but I did not meet him until we all moved into Con Thien. Doc Pinky from the First Platoon was Catholic, and he convinced me to attend mass with him. Growing up, I had attended mass with several of my friends, so I thought I knew what to expect, but mass at the Place of Angels was probably more like having mass with the Disciples. We were outside in the dirt; there was no choir or organ music, no collection basket, no ushers, and no chairs. The altar boys were Grunts in battle gear.

Father Greco was holding his first mass at the Place of Angels, attired in the vestments that one would see in the States. The Father was prepared to give Holy Communion, when we started to receive enemy artillery rounds. Everyone ran and dove for a trench line. I watch Father

Greco start for the trench, then stop and go back to the makeshift altar for the Holy Eucharist. A moment later, he emerged, and everyone saw the Father running for the trench with the Body of Christ in his hands. I was hooked.

I regularly attended mass with Pinky, and he soon became my sponsor as I started the process to become a Catholic.

A REPUTATION FOR INCOMING

Con Thien had such a reputation for receiving a constant pounding from enemy, mixed-caliber artillery, mortar, and rocket fire (up to 1,200 rounds in a day). But with the installation of a Counter-Battery Radar system,* that could quickly identify the enemy location and return fire, coupled with frequent B-52 and fighter jet bombing runs, the enemy was now limited as to how many rounds they could throw at us at any one time. Oh sure, we would receive a few mortar and rocket rounds every day just like we did at the bridge, but nothing like the shell-shocking barrages the place was famous for. I would have to say I was conflicted; on one hand, I was grateful for the lull, but there was a part of me that did want to experience the big-gun action just for the future bragging rights.

Careful what you wish for. On the morning of March 19, we started receiving 130 mm and 152 mm artillery rounds inside the perimeter (that is big shit). I know I had never experienced this large an artillery round before because the scream on the way in, followed by the explosion and ground shaking, was nothing like I had ever experienced. We all stood in our bunker; my eyes were glued to Captain Weede to monitor his reactions.

It was like being in one of those World War II submarine movies where the crew was just hanging on during a depth charge assault from an enemy Destroyer. First, you heard the screech from the incoming

---

* *Counter-battery radar—A radar system that detects enemy artillery projectiles fired by one or more artillery pieces. From their trajectories, it can locate the position on the ground of the weapon that fires it.*

round, then the explosion, followed by the earthquake, and that shocked your body and your entire environment.

Just like in the movies, the dust fell from the ceiling. The incoming rounds seemed as if they would never stop. Each round would leave a crater the size of a large Jacuzzi spa. When the day was over we had received only twenty-four of these large-caliber rounds, and I wanted no more bragging rights.

When the incoming was over, we conducted a damage and casualty survey from the Platoons. To my amazement, there was little damage and only a few minor injuries. I took a walk around with Gunny Sponenberg to check on the Platoons, and when we were overlooking the northern portion of the perimeter, I could see that some of the enemy rounds hit inside of our minefield and not inside our perimeter. I made a remark about what dumb shits the gooks were that after all these months they still could not hit the target. The Gunny replied, "That was no accident, Doc. They took out fifty feet of our outside wire and opened a clear path through our minefield." I stared at the minefield for a moment, swallowed hard, and then ran like a new puppy to catch up to the Gunny.

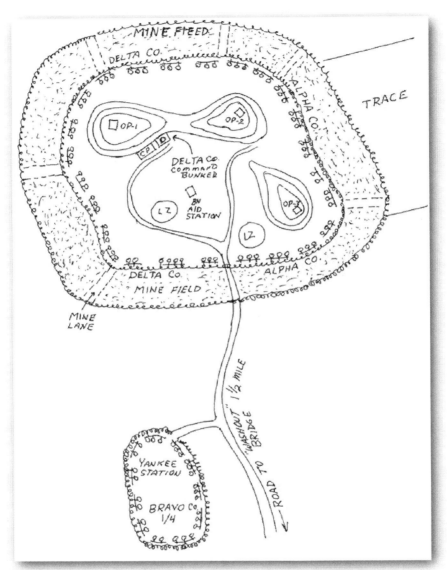

This is what Con Thien and Yankee Station looked like in March 1968
Mine Lane—A narrow corridor that was void of any mines to allow Marines access to the outside wire without having to go all the way around the outside perimeter. Hopefully, the Bad Guys didn't know where they were, but of course they did.

Leaving C-2 Bridge on my way to Con Thien. You can see the excitement in my face.

Moving into Con Thien, ten yards' separation, watch the tree line for the bad guys; expect incoming at any moment!

The correct translation is probably "the Hill of Angels," however,
I still prefer the name posted on the front door!

Delta Company's "Dymarker" bunker at
Con Thien, March 1968

Entrance to the Delta Command bunker

Looking northeast, fighting holes and living quarters for the Grunts in the foreground, three hundred yards of clear field of fire over a minefield in front of the fighting holes (thank you, Agent Orange). No matter where they were stationed, the Marine Grunt always lived the same. I am thinking of a word to describe their living conditions—yes, "shit hole" was the correct answer!

Walking south at Con Thien, OP-1 up hill on right, old ARVN or French minefield on right.

Near the 81mm mortars, looking at OP-1. A trench was always nearby.

Ten

*Theirs is not to reason why, theirs is but to do and
die: Into the Valley of Death rode the six hundred.*

—ALFRED LORD TENNYSON, CHARGE OF
THE LIGHT BRIGADE, 1854

A Visit by the Brass

During the first week in April, Captain Weede was taking a much-deserved R & R in Hawaii with his wife. In his absence, Lieutenant Muir was acting as the Company Commander. It was at this time that a two-star General landed in his helicopter, and after a meeting with the Battalion Commander, decided to visit the Delta Command bunker. Gunny Sponenberg yelled, "Attention on deck!" We all snapped to attention as this starched uniformed, spit-shined boots, puffed-chested General marched in and began to question Lieutenant Muir as to why he had not conducted any patrols north of the Trace or north of our perimeter at Con Thien.

I did not like the tone of his voice as he spoke to the Lieutenant. I felt like saying, "*Please tell me you have an objective that needs to be accomplished by sending us north. Please tell me this is part of a great strategy to march a small unit across the Trace into the arms of hundreds, if not thousands, of waiting enemy."*

Of course, I never said anything to the General because he would have sent me by myself.

A LITTLE HISTORY AS TO WHAT HAPPENED EVERY TIME WE CROSSED NORTH OF THE TRACE

As you may recall, the Trace was a six-hundred-yard-wide, six-mile-long bald strip designed to catch the enemy in the open should they attempt to cross the barrier. Funny thing about barriers is that they work both ways.

"Operation Buffalo." In July 1967, Bravo Company 1/9 walked into an ambush against two Battalions of NVA, about 1,200 yards northeast of Con Thien, in a location called "the Marketplace." The result of the two-week Operation was 159 Marines and Corpsmen killed, 345 wounded, and thirty-four Marines were missing (thirty-three bodies were eventually found, one never recovered). This operation ended with the defeat of the Ninetieth NVA Regiment, so it was deemed a success and "Operation Kingfisher" was launched.

"Operation Kingfisher." It had the same objective as "Operation Buffalo," and that was to "Stop the enemy from infiltrating across the eastern DMZ." It was estimated that there were as many as twenty-one thousand enemy soldiers in and around the DMZ, so let's send in a Battalion of Marines to stop the pesky little devils.

On July 28, 1967, as part of Operation Kingfisher, Battalion 2/9, supported by tanks, Engineers, and other attachments, was sent north of Con Thien, up Route 606, to make a "spoiling attack" into the DMZ. A spoiling attack was a tactic where we would attack them before they had a chance to attack us. Thus, we would spoil their attack. It could not have been a surprise attack because 1,200 Marines with tanks surely kicked up enough dust to be seen for miles.

Battalion 2/9 was to advance all the way to the Ben Hai River, which separated the two Vietnams. Then they were to turn east for several miles and then turn south to catch the NVA from behind. The Battalion arrived at the Ben Hai River with little or no contact with the enemy. However, because of poor intelligence and possibly hasty or poor planning from the boys higher up the chain of command, 2/9 found that a bridge that was critical for their turn east would not support the tanks, and they could go no farther.

The only option for 2/9 was to turn around and go back down the same road that they had come up on. In military tactics this is a NO, NO! The enemy was waiting for them on their return and ambushed 2/9 at three different points in their withdrawal. The Companies got cut off and isolated from each other and had to fight off attacks all through the night.

On the morning of July 30, 1967, the Third Battalion, Fourth Marines, were sent in to help extricate 2/9 and help bring them home. The Marine casualties for this little three-day venture were twenty-three dead and two hundred fifty-one wounded; the number of confirmed enemy killed was listed at thirty-two.

It was reported that we killed more gooks than they killed Marines. But in the end, we gained no ground, could not claim a victory, and did not shorten the war by a single minute. Nor did we accomplish a single strategy. As I have stated earlier, our brain trust in Washington and the Pentagon had a strategy of body count and attrition (they would run out of their Grunts before we would run out of our Grunts). If you were that Grunt on the front line, you just wanted to know that giving your life would make your family back home just a little safer. As dumb as we poor Grunts were, we all knew the answer.

"Operation Kentucky" commenced the last few days in November and continued most of December 1968. It probably had the most meaningful reason for having units on the north side of the Trace. The mission was for Delta 1/4 and the rest of the Battalion to cross to the north side of the Trace and provide screening and security operations in support of the construction of A-3 and its access road. On December 6, the entire Battalion came under heavy attack, which kicked off a monthlong slugfest with the NVA. At the end of December, A-3 was built, and 1/4 was moved to C-2 and the C-2 Bridge. The cost to 1/4 was nine Marines dead and one hundred thirteen wounded.

Back to the story about a visit by the Brass

Apparently, the General did not hear my thoughts or care about my feelings, because a few weeks later, Delta Company saddled up and moved out to cross the Trace. We were spread out on line about halfway across no man's land when we started receiving the familiar pop and zip of enemy small-arms rounds, just missing their targets. (You never hear the round that kills you, but then again, how do we know?) We all dropped in the shoulder-high elephant grass that now covered the once barren Trace.

Captain Weede called in a napalm strike while the Grunts smoked a few cigarettes. A short time later, an F-4 Phantom came on station and made a flyby to discuss the drop zone with the FAC (Forward Air Controller). He then circled around and got in position for a bomb run on the enemy target. We all stood up and watched as the jet swooped in and released the bomb a few hundred yards prior to the target. Once released, the projectile lost speed and almost tumbled in slow motion to its intended target. A second later it hit the ground, broke apart, spewed the volatile contents across a vast area, and then came the flash as the Napalm ignited.

From hundreds of yards away we could all feel the radiated heat from the jellylike flammable liquid that sucked the oxygen from the air and stuck to the skin, causing devastating burns. I cannot imagine how terrifying that must have been for the enemy Grunts.

After the bomb run, the enemy small-arms fire stopped, and we continued our move to the north side of the Trace. We were now where no Americans had been since the First Battalion Fourth Marines in December 1967 (except Marine Recon units).

Now here we were, one understrength company (185 Marines and seven Corpsmen), with no backup and no advanced artillery barrage to soften the enemy position. We were on a mission that seemed to have no real strategic or tactical benefit except to say we were not going to be intimidated by thousands of highly trained NVA soldiers that knew we were coming.

May I have an amen?

We swept through the area of the recent Napalm bomb drop and found only two dead NVA soldiers. I asked Gunny Sponenberg, "How in the hell did most of these little bastards escape the certain death that had just rained down on them?"

The Gunny replied, "Job security, Doc. No matter how many bombs are dropped on the enemy, it will always take a Grunt on the ground to finish the job."

We then came across an old two-thousand-pound bomb crater where one NVA soldier was standing at the bottom of the crater with his hands in the air and his AK-47 rifle at his feet. He appeared unhurt, so Captain Weede ordered him to climb out very slowly. We had a South Vietnamese Scout Interpreter with us who moved to the edge of the crater. I assumed he was going to speak to the enemy soldier, when all of a sudden he opened fire with his M-16, killing the prisoner. Captain Weede was shocked. Out of exasperation, he took his helmet off and swung it at the Scout, who jumped back with a smirk on his face. The smirk was quickly gone when a Marine stepped forward and threatened to blow the Scout's head off. I thought, "*Did the Scout hate the enemy so much that he just had to kill him, or was he sympathetic to their cause and wanted to silence him?*" We will never know.

The company started moving west on the north edge of the Trace when we all heard the familiar rapid boom, boom, boom, boom, and boom of an enemy artillery battery on a fire mission. The call went out, "In Coming!" Everyone jumped for the closest hole they could find. I looked around and saw an old family burial mound with a stone wall around it, and I thought I could make it there. Just then Gunny Sponenberg yelled at me, "Doc, get behind this tree!" I dived up behind the Gunny and landed in a position that any other time might have been considered inappropriate, especially for Marines. Then came the screech, followed by the explosions and overpressure, which blew me sideways, sucked the breath from my lungs, and sprayed my back with scalding hot earth. A second later, hot smoke and the smell of pungent burning gunpowder filled my lungs and burned my eyes—but I was alive!

Then another round of boom, boom, boom, boom, and boom, followed a few seconds later by the screech, explosion, and overpressure. One round landed in the old family burial mound that I initially intended to dive for. It blew the mound apart, showering the Gunny and me with countless generations of farmers.

I was lying flat on the ground with no cover. I could not stop thinking about what it would feel like with a direct hit that would surely turn me into "red mist." It was the first and last time that I ever experienced my knees knocking, and I thought, "Where in the fuck is our counter-battery fire to silence these sons-of-bitches?" Just then came boom, boom, boom, boom, and boom again.

After thirty rounds, it appeared that the barrage was over, and Captain Weede gave the order to pull back across the trace. When I heard his order, my first instinct was to get up and make a run for it, but I realized that I had wounded Marines to take care of and my panic quickly subsided. We only had three wounded Marines. Amazingly, no one was killed. The wounded were carried back to the south side of the Trace where we called in a medevac chopper and shipped them out. Confident that we had shown the enemy who was boss, we headed for Con Thien.

On our way back to the Place of Angels, three C-130 cargo aircraft came flying down the Trace, expelling a heavy mist behind them. They were flanked on each side by a fighter aircraft that flew at a much faster speed and had to continually circle around to provide the protection needed for the slower-flying airplanes. As the mist settled and wet our uniforms, I asked the Gunny what that stuff was.

He replied, "It's Agent Orange, and it is supposed to kill plants and not us. You will be one lucky bastard if this shit kills you in twenty years because it means you made it out of this shit hole. We are all going to die of something, Doc, and it will never be convenient!"

On the walk back to Con Thien, I was talking to a Marine who grew up on a farm in Bakersfield, and he informed me that he grew up spraying Agent Orange on the cotton crops to make the cotton bloom, and it was no big thing. Although he continued to say, "This shit was probably a lot more potent than the shit we sprayed on our crops."

When we got back inside the wire, the Vietnamese Scout was told to pack his shit, and he was gone. We were all relieved that we did not have to sleep next to a guy with questionable motives.

ANOTHER PROMOTION

On April 15, at twenty years and three months old, I was promoted to Second Class Petty Officer (a Sergeant if I were a Marine). I now held the position, title, *and rank* of Senior Corpsman of a Marine Rifle Company.

DELTA TO THE RESCUE

Two days after Delta Company was sent across the Trace in a failed attempt to mop up the estimated 21,000 NVA soldiers who occupied the DMZ, an Alpha Platoon stepped into some serious shit.

On the morning of April 26, 1968, a Platoon from Alpha Company was on a patrol about one thousand yards west of Con Thien and Yankee Station. At around 10:15 a.m., the Platoon observed two NVA soldiers in the open. The Platoon sniper took them under fire, killing one while the other bad guy made it into a tree line and disappeared. A 4.2-inch mortar mission was called in on his last-known position.

Shortly after 11:00 a.m., the Platoon set up a 360-degree perimeter. Their strategy was that each of the three Squads would take its turn and patrol a different sector while the other two squads would hold and act as a reactionary force in the event one of them made contact with an enemy force. The Platoon Lieutenant took the Second Squad and moved out to patrol the woodlands north of their position where the one NVA soldier had made his escape.

At 11:30 a.m., they entered the tree line and observed what appeared to be an abandoned enemy bunker complex. The Platoon Lieutenant advanced his squad on what was now a mission to search and destroy the bunker complex. As the squad closed in on the bunkers, the enemy sprung the ambush and opened fire with rifles, machine guns, and hand grenades. The squad radio was immediately knocked out of commission. Four Marines, the Lieutenant, and the Corpsman were killed, leaving four wounded Marines holding off what was initially estimated to be a Platoon of NVA. The squad was now completely surrounded and could not move because of extremely heavy grazing fire and chicom grenades. The four survivors set up a 360-degree defense to hold off the bad guys until reinforcements arrived.

Back at the Alpha Platoon perimeter the two remaining squads heard the small-arms fire, automatic weapons, and hand grenades coming from what was presumed to be the second squad's location. Unable to make contact with the second squad, the rest of the Platoon did what has always been done by fighting forces for centuries. They rode to the sound of the action. As soon as the Platoon swept into the wooded area to reinforce the squad, they immediately suffered the same fate. Radio transmission from the beleaguered Alpha Platoon now advised that the enemy had been reinforced by an estimated two NVA companies and that they were in desperate need of reinforcements.

Back at the Delta Company Command bunker, we were glued to the Battalion radio and listening to the escalating firefight. We were doing a little hand-wringing as we wondered who was going next. At 1:00 p.m., we got the order to saddle up the Second Platoon and the

Delta Command Group to respond to the struggling Alpha Platoon. We did a forced march out to the west and held up a hundred yards south of the wooded area. Captain Weede placed the reinforced second Platoon and the Command Group on line from east to west, facing the woods. It was going to be a dead run across open ground into the woods and the waiting guns of NVA, secure in their hardened bunkers. In an attempt to provide a little cover, white phosphorus artillery spotting rounds were called to create a little drift smoke over the open area that we were now going to attempt to cross.

While waiting for the smoke rounds to come in, we were crouched low to present a smaller target for enemy snipers. Harley Cowan, the Second Platoon Corpsman, slid up next to me with a smile on his face as if this was going to be a fun day. I was stunned. Here I am, about to shit myself, and Harley was smiling. Back at the base he was usually a very quiet, reserved guy, and now he seemed rather excited. I did not remember ever being this close to him when we were about to go into battle. Maybe he always enjoyed the excitement, and I just never noticed. I knew Doc Schindeler seemed to like the excitement, and so did Doc Ferguson. Most of the Marines seemed confident, but I never figured that Harley would be an adrenaline junkie.

Just then the screech and explosion of the spotting rounds landed between us and the woods, releasing a very disappointing volume of drifting white smoke that did not hide shit! The enemy must have been laughing and mocking us. I am sure I could almost hear them saying, "*Peekaboo, I see you,*" and I don't even speak Vietnamese. A few seconds later, Captain Weede gave the order, Gunny Sponenberg repeated the order up and down the line, and the Grunts started the charge.

I grabbed Harley by the arm and said, "Men are going to die here today. Be careful!"

Just then Gunny Sponenberg yelled back over his shoulder, "Let's go, Docs, it's time to earn your pay."

Harley smiled at me and said, "I'm fine. Don't worry."

And with that we were off on a dead run. As we closed on the tree line, the familiar pop, pop, pop sound of enemy rifle bullets breaking the sound barrier started zipping past our heads. We were so close now, my heart was pounding out of my chest. I could not stop visualizing what it was going to be like when we entered the tree line, and of course, my mind was only featuring the worst-case scenario. To add to my visualization, the head of the Marine running next to me exploded into red mist and spewed gray matter before us. In an instant, a sniper's bullet had ended his life as the rest of us charged on.

Am I the only one terrified here? Fear was never talked about; surely some of the Marines must be afraid. I had not gone through the same indoctrination as the Marines, but I wish I had. Would it have made a difference now? Do all these Marines truly believe, *"Ours is not to reason why?"* I can't ask them because I am not one of them. I am their Corpsman, and they depend on me. I must not show fear.

As we entered the woods, all hell broke loose. We were being shot at from three sides. Now I see several dead Alpha Platoon Marines just to my front. Just beyond them, I could see the gooks crouched in their bunkers, shooting at us from just above ground level. Corporal Spencer, a very large and tough black Marine, jumped into the trench line, attempting to gain access into the enemy bunker. Immediately, Spencer rolled back out of the trench holding his gut, screaming with pain from a bullet wound. I started to move forward when Doc Ferguson moved to the Corporal's aid.

I dropped to a crawl as the sound of pops and zips, grenade explosions, and machine gun fire filled the air. Men were screaming as close-quarter combat raged in every direction. The smell of gunpowder burned your throat, and now there was the all too familiar smell of wet rusty iron; it was the taste and smell of human carnage, of gallons of human blood being spilled across the battlefield.

"Corpsman Up," came a shout from the left, and Doc Cowan quickly moved in that direction. A second later, "Corpsman Up" was shouted again off to my right and fifteen yards ahead. I started my advance, but there were no lines of battle. There were good guys and bad guys in every direction. I hoped I was crawling toward some good guys.

I crawled forward and dived into a trench with three Marines. These Marines were not the Hollywood stereotypical square-jawed, muscle-bound, handsome leading men. These were scrawny, poorly fed, over-worked, sunbaked, filthy, and frightened eighteen-year-old boys. One of them had been shot through the neck, had instantly bled out, and his involuntary muscles were causing him to slowly gasp like a dying fish out of water. He was dead, and there was nothing I could do, but he was their friend. I pulled out a battle dressing and wrapped his neck. I asked one of the Marines to lay down covering fire and the other to help me get their friend out of the hole so I could drag him to the rear for more treatment and medevac. At least that is what I told them, because I knew their friend would be riding the tank back with the other dead Marines and Corpsmen when this day ended.

It was quite a struggle to drag a dead Marine and his rifle along with my Unit One (medical bag) back to the rear while crawling. Even though he probably weighed 140 pounds soaking wet, so did I. I would have asked for some help, but the Marines were a little busy at the time. There really was no rear, because the enemy had us pinned down from seemingly all sides. The bad guys maintained a heavy grazing fire from bunkers, using heavy machine guns and sniper fire. At 2:00 p.m., a Platoon from Bravo Company arrived with two tanks and was immediately greeted by the enemy ground fire.

Several gooks were holed up in one bunker, and they continued to engage the Marines with automatic weapons fire. Captain Weede jumped to the top of a nearby tank, directed the tank driver forward to the top of the bunker, and had him spin and crush the bunker, silencing their weapons.

More calls for "Corpsman Up" were heard across the battlefield, and the Docs continued to respond with their usual passion. After some time had passed, I was able to crawl over to a bomb crater where Captain Weede, Westy, and the Gunny were now lying. Captain Weede was constantly on the radio, talking with Battalion Command, and attempting to move Delta units around to gain the upper hand. It was almost impossible to stick your head out of the hole because of the withering gunfire. Harley Cowan rolled into the hole with us and was covered in blood from treating wounded Marines. The call for "Corpsman Up" was heard again, but the bullets popping over our heads were like a snare drum roll. Harley looked at me and said, "I got this!" and with that, he rolled to his hands and feet and started his climb out of the crater. Harley had just cleared the crest when we heard a pop, and Harley went down.

I reached out and grabbed Harley, pulling him back into the crater. He was screaming in agony as I searched his body for the wound. The blood was quickly flowing from a wound in his left groin area. I opened his belt then cut down through the front of his pants to expose the wound and tried to stop the bleeding. The bullet had hit him on the inside of his left leg where it articulated with the torso, struck the femur or pelvis, and created a hole that I could stick my fist in. The bullet had taken out the femoral artery and most likely the iliac artery. I pushed the first battle dressing into the hole and it disappeared into the cavity, then a second, and a third. Harley was losing consciousness from loss of blood and shaking his head back and forth saying, "Don't let me die, don't let me die." I pushed as hard as I could on the wound, hoping that the battle dressings would tamponade the bleeding. Harley continued drifting further away and now only mumbled through his pale blue lips, and then nothing.

Harley was dead!

Corpsman Harley Richard Cowan is honored on Panel 52E, Row 16, of the Vietnam Veterans Memorial.
Meanwhile the battle continued to rage. An AO (Aerial Observer) was now overheard directing helicopter gunships using rockets and machine gunfire on the enemy positions. Over Westy's radio, the AO quickly reported that several NVA were flanking our position. At that moment,

Gunny Sponenberg rolled over onto his back just as two NVA soldiers got to the edge of our crater.

I looked back over my shoulder, and there they were, two enemy soldiers not ten feet away. They were much like us—young, small, skinny, and panic-stricken. Why they hesitated I will never know. They probably had never seen an American up this close, and we had never seen them this close. Whatever the reason, the Gunny shot first. His Mossberg semi-automatic shotgun dispensed a mix of 00 buckshot and fléchette rounds that immediately erased their faces and sent them hurtling backward, inducted as the newest members of the NVA forgotten boys club.

At 3:30 p.m., the Battalion's Bravo Command Group (the second in command of the Battalion) along with Lieutenant Muir, leading the rest of Delta Company and two additional tanks, were committed to the action. As the remaining elements of Delta Company were leaving Con Thien, they came under fire by an NVA recoilless rifle that sent the Marines diving for the trenches. Several more attempts were made to exit, and each time the enemy replied with another round, returning them to cover again. After several of these exchanges, Lieutenant Muir, still standing in the open said, "Those Marines out there need our help," and with that, the Grunts sprang from their shelter and followed the Lieutenant on the double-time (dead run) while being chased by incoming rounds. Upon their arrival at the battle, the decision was made for all 1/4 elements to sweep the enemy from the battlefield. Lieutenant Muir quickly moved his Marines on line in coordination with the rest of the resources, and the push was started by every Marine opening fire.

The enemy did not give up ground easily and continued to return fire with a large volume of small arms, automatic weapons, and hand grenades as they pulled back. It was during this push that Lieutenant Muir was struck by an enemy bullet and went down. A fire team from the First Platoon quickly picked up their Lieutenant and placed him on the back of a tank while enemy bullets pinged off its side. The tank pulled back from the action and carried him to the LZ for medevac while the Marines continued the push. Finally, the enemy broke contact, making a hasty withdrawal as helicopter gunships and fixed-wing fighter jets continued to work them over as they attempted their retreat.

We had established an LZ, and the medevac chopper was on the ground. The wounded were being loaded when I was stunned to see Lieutenant Muir carried in. He had been shot through the forehead, a grazing bullet about one inch above both eyebrows. It had penetrated the skull, and gray matter was exposed. His eyes were open, he was conscious, but he was certainly not coherent. His hands were adjusting his belt and shirt as if he was squaring away his uniform for inspection. I covered his wound with a light dressing and started an IV of serum albumin (a blood volume expander).

To see this wonderful man in this condition broke my heart. I walked next to Lieutenant Muir while his Marines carried him aboard. They were as sad as I was because everyone so respected Lieutenant Muir. He was a Marine's Marine. He died of his wounds twenty-three days later on May 19, 1968.

Lt. James Muir is honored on Panel 63E, Row 14, of the Vietnam Veterans Memorial.

Shortly after the medevac chopper lifted off, Staff Sergeant Whyte was brought to the LZ. His facial wounds were such that Doc Walker had inserted a plastic oropharyngeal airway in his mouth and throat so he would not drown or choke to death on his own blood.

The tide had finally turned, and the Marines swept the area and recovered all our wounded and dead. Seventy-two NVA kills were confirmed, and that was important to those in the rear. The battlefield was riddled with discarded enemy weapons, and a bunker was discovered that housed many RPGs (rocket-propelled grenades), but time did not permit their destruction.

There were only two Platoons protecting all of Con Thien. With nightfall at hand, Staff Sergeant Whyte was loaded on the back of a tank with the other wounded and dead Marines and Corpsmen, and we started our slow walk back to Con Thien. For seven Marines and two

Corpsmen, their ambitions, their dreams, and their lives were now over. Seventeen more were wounded, and still I was amazed that the numbers were not much higher given the day's events. I was covered from head to toe in dried blood, and now my uniform crinkled when I walked as if it had been heavily starched.

As we approached the main gate, we were greeted by our Battalion Commander, Lieutenant Colonel Deptula. The Colonel had served as a Grunt Platoon Lieutenant in Korea and was no stranger to firefights. I must have looked like quite a sight as he looked me up and down. He made eye contact and said, "Outstanding job, Marine."

Meaning no disrespect, I quickly answered back, "I am not a Marine, sir. I'm a Corpsman." I think the Colonel then realized that the blood I was covered in was not that of the enemy but of his own men. His slight smile of a warrior's approval quickly turned solemn. He nodded with understanding, and I continued on.

The dead Marines and Corpsmen were gently placed in the sandbag-protected holding area, next to Con Thien's main LZ, to await their flight out. The holding area and LZ were only twenty to thirty yards from the Battalion Aid Station where our Battalion surgeon was stationed. The Navy doctor had only been in country for two weeks, and I had not had a chance to meet him.

I walked into the Aid Station bunker and introduced myself. Tears filled my eyes as I asked him for a favor. I wanted to come out to the holding area and look at Harley to see if I could have done anything to save his life. The doctor placed his hand on my shoulder and said, "Let me get a flashlight, and let's take a look at your friend." It was dark as we entered the holding area. I identified Harley and showed the doctor the wound area.

In those days we only used rubber gloves to protect the patient from contamination; not much thought was given to being protected from the patient. The doctor dug right in and removed several of the battle dressings from the gaping hole. Then stood up and said, "Doc there was nothing anyone could have done. He could have been on the operating room table, and we would not have saved him. I am so sorry." With that, I thanked him, and he walked back to his bunker.

I said a prayer over Doc Harley and the rest of the casualties, got off my knees, and was walking out of the enclosure when something caught my eye on one of the bodies. It was a Rolex watch strapped to the arm of a lanky, redheaded, freckle-faced dead Marine. I flashed back several months earlier to the vision of a grab-ass session in the back of a deuce and a half that struck the dud antitank mine. The other Marines were busting his balls for being a rich kid who did not need to be there. He had wanted to see action over the objection of his dad.

That was almost more than I could take. I said my good-byes to all the forgotten boys and walked back to my bunker.

It was very quiet that night—none of the usual bullshitting and grab-assing. We all completed our duties and then pretty much kept to ourselves. I was so exhausted I rolled into my bunk, still in my bloody clothes, and soon I was sound asleep.

AFTER ACTION

If there is one happy note to this story, it is that while researching information for this book, I was able to contact Staff Sergeant Whyte, who survived his wounds. This tough old Marine endured three brain surgeries and retired from the Corps as a Gunnery Sergeant.

The Gunny advised me that he and Lieutenant Muir were both sent to the US Naval Hospital Guam after they were wounded. Although the Lieutenant never regained consciousness, the Gunny visited Lieutenant Muir and held his hand every day until his passing.

Semper Fi, Gunny Whyte, and God bless you for your service!

THE END OF APRIL AND STILL NO RELIEF

Since the Marines took over the defense of Con Thien, back in May '67, no unit had to stay there for more than thirty days. For six weeks, 1/4 had been taking a beating, and there was still no word about our relief.

It appeared that the NVA attacks on the large population centers during the Tet Offensive were not the success that the North had hoped and planned, and the local population did not rise up to riot and overthrow the South Vietnamese government. Additionally, the North Vietnamese Army sustained staggering losses of equipment and manpower with little return on their investments. So it appeared that they were going to resume their concentration on clashes with the American soldiers in hopes of running up our death toll and creating dissent back home. As history showed, that was the best strategy.

The last half of April saw an increase of incoming mortar, rocket, and artillery rounds. There was an increase in enemy sightings and shootouts with our day patrols and night ambushes. Many nights saw explosions along our outer perimeter, resulting in the discovery of large gaps in our barbed wire the next morning. This would create the need for Marines to go out and patch the damaged sections of outer wire, leaving them vulnerable to mortar and sniper fire.

WE HAD SNIPERS, TOO

One night I was up in OP-1 with Lieutenant Carolyn, looking through the Starlight Scope. This night we were blessed to have a sniper with us who had a night-vision scope mounted on his rifle. He was there to search our outside wire and try to kill the little bastards before they could blow another hole in our defenses. The sniper and I were searching back and forth across our northern wire, when the sniper spotted three NVA soldiers approaching the wire. He directed me to the location, and through my scope, I could see that they were putting together a Bangalore torpedo.

The Marine sniper said, "Watch the gook on the left, Doc."

Bang went his rifle as it spit out the message of death. A nanosecond later, I observed mist come from the head of the gook on the left as his head snapped back. The other two soldiers were frozen with disbelief. It was pitch black, and no one could possibly see them.

The sniper whispered under his breath, "Say good-bye to the gook on the right."

Bang, the rifle reported again, followed a second later with the now familiar mist and the snap of the head, and he was gone. The remaining soldier, now a believer, quickly aborted his mission and disappeared into the elephant grass.

"Doc" Harley Richard Cowan died April 26, 1968.
This Hero is honored on
Panel 37E, Row 31 of the Vietnam Veterans Memorial

Gy. Sgt. Carl Sponenberg left, Lt. James Muir,
our second in command of Delta Company, right. Enjoying that
ice-cold beer I told you about. Each was a Marines Marine! The Gunny
rotated home safely. Lieutenant Muir was just a few days away from death.
**Lt. James Muir is honored on Panel 63E, Row 14,
of the Vietnam Veterans Memorial.**

Old French and ARVN minefield in foreground with a fence around it so Marines would keep out. Battalion Aid Station and Battalion surgeon bunker middle left, wooden walkway to casualty evacuation and helicopter landing zone middle right. This was called the "Valley of Death" at Con Thien.

Captain Weede doing some amazing Captain Shit.
How did he get that little ball in the cup?

OK, maybe Bill Chastain had three beers and
now he thinks he is as smart as Captain Weede.
He never did swing the little ball into the cup.

Eleven

*The only thing more accurate than incoming
enemy fire is incoming friendly fire.*

—M<small>URPHY'S</small> L<small>AWS OF</small> C<small>OMBAT</small>

J<small>UST ANOTHER DAY IN HELL</small>

A little before 7:00 in the morning on May 1, a Platoon-size patrol from Alpha Company (about forty Marines) made contact with NVA solders just outside our northern wire. The Marines took the enemy under fire with M-16 rifles, machine guns, and M-79 grenade launchers. The rest of Alpha Company quickly reinforced the Platoon, and 81 mm and four-deuce mortars were called in on the enemy position. An Aerial Observer came on station and called in fixed-wing fighters that strafed the enemy lines and then engaged a Platoon of NVA who were coming in from the north as reinforcements. The bad guys broke off contact and melted into the elephant grass. Alpha swept through the enemy position and found fourteen dead NVA. They also discovered a tunnel and command-detonated mines facing toward our outer concertina wire. It appeared that the NVA were set up to ambush the Marines when they came out to patch the wire that had been blown the night before. Alpha suffered four WIAs.

At 8:30 a.m., OP-1 started receiving sniper fire from a gook in a tree five hundred to six hundred yards due west of our position. A 106 mm Recoilless Rifle fired one round with a direct hit that observers said resulted in body parts being sprayed in all directions.

About 10:15 a.m., the Forward Artillery Observers (FOs) were busy directing artillery fire in support of Alpha Company, north of Con Thien, when suddenly BOOM, a large explosion occurred inside the perimeter, in Third Platoons sector, that rocked the entire hill. Screams of "incoming" could be heard outside our bunker and then, BOOM, a second explosion shook the bunker again. We all looked at one another, and Corporal Whiteleather remarked, "That is some big shit they're hurling at us!" BOOM, came a third round and more screams outside.

Over the radio came a shout, "Check your fire, check your fire! You are impacting inside our perimeter!" An FO reported it was friendly fire, and the fire mission had been canceled. Another report over the radio, Third Platoon had taken casualties. Captain Weede dashed for the door with Westy at his side. I grabbed my Unit One and followed. We ran down the road through the Valley of Death with one eye on the trench line that ran next to the road, just in case.

We reached the Third Platoon Dyemarker bunker, and as we came around the corner, I was not prepared for what I saw. One Marine's mangled body laid out in the open, and lying there at the entrance to the bunker was the broken body of S. Sgt. Dan Youmans. Sergeant Youmans was the one who kicked me in the ass on the foiled ambush back at CAC-3 and probably saved all our lives that night with his quick actions. He was so well respected, and now that I am old, I can say loved by everyone. His death shook the Third Platoon Grunts to their core.

Captain Weede turned to Westy and said, "Let's get them covered and get some Marines from the First Platoon to handle the bodies." The Captain then turned to the Third Platoon Lieutenant, Lieutenant

Murphy, and advised him to get his Marines away from the site; we would take care of their two Marines.

I stayed with Sergeant Youmans until the First Platoon Marines arrived and placed him in a body bag. I then accompanied him to the sandbag-protected holding area next to the LZ. When the Marines left, I was there with both bodies. I took my Catholic study material from my left thigh cargo pocket and was about to read a "Hail Mary" and an "Our Father" prayer when Father Greco arrived and asked if he could join me.

The Father administered last rites, and then I followed him in a prayer. At the conclusion, Father Greco blessed me and both Marines, and then he walked out. I placed my hand on the chest of Sergeant Youmans and said my good-bye to a friend and a lifelong mentor.

S. SGT. DAN RANDEL YOUMANS IS HONORED ON PANEL 53E, ROW 43, OF THE VIETNAM VETERANS MEMORIAL.

HOW DOC WALKER REMEMBERED THE INCIDENT

In his book the *The Banyan Tree*, Doc Walker remembered, "Sergeant Youmans had just completed a routine morning briefing, and the squad leaders had just left our bunker and were heading back to their respective areas to brief their own men on the details of the meeting. Suddenly there were several thunderous explosions outside our bunker, and these sounded bigger than anything the enemy had ever thrown at us.

"Sergeant Youmans jumped up from his chair and told us to stay in the bunker, then grabbed his helmet and flak jacket and ran out the narrow corridor of our bunker. Doc Livingston had been injured during incoming the week prior, and his replacement, Doc Tweety, Sergeant Randle, and I were putting on our gear when we heard someone yelling, 'Corpsman! Corpsman!' We all ran out, only to see Sergeant Youmans running toward us yelling, 'No! No! Get back in the bunker!' Tweety, Sergeant Randle, and I dashed back inside. We barely made it into the bunker when another round hit right in our doorway, and I feared the bunker might collapse. The entire bunker was filled with a choking dust cloud, and we all ran for the back doorway as more rounds were hitting around the bunker. I was sure all of us made it to the safety of the bunker.

"Sergeant Randle noticed that Sergeant Youmans was not with us, and he ran back to the front doorway to check on him. When he returned, he said, Sergeant Youmans has been hit! I slipped my medical bag off my shoulder and started toward him when he put his hand on my chest and pushed me back. He said, 'It's no use, he's dead.'

"I ran out the back entrance and ran around to the front entrance. I found Sergeant Youmans lying facedown. There was nothing I could do medically for him. The nature of his wound was so sudden and severe that I'm sure he did not suffer for even a second. I felt totally devastated and had to walk away from the area while some Marines placed them in body bags and carried them away.

"I must have walked completely to the other side of the base, and I did not come back for a long time. I didn't talk much for the next day or two because this one really hit me hard. The next afternoon we packed up Sergeant Youmans's belongings, including a picture of his family, which hung above a small makeshift table between his chair and bunk. The next day the Chaplain came over to our area and we had an informal memorial service for the two Marines."

FRIENDLY FIRE

It was later confirmed that we were hit by friendly fire from the Fourth Battalion Twelfth Marine Artillery Regiment. It seems that one of their 155 mm Howitzers made a slight deflection error. Later that afternoon, a Lieutenant from the artillery battery came out, did a crater analysis, and concluded, "Yep, it was ours." The Lieutenant apologized for the error and then departed.

A LONG NIGHT AHEAD

The early morning of May 2 literally started out with a bang. Fourteen rounds of 82 mm mortars impacted inside the Place of Angels, killing one Marine and wounding two. Counter-fire was initiated with artillery, 81 mm mortars, and Dusters on the suspected NVA mortar sites.

At around 7:30 in the morning, a Bravo Company road sweep was fired on with small arms from the tree line. A firefight ensued that brought out a Platoon from Charlie Company with three tanks from the C-2 Bridge. One Marine was wounded. An hour later Op-1 observed bad guys moving at several locations northwest of Con Thien, mortars were called in on their positions. Incoming mortar and artillery fire, followed by our counter-fire, continued throughout the day with many sightings of NVA soldiers.

Toward the time that most adults back home would call cocktail hour we received a message from the intelligence unit that they had received an Alpha-rated warning that a large NVA ground force accompanied by tanks would attack Con Thien that night, and they might use gas. I swallowed hard and asked Captain Weede what an Alpha-rated intelligence warning was. The Captain replied, "Doc, it is as good as seeing them in the wire."

A few minutes before midnight, the Grunts on the line reported three large explosions on the outer wire, which all three of the Ops confirmed. The wire had been blown on the northwest, north, and northeast. The listening posts were called in and Con Thien went to 100 percent alert (that means every available man is awake and on the line). Fifteen minutes later, we started receiving 82 mm mortar and artillery fire, which usually signals the attack is imminent.

Our 81mm mortars started firing illumination rounds in anticipation of the sapper squads that would lead the charge. Four-deuce mortars were firing counter-mortar missions on the suspected enemy positions. Then it went quiet. Hour after hour the night dragged on. An hour seemed like a week as we sat there peering into the darkness while the shadows from the illumination rounds created dancing figures on the elephant grass that elicited an immediate response from the hair-triggered Grunts on the line.

All night sporadic rifle and machine gun fire could be heard all around the perimeter, and thank God, it was all ours. In the forty-five years since that night I have enjoyed some amazing sunrises, but seeing the sun come up on the morning of May 3, 1968, is still among my favorites.

FRIENDLY FIRE IS NEVER FRIENDLY

Midmorning on the fourth was met with the sighting of a delta-wing aircraft rolling in from the north and firing several missiles, followed a second later by the screaming sound of the projectiles coming in and the earthshaking boom of their impact at the counter-battery radar unit near OP-3. Five unlucky Grunts were filling sandbags at that location. One was killed, and the other four were severely wounded.

At first, it was thought that it was a Russian Mig-21, but later it was confirmed that it was just another friendly fire incident. Apparently, an American fighter jet's electronics picked up a radar signal going out from the Counter-Battery Radar Unit at Con Thien, thought it was an enemy Surface-to-Air missile site (SAM site), and fired a counter-missile strike.

THE ENEMY WAS ALWAYS SO CLOSE

At quarter past four in the morning on May 8, an Alpha Company ambush was moving into position just east of our outside wire when they made contact with an NVA squad. The patrol returned with rifle fire and M-26 hand grenades, then broke contact and returned to the perimeter with one minor WIA.

THE DINING EXPERIENCE AT THE PLACE OF ANGELS

Napoleon coined the famous phrase, "An Army travels on its stomach," but Commanding Generals dating back prior to the Roman Empire understood the need for decent food supplies and the impact that nutrition had on the health and morale of their Armies.

During the Revolutionary War, feeding the Continental Army was a constant problem. There are numerous stories about our soldiers having to resort to boiling their boots for nourishment. Ah, the aroma of boiled boots drifting through the campsite surely had to increase the hunger pangs and salivation as the soldiers anticipated their evening meal. This lack of rations, along with poor living conditions, resulted in staggering accounts of disease, death, and desertion among Washington's troops. The US military has been on a constant quest to improve the soldiers' rations ever since.

The hot cafeteria food (A Rations) that you would find at the large military bases in the rear areas was just not practical or deliverable to the Grunts in the field. The enemy, for some reason, would not cooperate and stop shooting so we could eat supper. Long before World War I, our military has been attempting to improve the individual emergency food rations that the Grunts carry with them in the field.

In Vietnam, one meal weighed 2.6 pounds and supplied 1,200 calories. Three of these meals made up one day's ration of 3,600 calories. The one-day rations tipped the scale at 7.8 pounds and left little room in your pack for much else. If you were going out for a three-day operation, you were taking 23.4 pounds of food (a loaded M-16 rifle only weighed 8.7 pounds).

There were twelve meals to tantalize your palate, only eight if you were Jewish:

1. Beef Steak
2. Ham and Eggs Chopped
3. Ham Slices
4. Turkey Loaf
5. Beans and Wieners
6. Spaghetti and Meatballs
7. Beefsteak, Potatoes, and Gravy
8. Ham and Lima Beans (affectionately referred to as "Ham and Motherfuckers")

9. Meatballs and Beans
10. Boned Chicken
11. Chicken and noodles
12. Spiced Beef

Needless to say, no Marine ever went into the field with full rations. They would mix and match their favorite cans of meat choices, fruit choices, and crackers and spreads, and eliminate the excess weight of the shit that they hated. The word favorite might be a bit strong; it was more like the choices that they could still choke down.

I have always been an "eat to live" type of guy, and when I first started eating the C-Rats back at the C-2 Bridge, I found them a welcome change from the hot meals served at C-2 and back at Dong Ha. However, eating three of the same twelve choices day after day, the monotony would finally get to everyone. When a new case of C-Rats was opened, the Sergeants would dump the case upside down to hide the labels. Everyone had to pick out three meals blind. If you were the unlucky bastard to draw "Ham and Mother," it was like drawing the "old maid" in cards.

Some Grunts were the "live to eat" type and had spices sent from home. They had recipes that combined a little of this and some of that, along with some hot sauce and spices, which resulted in some pretty good-tasting chow.

The Grunts and Corpsmen of 1/4 went eighty days at Con Thien, all on C-Rats, and we never took a bath.

A NAP HE WILL NEVER FORGET
PFC (Private First Class) Ron Washington had just come to Delta Company that afternoon. A recent graduate from Advanced Infantry Training at Camp Lejeune, North Carolina, Ron had spent his entire life in the predominantly black community of East Saint Louis until receiving his notice from Uncle Sam that it was his turn to serve. His basic and advanced training had been a culture shock on several levels.

The Marine Corps training was a shocking experience for everyone, but for PFC Washington, it was also the first time that he had ever had any extended conversations with whites, much less sleeping in the same room with them. During the weeks of training, he had made friends with many white, Mexican, and other black Marines, but now he was alone again and new in the company of battle-hardened Grunts.

Private First Class Washington was quickly introduced to his Platoon Lieutenant and Staff Sargent. Then he was sent to his squad position on the west perimeter of the Place of Angels. It was late in the evening by the time Ron met the members of his squad, ate his C-ration of Ham and Mothers (obviously, being the new guy, you were not in the running for one of the better meals; instead, you received the worst of the lot), cleaned his rifle, and stowed his gear. Exhausted from the time changes and the many days of travel, he barely had the energy to blow up his rubber lady (air mattress) and roll into the dirt shelf he would call home. As tired as he was, Ron's brain would not shut down and continued to review the possible scenarios that laid ahead for him over the next thirteen months.

It seemed like only a few minutes had passed when a Marine shook Ron awake and informed him that it was his turn on watch. Clearing his head, he rolled out of his shelf, grabbed his rifle, and stumbled out of the bunker into the trench line that encircled the perimeter. The night air was hot and heavy, which enhanced the fragrance of sweat and red clay, mingled with the scent of decaying jungle foliage. The sound of mosquitoes buzzed in his ears. There was no break-in period for new arrivals, no welcome-aboard party; he barely had time to tell them where he was from.

Once outside, his Fire Team Leader said, "Stand here and keep your eyes moving from our outer wire to that tree line farther out, and then back again. If you see any movement, or you just think you might have seen movement, give someone a nudge and a whisper. Do you understand?" Ron shook his head in the affirmative, and with that, his team leader disappeared into the bunker.

Ron rubbed his eyes to clear his vision and strained to make sense of the dark shadows that played out before him on the cloud-covered moonless night. The darkness and quiet were only occasionally interrupted by the thump of a distant mortar tube followed by a crack as a flare ignited high overhead, deploying a small parachute, and slowly drifted toward earth, providing a minute of precious light that gave a little clarity to the vague shapes he had been observing.

Ron strained to stay awake and fought against heavy eyelids that begged him to let them close for just a few seconds. He knew if he did, his eyelids would never open, and a firing squad could lay in his future; at least that was his fear.

What seemed like an eternity slowly passed, when one of his squad members tapped him on his shoulder, whispering in his ear, "I will wake our reliefs." A few minutes passed when the plastic poncho that covered the entrance to his bunker pulled back and another Marine stumbled out into the night. Ron scarcely had time to roll into his shelf when he was shaken awake by his squad Sergeant. "Rise and shine, ladies. We leave in an hour." Ron's fire team leader advised him that the entire Platoon was going out on a patrol, so quickly eat, shit, and saddle up.

The Platoon cleared the Angels gate by six in the morning, headed south toward the C-2 Bridge for a few hundred yards, and then turned east toward the tree line into what could only be considered a jungle. Rifles locked and loaded and at the ready, everyone was on hyperalert and knew they had just entered the most dangerous real estate on earth. Making contact with a well-equipped, well-trained, and very experienced and determined enemy was their mission for the day, and they all hoped they would return disappointed.

By noon the sun was hot and high overhead. The temperature was near one hundred degrees as they reached the midpoint of their patrol. The Platoon Lieutenant passed the word to break for lunch, but no heat tabs could be used to warm rations, and they were to make no noise. Everyone moved off the trail and spread out in an oval facing outward. Ron fumbled with his "John Wayne" to open another can of "Ham and

Mothers" (you knew that was coming) Ron took one taste of the fat-congealed lima beans and then set them to one side. He snuggled down into the grass and munched on his cheese and crackers.

Ron's eyes popped open and he thought that he must have dozed off for a few seconds. Clearing his head, he sat up and looked around. The sun was now much lower in the west and he could see no other Marines around him. It was so quiet that he could hear the rapid increase of his heartbeat in his ears. He now stood in a crouched position and moved out onto the trail and still could not see any other Marines. His pulse now raced, and his heart started to pound out of his chest. His mouth became so dry he could not move his tongue.

Ron moved up and down the trail where just a few minutes prior forty Marines surrounded him, and now there were none. How did this happen? Where did they go? Is this just a horrible dream? He quickly figured that they came in from this side of the trail and probably went out that side of the trail, and he took off running in hopes of catching them.

Blind with fear, Ron was running faster than he had ever run during his high school track days. Putting his hands up to clear his way only slowed his progress so he lowered them to the power position and let the palm leaves and branches slap his face as he ran full-out up the small trail.

Ron did not hear the engine of the aerial observer aircraft overhead, nor did he hear the spotter rockets impacting near him with the intent of drawing his attention. Ron was on a dead run to North Vietnam and did not know it. He also did not hear the wop, wop noise of the Huey that landed a few yards to his side in an attempt to pick him up. No, Ron was on a dead run to get there but did not know where there was.

The Huey lifted off again and this time set down directly in the path of Ron's travel. The door gunner stepped out of the chopper and opened his arms in an attempt to catch Ron in his flight for safety. A few seconds later, Ron hit the door gunner like a fullback headed for the goal line, driving him against the side of the chopper. Fortunately, the door gunner had played football, and after the initial contact, he had rolled Ron to one side and brought him to the ground hugging him and shouting, "You are safe, Marine! Get your ass on this chopper, and let's get the fuck out of here." With that, Ron was shaken back to reality, jumped on the chopper, and they were off to Con Thien to reunite him with his Platoon.

A few minutes later, the chopper touched down on the LZ at Con Thien, the door gunner shouted, "This is where you get off," and with that, he grabbed Ron by the arm, pulled him into the doorway, and then pushed him off the aircraft as they lifted off.

The Platoon Staff Sergeant was there to catch him. Putting his arm around Ron's neck, pulling him into a bear hug, he shouted above the chopper's blade rotation and engine noise, "It is a good thing the gooks don't have any black soldiers because that Huey would have shot you if you were any other color. Welcome home, Marine. I don't suppose you will fall asleep on watch anytime soon, and I can assure you that your squad leader and fire team leader will not ever fail to take a head count again."

As they reached the Platoon lines the Staff Sergeant slapped Ron on the back and said, "Welcome to the Platoon, I hope you enjoyed your first two days because these will be the easiest. We will talk about you leaving your rifle behind later." With that, the Sergeant pushed Ron toward his bunker and walked off.

A QUICK WORD ABOUT "DEAR JOHN"

A member of the Armed Forces who is deployed in a combat zone is under a lot of pressure and needs to keep his head in the game. Any negative distractions from home can have devastating consequences to the individual and to those around him. One of the worst disruptions seems to be the "Dear John" letter. In many cases, it can result in changes in attitude, causing reckless behavior. Many Grunts received these letters, and I often wondered why the girlfriends or wives couldn't just string the poor bastard along until he got home and then deliver the bad news.

SOMETHING NEEDED TO BE DONE ABOUT THE CONSTANT DESTRUCTION OF OUR OUTER WIRE

Night after night the enemy would blow holes in our outer concertina wire, which required a Marine work party to go out and make repairs the next morning, leaving them exposed to snipers and mortar attacks. It was decided that an ambush would be set up just outside our wire to catch the bad guys as they attempted to blow another hole.

A squad of fourteen Marines and Doc Walker from the Third Platoon got the assignment. Just after dark, the squad went out. They spread out on a line in ankle-deep grass, facing toward Con Thien, about three hundred feet west of our outer perimeter wire. Doc Walker said later that he was the last man on the left side of the line of Marines.

A little past midnight, enemy soldiers were spotted through the Starlight Scope, and a moment later, the entire squad could see their silhouettes as they approached. The word was passed to hold your fire and allow the enemy soldiers to get trapped between the squad and the concertina wire. A radio message was sent to us at Delta Command and relayed all along the line to take cover in anticipation of incoming friendly fire when our ambush was sprung.

Doc Walker said, "I could see that they were carrying Bangalore torpedoes along with AK-47 rifles and they appeared to be coming straight for me. I was becoming so nervous as they approached, I was sure if they couldn't see me, they must have heard the grass shaking. I had my .45 drawn and a round in the chamber as they walked not more than five feet to the left of me. After they passed me, they split up into two groups of three soldiers."

Captain Weede had moved to OP-1 and was looking through the large Starlight Scope. He was talking with the squad leader and advising him as to when the enemy would move into the kill zone. The Captain said, "Now," and the squad leader gave the order to open fire. The night erupted in a blaze of red tracers and muzzle flashes from fifteen weapons.

The enemy was caught by complete surprise. Illumination rounds lit the sky as the squad swept the area as they moved toward our perimeter's outer wire. A quick body count revealed at least three NVA were killed. A radio message came in that the squad had several minor wounded, they were coming through the outer wire, and to hold fire. Captain Weede ran to the perimeter to meet the squad, while I ran to the aid station to help prepare for the arrival of casualties.

Two Marines were brought into the aid station and I assisted the Battalion surgeon with the examination. We were relieved to find that they both had received minor lacerations from the razor-sharp concertina wire as they attempted to cross back inside our outer perimeter.

The next day a patrol was sent out to look at the ambush site, and they found that the enemy bodies had been removed. It was not a giant victory, but the destruction of our outer wire stopped for a while.

What didn't stop was the constant sniper, mortar, and artillery fire. Five to eight times throughout the day we would receive from one to twenty-five rounds of mixed-caliber ordinance. Some of these rounds were airbursts that exploded a hundred or so feet above the ground and were designed to send shrapnel raining down on Grunts in the open or hiding in a trench.

Other rounds were delayed-fuse ordinance that were designed to explode a few seconds after they had burrowed themselves into your bunker. The delayed fuse was always the worst because you would hear them come in with a thud, and the explosion would follow a second or so later. The Dyemarker bunkers were not designed to withstand a delayed fuse, and your mind would play out what it would probably look like as the big artillery round joined you deep in your bunker, leaving you no time to even kiss your ass good-bye.

THE BOYS LOST THEIR ADULT SUPERVISION

Sometime around the first of May, Gunny Sponenberg left Delta and went back to the world, and with him he left a big hole in my heart. He was such a force in our company. If you looked up the definition of Marine Gunnery Sargent in the dictionary—OK, you know the rest. On

May 8, Westy and Captain Weede rotated out of the Company and I felt I had just lost my family. I was now a foster child with a new family. All nice and competent Marines, but they were not my real family.

Baptism and First Communion

On May 18, 1968, I was baptized Catholic and received First Communion from Father Evan Greco at the Place of Angels. My witness and sponsor was Michael Pinckney (Doc Pinky). Many Marines and Corpsmen received their last rites at the Place of Angels, but I may have been the only one baptized.

My first confession was heard by Father Greco while standing next to a Water Bull (a four-hundred-gallon water trailer). The Father asked me to spill my guts as to the sins that I had committed during my entire life as a non-Catholic. I blushed with embarrassment and asked, "Don't you usually give confession behind a screen to hide the identity of the repentant?"

Father Greco smiled and said, "Yes we do. But, Larry, I know who you are. Would you feel better if I turned my back?"

Now I was even more embarrassed and agreed to continue. When finished, I realized that I was a bigger geek than even I thought I was. My biggest crime was stealing a nickel bag of M&M's from the Rosecrans Market while under the tutelage of my older brother. Maybe I should have lied to spice it up—but what kind of turd would make shit up during his first confession? Most people are trying to hide shit. OK, maybe I do cuss more than the average guy on the street, but not more than the average Grunt in Vietnam.

A close call or a blessing of sorts, I still don't know the answer

The next morning around half past ten, we heard a call from our First Platoon on patrol a thousand yards east of Con Thien just south of the

Trace. They had just made contact with an estimated ten to fifteen NVA. A few minutes later, an Aerial Observer reported that the enemy had been reinforced with another fifty to sixty soldiers, and the game was on.

The First Platoon was under heavy rifle and machine gun fire and at least one .50-caliber machine gun. The Platoon Staff Sergeant came on the radio and announced, "I need another Corpsman up here. This one has had it." I was stunned by his comment. The Sergeant was fairly new to the Platoon, but he was talking about my friends Doc Schindeler or Doc Pinky as though they were spoiled vegetables.

Our new Company Commander ordered us to saddle up; we were going to reinforce the First Platoon. I was already saddled up and ready to go. The temperature was already over 120 degrees with very high humidity, so I carried five canteens of water in anticipation of incurring many heat-related casualties. Halfway through our forced march, my assumption was validated, as a half dozen Marines fell out with heat exhaustion. A hasty squad size perimeter was set up around an LZ while the rest of the Company continued their march. I requested a medevac chopper that came in and extracted the heat casualties, and we quickly rejoined our Company.

It was not hard to find the First Platoon; you just needed to follow the sound of the rifle and machine gun fire and the explosions from the grenades. The American M-16 rifle had a smaller-caliber bullet than the Russian AK-47, and the report from the two muzzles was distinguishable from a distance. There was also the distinctive sound and slower rate of fire coming from a much-larger-caliber machine gun. It sounded much like our Ma Deuce (M-2 .50-caliber Browning) but we did not have one out there. The sound from that big gun increased your pucker factor by a couple of notches because its bullet could penetrate just about anything you could hide behind.

As Delta Command with the Second and Third Platoons got close, the pops and zips started coming our way, and it was a crawl from then on. We linked up with the First Platoon and quickly established a defensive perimeter. Enemy rifle and machine gun fire grazed just over our heads. I met up with Doc Schindeler, and he advised me that he had just medevaced Doc Pinky, who was one lucky son of a bitch. Doc Pinky had been hit in the front of his helmet by a large-caliber bullet (possibly a .50-caliber round). The bullet went through the front of his helmet, took off part of his ear, knocked him out, and exited the rear of his helmet. His hearing was probably destroyed on that side, but he was alive.

By 1:30 p.m., Bravo Company joined the fray along with the Battalion Command Group and five tanks. "OK, you sons of bitches, WE now have YOU outgunned." Bravo and the five tanks moved along the south edge of the Trace, and using the five .50-caliber machine guns and their five 90 mm cannons, they swept into the enemy positions.

The enemy quickly broke contact with us, but the Aerial Observer brought in fixed-wing fighter bombers that fired rockets, guns, and napalm on the retreating foes. At around five o'clock, the enemy now gone, both companies pulled back to a clearing and set up a perimeter to give us a chance to regroup and catch our breath.

Everyone was exhausted and dying of thirst. God bless those tankers, for they brought out plenty of water, and we all sat around and gulped that wonderful liquid that tasted even better than an ice-cold beer. While rehydrating and gaining strength for the long hot walk back to the Place of Angels, we started receiving incoming 60 mm mortars. It was the first time that I did not see anyone run for cover. We all just sat there, too tired to move, and decided to take our chances. Counter-battery fire from Con Thien quickly silenced the mortars and amazingly, we took no casualties.

We got back inside the wire just as darkness fell. I had Pinky's bullet-riddled helmet with me for part of the afternoon but with all the activity and excitement, I lost contact with it and never did find it again. Nor did I ever find out what happened to Pinky. I never heard from my Catholic sponsor and witness of just one day, ever again. His name is not honored on the Vietnam Veterans Memorial, so I can only hope that he has enjoyed a wonderful and prosperous life.

S. Sgt. Dan Randel Youmans was killed by friendly fire on May 1, 1968.
**This hero and my savior is honored on Panel 53E,
Row 43, of the Vietnam Veterans Memorial.**

May 1968, Baptism and First Communion into the Roman Catholic family by Father Evan Greco at the Place of Angels. Witness and sponsor Michael ("Doc Pinky) Pinckney (on the right) was shot in the head a few days later, and I have never known his fate. Pinky, if you are out there, give me an e-mail.

Twelve

It is fatal to enter any war without the will to win it.

—General Douglas MacArthur

Another battle at Phu Oc

A little before daylight on May 22, India Company 3/3 set out from Fire Base A-3, located about three miles east of Con Thien. Their mission was to establish a series of ambush positions south of the Trace between A-3 and Con Thien. Around 6:30 in the morning, the point element was about eight hundred yards southwest of A-3 when they sighted a small group of NVA approximately one hundred yards to their front. The enemy was taken under fire by company snipers. The enemy returned fire with small arms, hand grenades, and 60mm mortars. India's point was pinned down, and the rest of the company started receiving incoming mortars as they advanced to reinforce their point position. Around eight in the morning, Lima Company 3/3 was dispatched to reinforce India Company. On their way out of the gate at A-3, Lima was hit with enemy artillery, severely wounding six Marines (clever little bastards, wouldn't you agree).

At ten past eight, India attempted to disengage but the enemy counterattacked and kept the fight going. Helicopter gunships were

145

requested and came on station thirty minutes later. With the help of Lima Company and the gunships, the enemy finally broke contact and retreated southwest into the heavy jungle canopy. Throughout the rest of the day, both India and Lima 3/3 made sporadic contact with small enemy units and were on the receiving end of constant artillery and mortar fire.

Around noon, Bravo Company 1/4 departed Yankee Station aboard eight tanks moving east along the southern edge of the Trace to exploit contact made by India and Lima 3/3. Bravo Company halted their advance and dismounted the tanks about two thousand yards east of Con Thien. Using the south edge of the Trace to anchor their left flank, the Bravo Company Commander, Capt. Robert Harris, spread his Marines out south on the old abandoned portion of Route 561. Alpha Company 1/4 was brought out and had moved about seven hundred yards east of Bravo's position and set up with their backs to the Trace in an east-west posture, facing south toward the suspected enemy position. The tanks that delivered Bravo Company continued east on the Trace and sat in with Alpha Company to help block the enemy retreat and to ambush the little bastards when they attempted to flee north.

By four in the afternoon, the trap was set. Bravo Company 1/4 was on the west side of the enemy's suspected position, India and Lima 3/3 were on the east side, and Alpha 1/4 was on the north to block their escape. You cannot handpick a better killing position to have your enemy trapped in. At 4:10 p.m. Captain Harris and his Bravo Company received the honor to sweep the enemy from the battlefield. Bravo Company, strung out on line, stepped off into the thick jungle canopy and dense undergrowth, moving east to squeeze the enemy between them and India and Lima. What Bravo Company did not know was the NVA were waiting in camouflaged bunkers that protruded only a few inches above the ground. They had positioned the bunkers so the Marines would have to cross a wide-open abandoned rice paddy to get to them. The enemy was well trained and disciplined and held their fire until the Marine point man was but a few yards from their guns. The NVA sprung the ambush, killing the Platoon Lieutenant and the Radioman instantly along with several other Marines from the point squad. Captain Harris quickly responded by leading his two remaining Platoons into the fight to rescue what remained of the First Platoon. Captain Harris was killed during the push forward, causing the two remaining Platoons to circle the wagons where they fought off several counterattacks while enemy mortars fell on their position. In less than a half hour, almost every officer, Radioman, and staff NCO from Bravo Company had been killed or wounded.

Alpha Company now left their position, started moving south to assist Bravo, and also came under heavy enemy fire, followed by incoming artillery and mortars.

Around five in the afternoon, Delta saddled up, and they we were sent out to reinforce the beleaguered Alpha and Bravo Companies. The temperature was way above a hundred, not a puff of wind, and the air was so thick you could cut it with a knife. I loaded up with five canteens of water and a bandoleer of battle dressings in addition to my Unit One. We went out on almost a run to connect with Alpha and Bravo, with the intention to make contact while it was still light. Several Marines from Bravo Company were sent out to meet us and guided us into their position. As we approached the rear of Bravo Company, we started to receive heavy enemy small-arms fire.

Our new Company Commander moved the Delta Marines into position to assist the Bravo Marines, and I moved to the medevac area where there were numerous wounded Marines waiting for evac. Choppers were inbound and if there was another Doc there, I did not realize it. They were very busy keeping Marines alive farther up in the action (when I say farther up, I am talking maybe twenty-five to fifty yards). While attending to the wounded Marines, I could tell that we were close enough to the enemy that their bullets were still supersonic as they POP, POPPED over our heads.

While moving and treating the wounded, everyone stayed in a very low crouch, hoping that it was low enough. I could hear the rotor blades of the copters on final approach. I only had a few seconds to make a quick triage of who would go and who would stay. In the heat of a battle every rifle is important; the minor wounded would be bandaged and returned to the battle. The more severely wounded were flown out as soon as possible. The dead Heroes were either flown out if there was room in the chopper, or they would ride the tank back to the base and be flown out later to Graves Registration to start their long, lonely, and quiet trip home to their families.

It was almost dark when the first chopper landed. Four Marines grabbed the first body they came to and started to run to the copter. I stepped in front of them to slow them down so I could quickly make a triage assessment. The head of the Marine they were carrying rammed into me and the jagged edges of what little remained of the lower portion of his skull poked deeply into my abdomen. The blood and brain matter from the dead Marine soaked instantly into my shirt and felt cool compared to the sweltering temperature on the late afternoon. I turned the Marines around, and we went back to the collection point and exchanged the brave and heroic Marine for another hero that just might survive the trip.

It was getting late, and Bravo still had two squads pinned down, but Alpha Company was closing in to extract them. The intense fighting went on and on for hours. Finally, the trapped Bravo squads were rescued. At about 9:30 in the evening, contact with the enemy was finally broken off, and the Battalion moved back west and set up a defensive position for the night. All the casualties were finally evacuated except for a few of the KIAs. The day ended with sixteen Marines killed, seventy-six wounded. Six dead Marines had to be left behind along with two missing. I could not stop thinking about the black Marine who fell asleep on a lunch break while on patrol and how frightened he was, and now we had two Marines unaccounted for and, if alive, I could not imagine how terrified they must be. I hoped they were together.

Bravo Company lost two PRC-25 radios, which compromised the Battalion and Company frequencies, shackle sheets* for unknown dates,

---

* *Shackle Sheets—A list of codes used to decipher orders received over the radios that could not be transmitted in the clear.*

and one map with Regiment Thrust Points. It was estimated that our Marine Companies received between 450 and 550 mixed-caliber artillery and mortar rounds during the first day of battle. I couldn't help but think of the letters I had received from home telling of how General Westmorland was spouting off about the ass-kicking we were giving the enemy and how they were losing their will to fight after their staggering losses of the Tet Offensive. Someone should have told these little bastards we fought today about their lack of will to fight.

Delta Company Command set up for the night in a small Catholic Church with only two partial walls still standing, and it reminded me of the heavily damaged buildings in one of the old World War II movies. The Platoon Marines configured a perimeter in a circle with the church in the middle. The perimeter Marines got busy digging fighting holes, but the church floor did not lend itself to digging. I quickly spotted a small artillery crater just inside a collapsed pile of debris, jumped in, and made it my home for the night.

Earlier in the day I had dispensed all my water to needy Marines and had only enough time to refill two of the canteens from a small pool of standing water in an abandoned rice paddy. As I submerged the canteen below the waterline, obvious chunks of particulates poured in. I dropped several halazone purification tablets in on top, screwed the lid back on, and gave the concoction a good shaking. I could only hope that the halazone would kill whatever was in there. I was so thirsty that either way I was going to drink it after the recommended one-hour wait time.

The heavy jungle foliage came almost up to the walls of the church and eliminated any meaningful field of fire, should the enemy launch a counterattack. Because of this lack of visibility, the listening posts were put out only a few yards in front of our lines. The night was very dark, and as I laid there in my hole, I thought that if everyone would just shut the fuck up, the enemy would probably not be able to find us.

There was not much sleeping going on because of the imminent danger of an enemy attack and the thoughts about what tomorrow would bring. Exhausted, I snuggled down into the artillery crater as hundreds of mosquitoes attempted to eat me alive. The evening temperature felt as if I were in a sauna, causing my sweat to turn the dirt into mud, caking my clothing and exposed arms.

My flak jacket held in my body heat and just added to my misery. I so wanted to unzip it and release the trapped heat, but I could not. Many Marines would leave the flak jackets unzipped to allow air circulation, but I had seen way too many men pay a high price for exposing their chest and gut to flying shards of shrapnel from exploding ordinance. I was sure that several of the Marines I had treated today had fallen victim to this breach in personnel security.

WE FINALLY DECIDED TO NOT PLAY FAIR

Apparently, I was not the only one who thought the day's activities did not go very well. The gang in this hood were a tough bunch, and they were not going to give up the playground easily. This playground was named Phu Oc, where several major clashes between the Marines and the NVA had been conducted, including the ass-kicking that 2/4 received back in September '67 when they walked into a Battalion-size ambush.

Names like "Phu Oc" and "the Marketplace" sent shivers down the spines of every Marine in Leatherneck Square because of the stories told by the survivors. Much like when the Earp brothers and Doc Holliday decided to go over and pay a visit to the McLaury and Clanton brothers at the OK Corral in Tombstone, Arizona. The Earps just knew there was going to be a fight, and neither side was assured of survival that afternoon.

The Regimental brass estimated that there was at least a Battalion of NVA dug in at Phu Oc, so to counter their numbers, Battalions 1/9 and 3/9 were lifted in by helicopter to bolster our strength. We now had two companies from 3/3, three companies from ¼, and four companies each from 1/9 and 3/9. I am talking twelve companies in all, for a full Marine Regiment. Always in the past, if we went up against a squad of bad guys, we would respond with a squad. If they reinforced with a Platoon, we would send out another Platoon and so on and so on. We always had to break contact before dark to get back and protect our base.

This time we had Con Thien covered, so that was not a worry. We had approximately 2,500 Marines plus tanks, helicopters, fixed wings, spotter aircraft above, and artillery units standing by to shoot big shit at the bad guys at our command. In addition, we probably had a Bird Colonel and his staff at the helm, all against a possible six hundred NVA.

We must have had a change at the top of our command, because for the first time, we were using overwhelming firepower. I am talking the Earp brothers and Doc Holliday being reinforced by Bat Masterson, Kit Carson, Wild Bill Hickok, and for you younger readers, the Iron Man and Thor all going up against the McLaurys and Clantons at the OK Corral. Shit, even I was optimistic!

The plan was for 3/9 to be positioned south of Phu Oc as a blocking force. Battalion 1/9 and Alpha 1/4 were positioned north of Phu Oc, and Alpha had the honors of making the push from the north into the enemy position (not sure if honors is the best term, but they picked the short straw, and life can be a bitch). Battalion 3/3 would block on the east while Bravo and Delta blocked from the west. I do not know who developed this plan but it was a different plan than ever before and it would change my thinking forever.

Early on the morning of May 23, we woke up the enemy by pounding their position with artillery and air strikes. It's an age old tradition dating back hundreds of years to soften up your enemy prior to your major ground attack. At around 8:00 a.m., Alpha Company 1/4 with five tanks stepped out on their move south to engage the foe waiting for us at Phu Oc. Almost immediately, Alpha started receiving sniper fire from these tough little bastards who had been pounded all morning. Alpha called in more artillery and air strikes on the enemy positions, and this time good things started to happen.

Approximately 150 NVA made a break out of the tree line and fled north toward the Trace. Alpha immediately took them under fire with rifles, machine guns, M-79 grenade launchers, tanks, and artillery. Three artillery batteries were firing simultaneously, along with 60 mm mortars from Alpha Company. The NVA became confused and panicked, and they began running into one impact area after another.

Tanks fired canister and beehive rounds into the disoriented enemy. The enemy must have known that they were boxed in, and there was no way to avoid an ass-kicking because more of them abandoned their positions and headed for the exit. Bravo and Delta 1/4 took them under fire as well.

The enemy attempted to fire mortars on our positions, but tanks quickly identified their positions, took them under fire, and destroyed them both. Aerial Observers circling overhead called in air strikes on the retreating NVA, killing them all. The units at Con Thien even joined in on the turkey shoot as the bad guys were caught in the open.

Artillery and airstrikes continued to pound the enemy positions dug in at Phu Oc, ahead of Alpha Company's approach. Alpha swept into the area where Bravo Company had been ambushed the day before. Only this time, we had been doing the killing. When Alpha entered the enemy bunker complex, it was deserted except for piles of their dead. Alpha was able to recover the six Marine bodies who had been killed the previous day and the bodies of the two Marines who had been reported as missing.

All the equipment had been recovered except for the two PRC-25 radios. The day ended with only five more Marines wounded and no deaths. The rest of the afternoon was spent consolidating the area and evacuating the wounded and the recovered dead. Toward evening, 1/4 and the Battalion Command Group moved about five hundred yards southwest of Phu Oc and set in for the night. This night, fuck the mosquitoes, the sweat, mud-covered arms and clothing, and thirst, I slept like a baby.

THE STORY CAN ALWAYS GET WORSE

The Battalion awoke on the morning of the twenty-fourth and again patrolled the area to ensure that the enemy had cleared out. By the afternoon, the action was declared over and Bravo Company was released to return to Yankee Station for a much-needed rest.

Alpha and Delta along with the Battalion Command Group were to stay out for another night. This is when I first heard the rumor that the Bravo Company Captain's relief had arrived, and the good Captain was due to rotate home in less than a week. It was not even necessary for him to be on this engagement, but he insisted on going along to tutor his new replacement.

Every death is sad and grates on your emotions, but when you see the "Skipper" of your ship killed, it instantly destroys the morale, and that is what happened to Bravo Company.

Marine Capt. Robert Eugene Harris is honored on Panel 65E, Row 10, of the Vietnam Veterans Memorial.
On July 12, 2014, forty-six years later, a note is written to Captain Harris on the Vietnam Memorial Fund website. It reads, "You will always be my hero the love of my life and the father of our children. You chose to go with your men that day on May 22, 1968. I thought you were on a plane to come back to me. Once a Marine always a Marine, you were concerned about your men. I will always love you, and someday we will be together again. You have left behind a loving wife, two sons, and three grandchildren. I always tell my grandchildren about you. Jacie is five years old. She says she will put flowers on your grave when I go to heaven to be with you. We love you and miss you, Jeannie."

The Captain was the love of her life and she never remarried.

I apologize to you Mrs. Harris but I must make a small rant.
In April 2016 I had a phone conversation with Mrs. Harris and received her approval to include her message that she left to her Captain on the Vietnam Veterans Memorial Fund web site (the one you just read). During the conversation she told me that shortly after the news of the Captain's death she received a phone call from a draft dodging coward

(my words not hers) that advised her that the Captain got what he deserved and that he should have never been there in the first place.

On another occasion she was at the cemetery visiting the Captain when another coward approached her and relayed a similar message.

I do not care if you are a conservative or a progressive, should a wife and mother be subjected to this kind of harassment because her husband gave his life to his Country?

The death benefits during the Vietnam War were ten thousand dollars and Mrs. Harris became the sole provider for her family for the rest of her life.

To Mrs. Harris and your family

Mrs. Captain Harris, God bless you, your family, and Captain Harris. I will never forget, and I write this tribute so MY family will never forget your husband and what he did for his Marines, for Bravo 1/4, for the Marine Corps, and our country. "Semper Fi."

The battle for Phu Oc was over again

No further contact with the enemy was made, and Alpha and Delta Companies returned to Con Thien on the morning of May 25. The final toll of the four days of action resulted in twenty-three Marines killed and seventy-eight wounded. The enemy lost at least two hundred twenty-five dead, and we took three prisoners.

While we were out in the field for three days, Hotel Company 2/26 along with forty-two Marines from the 1/4 rear area at Dong Ha were brought in to defend Con Thien.

Talk about being out of the frying pan and into the fire

We had no sooner gotten back to the Delta Company Command bunker when our new Company Skipper was called to a meeting at the Battalion

Command Post. He was gone for an hour or so, and when he came back, he had a "shit-eating" grin on his face. He called for a meeting of the Platoon Commanders and the Staff NCOs, and he could hardly contain himself while waiting for the Platoon leadership to arrive.

Once they were all present and settled in, the Company Commander started the meeting. "Gentlemen, I have some great news. Our new Third Marine Division Commander, General Davis, is changing the Division strategy from defensive to offensive. There will be no more of this 'McNamara Line' bullshit, where we set in these Strong Point positions and wait for the enemy to attack us. We are now going to do what the Marine Corps does best, and that is to attack the enemy in his backyard."

The Lieutenant continued, "Intelligence reports indicate a large number of NVA are massing near the Laotian border south of Khe Sanh. They are building a road and staging materials with the probable objective to infiltrate southern Quang Tri Province and possibly the provincial capital of Hue. The new Third Division strategy calls for a large-scale air-mobile offensive. The new mission is called "Operation Robin," and it is very straightforward. The Fourth Marine Regiment will be inserted by helicopter to interdict and destroy the road and any NVA and materials that we find. To accomplish this mission, a series of Fire Support Bases (FSB) will be established on hilltops very near the Laotian border."

I looked around the room and saw nothing but satisfaction. I swallowed hard and thought I was back at CAC-3 when Captain Weede proposed dropping leaflets begging the NVA to attack us. What is it about these Marines that elicits a fucking "smiley face" response when they hear that we are going to go attack a numerically superior force of bad guys? It seemed to me that we had plenty of trouble right here over the last couple of days; the NVA were not some poorly trained and poorly equipped bunch of misfits with low morale. From what I had seen, they were very tough and determined little bastards and should not be taken lightly. While the Marines were excited, I kept thinking that I should order up a shitload of battle dressings for these crazy Heroes.

The Lieutenant further informed us that Delta Company was moving out of Con Thien the next day and was going to be moved to the "Rockpile." From there, we would be airlifted to establish one of the new Fire Support Bases.

I thought, *"Holy shit, there is no way that we will be able to mass enough Grunts to overwhelm the NVA like we did at Phu Oc. This time just who would play the part of Wyatt Earp?"*

THE PLAN

The plan was, on May 25, Bravo Company was to be choppered to the Fourth Marines and moved from Yankee Station to Camp Carroll. On May 26, Delta and Alpha were to be transported to the "Rockpile." One Platoon from Alpha would be assigned to Bravo Company to help protect Camp Carroll. On May 27, 1/4 Battalion Command Group would assume command of Camp Carroll while Charlie Company would occupy four positions along Route 9. Battalion 2/26 would assume the defense of Con Thien.

AND THEN CAME SOME GOOD NEWS, JUST FOR ME, NOT THE GRUNTS

I was pondering my future and playing a mental simulation in my mind of the battles that lay ahead in the next few weeks, speculating on my odds of survival. Just then, I looked across the bunker and suddenly realized there was yet another new guy reporting for duty. Just who was he replacing? I looked him up and down and then gazed at his collar insignia and realized he was a second class Corpsman. At that moment, the Company Commander said, "Doc, I want to introduce you to Doc Marty Romero. He is your replacement. You have been transferred to the Third Medical Battalion in Phu Bai. Take as many days as you need to brief him on his duties."

All I knew was that Bravo Company was moving to Camp Carroll, which was on my route to the loving arms of the rear area. Going with

Delta Company to the Rockpile was on the road to yet another battle. I advised my Company Commander that everything that my replacement needed to know I could wrap up prior to Delta leaving for the Rockpile. I knew time was short and there was a lot of information that I wanted to pass on to Doc Romero, so we immediately got busy.

I was taking Marty around to the Second Platoon position on the north side of the perimeter to introduce him to his Corpsmen when we started receiving 122 mm rockets into the Third Platoon area on the south. Following the trench lines down through the middle of the base, Marty and I reached the Third Platoon area.

At least nine rockets had hit the area. Several of them actually struck inside the trench line that Docs Walker and Tweety were hiding in. How they were not killed can only be described as "a gosh darn miracle." It probably deserved stronger language, but it just might have been divine intervention, and even I am not that stupid.

Several Marines were seriously wounded and were medevaced out. Doc Walker and Doc Tweety suffered some minor injuries and were taken to the Battalion Aid Station for an exam by the Battalion surgeon. Both had sustained severe ear damage as a result of the overpressure of the explosion and the next morning they were sent by jeep to Dong Ha and then off to Da Nang for more definitive treatment.

Several more Corpsmen were requested from the rear to replace Docs Walker and Tweety, and I continued the tour with Doc Romero. The next morning was May 26, and all of Delta and Alpha Companies were up early, packed up, and ready to move out to their new home at the Rockpile.

I accompanied them as far as Camp Carroll, jumped out of the back of the deuce and a half, and shook hands with Doc Romero and the Company Commander, wishing them the best of luck in the coming months. As the convoy pulled away, I waved good-bye to the rest of my Delta family, which was now mostly full of new faces. I picked up my seabag and went looking for a temporary place to sleep for the night.

Camp Carroll was one of the largest of the nine artillery bases constructed along the DMZ and could accommodate up to two thousand soldiers and

Marines along with sixty to eighty artillery pieces, including twelve of the Army's M107 175 mm guns. The M107 was the most powerful American field artillery piece at the time, capable of sending a 150-pound projectile twenty miles and could return fire on any enemy gun that could reach us. Camp Carroll was considered a foreword base but not the same foreword as Con Thien. Hell, this place had a chow hall, and you didn't need to sleep in a bunker. It was almost like being in the rear, if you asked me.

I was assigned to a bunk in a "hooch" with other 1/4 Corpsmen that were rotating out of the field, along with corpsmen who had just arrived in country. I could not help but think back to Doc Hal Jones, that bigger-than-life Doc who told us all those stories, then lost his life in the copter crash on his way to see his wife in Hawaii.

Now, almost six months later, here I was in the same position with the new guys wanting to know what it would be like when they got to their Marine units. I was the highest ranking Doc in the room and probably the biggest bullshitter of the bunch, so I probably told the most stories. Soon, the other old-timers joined in and, just as Doc Hal Jones did to us, the new guys were like children around a campfire, hearing their first ghost story. We scared the shit out of them that night; however, the difference between the ghost stories and the stories that we told was that ours were the truth.

The next morning I went to the chow hall and had scrambled eggs, bacon, and potatoes that tasted out of this world. It was the first real food that I'd had in eighty days, and forty-five years later, breakfast with eggs and bacon is still my favorite meal. After breakfast, I packed up my shit, and with several other Docs, caught a ride to Dong Ha where we turned in our pistols and other gear at the 1/4 rear area, received our new orders, said our farewells, and all went our separate ways.

I caught a flight on a C-130 aircraft taking wounded Marines from Delta Med at Dong Ha to the Third Marine Medical Battalion at Phu Bai. The Medical Battalion was attached to the Phu Bai airport, so when we landed, the aircraft was able to taxi right up to the front of the emergency room. The rear ramp was barely lowered when we were instantly greeted by a Second Class Corpsman who stepped aboard and started to triage the wounded as they were being carried off the aircraft.

He would read the wounded Marine's paperwork, do a quick patient assessment, and then quickly shout, "Take this Marine to station fifteen, take this Marine to station three, take this Marine to station eight, "and so it went until the stretchers were gone. Some of the patients were walking wounded, and the Doc would instruct them to walk to one of the various specialties within the hospital (minor surgery, EENT, medical ward, etc.).

In just a few minutes, the aircraft was empty, and all the wounded were being treated. I stood there for a few minutes in total amazement at just how competently this twenty-year-old Corpsman handled this very difficult task. After a few minutes of taking it all in, I went off to locate the administrative office to report in and receive my new assignment.

ROBERT EUGENE HARRIS
KENTUCKY

Capt. Robert Eugene Harris was killed in action on May 22, 1968.
This Hero is honored on Panel 65E, Row 10,
of the Vietnam Veterans Memorial

Thirteen

In the Rear with the Gear

Thank goodness, many years ago, I had a preceptor,
for whom my admiration has never died, and he had
a favorite saying, one that I trust I try to live by. It
was: always take your job seriously, never yourself.

—DWIGHT D. EISENHOWER

BACK TO PHU BAI

On June 2, 1968, I reported for duty at the administrative office of the Third Marine Division Medical Battalion, which at the time was located next to the civilian airport near the city of Phu Bai. The clerk at the desk offered me several positions that were available, including the emergency room, but I needed a break from seeing heroes mangled, disfigured, and clinging to life, so I opted for a position in the medical supply unit, which was as far removed from the ER as I could get. I was assigned to a hooch, and off I went to stow my gear. Then I reported to the supply unit.

When I entered the hooch, I was greeted by "Kim," a young Vietnamese girl who was around college age. She was cleaning the hooch and collecting laundry from the bunks of my fellow hooch mates, who were all at work at the time. Each girl who cleaned the hooch was called, "A House Mouse." There were ten men to our hooch, and Kim cleaned and did laundry for us for ten dollars a month for each occupant. We did not pay her in US dollars, but instead we used military payment certificates (MPC). Kim could then take the MPC and exchange it for South Vietnam piasters. One hundred MPC dollars a month converted up to double the value of the piaster and made Kim a very good wage earner for her family. And, NO, there were no scandalous Hollywood stories of Kim being forced into sex or even offered sex. She was a very sweet Catholic girl who attended college in the ancient city of Hue, and I hope she survived the Communist takeover and now has a good life either in Vietnam or here in the United States.

I stowed my gear and made my bunk, which, by the way, actually had a thin mattress that I could hardly wait to sleep on that night. I headed off to the supply unit to introduce myself to the new crew. When I got there, I introduced myself to three or four guys and a Chief Petty Officer who was the senior enlisted officer for the supply unit. I was informed that the Third Marine Division was moving all its forces into northern I Corps and the Third Marine Division Medical Battalion was moving from Phu Bai to a new base, farther north, at Quang Tri.

The warehouse was a beehive of activity, loading trucks with medical supplies for the move to our new facility. With no time to waste, I jumped right in and started removing supplies from the warehouse shelves, placing them into boxes, labeling the contents, and placing them into larger boxes to be lifted by forklift onto the trucks. We worked until the chow hall was about to close, then rushed over to eat, then off to the EM club (enlisted man's club), grabbed a couple of beers each, headed back to the warehouse, and continued to work late into the evening.

ACCIDENTS DO HAPPEN

The next morning we were up by six o'clock. We hit the chow hall for a quick breakfast, and we went back to the warehouse. Sometime in the afternoon, I was breaking down a large wooden shipping container, using a short-handled sledgehammer. To get a better angle for my hammer strikes, I climbed into the crate with the intent of forcing the shoulder-high sides of the box outward. I lined up my hammer on the intended impact point, drew back, and with all my might swung the hammer forward. The head of the hammer just missed the intended target and continued over the top of the box, pulling the handle from my hand like a missile leaving its launch pad. One of my new work mates had the misfortune of walking by at that exact moment, and the hammer struck him on the right side of his head. Bones was his nickname and not because he was skinny. He was a hulk of a man who would have made two of me. The hammer hit with a thud, turning him in my direction, and almost cartoonlike, he staggered sideways and said, "You mother fuc" but his lights went out before he could finish the complete phrase.

I jumped from the container, ran to his side, and checked for a pulse. Thank God, there was one, but Bones was not responsive. I yelled for help, and several other Corpsmen came running. As humiliating as it was, I explained what happened as we loaded him into the back of a truck and ran him up to the emergency room. Bones was awake by the time we arrived, but the doctor wanted to keep him overnight for observation. We stayed with him until we were certain he was wide awake and out of danger. Then we went back to work. Driving the truck back to the warehouse, one of the guys suggested that my new nickname should be friendly fire. After work I went back to the ER to check on Bones and to apologize profusely. I advised him of my new nickname, which brought out a much-welcome chuckle. Bones was back to work by noon the next day with no permanent injuries, and fortunately, my nickname only lasted for a few more days.

WHEELS UP FOR QUANG TRI

Within a week, the last truckload of medical supplies joined a convoy heading north to Quang Tri, and the four of us hitched a flight on a

C-130 from Phu Bai to our new home where we immediately started unloading all the boxes we had loaded a few days prior. I finally got to meet the rest of the warehouse staff. There were four or five Corpsmen, including myself, assigned to the warehouse, and our job was to take a supply order that came in from the hospital, pull the supplies from the warehouse, and deliver the supplies to the various wards and units. Additionally, there were four or five enlisted personnel who worked in the office portion that processed the paperwork and ordered supplies to restock the warehouse shelves. A Navy Lieutenant and a Navy Chief Petty Officer were in charge of the entire process.

Not every Corpsman in our supply unit had seen combat with a Marine rifle company. Many, because of their clerical skills, had been assigned here from their very first day. We never really talked about who had or who had not been "in the shit." One day though, it was so hot that we were working with our shirts off, and I could not help noticing one of the Corpsmen had a perfectly round silver half-dollar-size scar on his left upper chest just below his collarbone and a slightly larger matching scar on his left upper back. Both scars looked as if someone had left a burning hot cigar in contact with his skin for several minutes.

I just had to ask how he had got the scars. Jim responded that he was a Corpsman with 3/4 and his Platoon was in a firefight. He remembered a Marine fifty yards to his front had been shot through his gut, the AK-47 round went through the Marine and through the Marine's canteen where the bullet picked up a blood-and-water vapor trail. Jim continued, "I remember being in a crouched position, and I could see the bullet's pink vapor trail coming straight at me. It seemed like I was caught in slow motion, and I knew I was going to be hit, but there was not enough time to move out of the way. A second later, I felt the thud. The bullet went clean through and did not hit any bones or major vessels. I was one lucky son of a bitch."

I could not help but be a little envious. Just thinking that he had a Purple Heart that resulted in no disabilities, and a wound that, when his shirt was off at the beach, at some lake, a backyard pool, or better yet a romantic interlude, someone would surely inquire as to how he got those scars. If it were me I would calmly gaze down and say, *"Oh, this little thing? Let me tell you how this happened."* Of course, there would have probably been a smidgeon of bullshit thrown in, and depending on the audience, the story would have a variable start with a flexible ending, but that's just me.

LIFE CAN BE A SLIPPERY SLOPE

One day a monsoon storm rolled through that exposed several leaks in the roof of our new Butler building, which posed a contamination risk to our medical supplies. It was impossible to trace the drips and leaks back to their origin, so I volunteered to go up on the metal roof with a caulking gun and put a dab of sealant on the rivets in the suspected area.

The peak of the "gabled" roof was near twenty-five feet high, and I used an extension ladder to climb onto the ridge. The rain was still coming down as I walked along the ridge to the spot where we determined the leak was probably coming from. The plan was that I would start applying sealant on the rivets while several guys maintained vigilance on the leak from the inside. If I was lucky enough to caulk the aberrant rivet, the leak would stop and my job would be finished.

I started applying sealant to the first row of rivets closest to the ridge, where my footing was the most stable, and moved along the ridge for a distance of ten feet. Then I reached down to the next row of rivets and worked my way back to the start. When I finished the second row of rivets, the third row was just out of my reach, which necessitated my stepping off the ridge and onto the sloping metal roof sheeting.

Keeping my left foot firmly on the ridge, I tested the adhesion with my right foot. Feeling satisfied that the roof was not too slippery, I stepped off the ridge with both feet and immediately my feet went out from under me, my back slammed onto the roof, and then I began a slow slide. I tried to spread out and lay perfectly still, but I kept sliding, and the edge of the roof was getting closer, so I switched to frantic flailing with no better results.

Now helpless, I anticipated sliding off the edge of the roof, falling twenty feet, landing on my back, probably ending up paralyzed from the neck down! What bullshit this was. I just came out of combat without a scratch, and now this is how I am going to go out?

I let out a scream in frustration, and yes, probably more out of fear as I went over the edge. I was in a free fall for about five feet when my back bounced off a stack of empty medical supply storage cases that sprang me forward, where I fell another three feet, landing on my chest on more empty cases. Then I rolled off and landed on my feet, standing up.

A moment later, two Marines came running around the side of the motor pool. Seeing me, one of them asked, "Doc, did you hear someone scream?"

I replied, "No I didn't hear anything."

The Marines turned and started walking back to the motor pool, and I could hear one saying, "I could swear I heard a woman scream."

I did not ascend the ladder to attempt further caulking.

SO WHAT DID WE DO WITH OUR TIME OFF?

Our new hooch at Quang Tri was the same typical half-inch plywood sides and corrugated tin roof that was seen at every military instillation in Vietnam. Unlike Phu Bai, we had no "House Mouse" so the cleaning was up to us. The hospital had a laundry, and one of my hooch mates ran it. We would throw our dirty clothes in net bags that had our names on them, and the clothes were washed and dried in the bag and returned to us.

After work, there was not much to do. You could go to the enlisted man's club and watch drunken Corpsmen and Marines compete to see who was the quickest at biting open a can of beer, squeezing the contents down their throat, and throwing the empty can against a wall. I swear the record was less than three seconds. I am sure it was something to be very proud of, but back then I was not much of a drinker, yet.

There was always a card game going on somewhere, and it was very easy to lose a month's pay in a single night. But not to worry; the winners were always ready to lend you your money back until payday at an interest rate as high as 40 percent. Volleyball was a big sport. The rules were pure jungle ball with a lot of shit talking, and the losers bought the beer. I was a fair player but a great shit talker.

There were the occasional USO shows that came through to entertain the recovering wounded and sick Marines but never the caliber of a Bob Hope show. These acts were more on the level that you might see at some local "shit-kicker" bar on the outskirts of some small town back in the United States. I am not complaining. God bless the USO and the singers and dancers who risked coming so close to North Vietnam.

In addition to our regular daytime warehouse duties, at least once a week, we were also responsible for standing after-hours duties in the hospital. I would usually wind up working in the Emergency Room or what they called the Minor Surgery Unit, where we got to clean out and suture up small wounds. Having assisted many doctors with suturing when I was working in the operating rooms back in San Diego, I found this duty to be quite rewarding.

JUST WHEN YOU THOUGHT YOU HAD SEEN EVERYTHING

One evening I was in the Minor Surgery Unit when a Marine came in with a god-awful infected burn on his right forearm. The burn was about three inches long, a half inch wide, and a quarter inch deep with a yellow, puss-filled scab that caused his entire forearm to be swollen. I asked the Marine just how he got the burn and was dumbfounded at his answer.

The Marine indicated that he and another Marine were playing chicken by facing each other, placing their forearms tightly together, then taking a lit Pall Mall cigarette and dropping it in the crack between the two arms. The first one to pull away was the "chicken shit." The Marine went on to tell me that neither one quit so they both held their positions until the cigarette burned itself out.

You tell me, would two men do that, or were they boys who were lacking adult supervision that night?

I advised the Marine that the cigarette burn was nothing compared to the pain he was going to feel when I scrubbed the scab off to wash out the wound.

After the scrub down, bandage, and a butt full of penicillin, the Marine agreed that the cure was much worse than the cause.

I am sure that he had a major scar from the burn, and I have often wondered how he explained the scar to his son and grandson. I can just hear him now, *"There I was, gooks on my right, gooks on my left, and so on and so on."*

THERE IS ALWAYS A JOB WORSE THAN YOURS

Sometimes we were just used as litter humpers who carried wounded Marines off the choppers and into the ER. Most of the incoming choppers were bringing the wounded and dead straight from the field. Once the wounded were removed, the dead were taken off. Many of the dead had been in the field for days where they had been exposed to one hundred plus degrees. The stench and the sight of our mangled and bloated brothers was almost overwhelming, and many times it resulted in gagging and retching.

We would carry the bodies to "Graves Registrations," which was housed in a building just off the helicopter landing pad but separated from the hospital buildings. In this small building, a group of Marines was tasked with starting the identification and recording process of the dead Marines and Corpsmen. As we carried the bodies through the door, we were instantly confronted with a picture out of a very gruesome horror movie. We were instructed where to set down the new arrivals in what appeared to be an already overcrowded venue. I am not sure what procedures were in place to process the deceased and start them on their journey home, but I knew that there was one job I was not suited for and did not care to know much more about.

Our House Keeper while in Phu Bai what
a sweetheart, a good Catholic girl that
I hope made it to the US.

The lead Corpsman from the Emergency Room
would triage the wounded Marines as they came
off the aircraft as to which station in the ER they
would go to. You never wanted to be taken to "Station One."

OK, so the USO never sent Bob Hope
this far north.

Some chicks remain a "two at two."

Fourteen

LZ LOON

*If you are short of everything but the
enemy, you are in the combat zone*

—*MURPHY'S LAWS OF COMBAT*

A REUNION SOONER THAN EXPECTED

One evening soon after I arrived at Quang Tri, I was assigned to evening duty in the Emergency Room. Several other Corpsmen and I were just signing in when we received the word that a chopper was inbound with wounded Marines as a result of a massive firefight near Khe Sanh.

Several other Corpsmen and I followed the Senior Corpsman from the Emergency Room out to the chopper as it landed. The Senior Corpsman was the first on the chopper as the back ramp came down and he started his usual triage procedure and shouted out which station in the ER to take each Marine, "This Marine to station five, this one to station two, this Marine to station one," and so it went.

We would quickly carry the stretcher to the stations and then hustle back out for another wounded Marine. After the stretchers were off-loaded, then came the walking wounded. That is when I spotted my

170

Delta Company replacement, Doc Marty Romero, come walking down the ramp.

Marty spotted me and said, "Hey, Doc, I never thought I would see you again."

I walked with him to the ER and asked, "What the fuck happened?"

He replied, "The gooks kicked our ass. I just flew in with these Charlie and Delta Marines to try to keep some of them alive during the flight here." With that, we entered the ER and jumped in, helping the ER staff with all the wounded.

The next evening I saw Doc Romero walking toward the EM Club, and I joined him for a beer. We sat down at a table, and he filled me in on what happened to Delta 1/4.

LET ME FIRST SET THE STAGE FOR YOU

Major General Raymond G. Davis was the newly appointed Third Marine Division Commander (two stars on his collar). The General wanted to make a statement to the NVA that there was a new sheriff in town and the static perimeter, hide behind barbed wire, minefields, and clear fields of fire, come-get-me bullshit was over.

This new sheriff was going to have his posse hunt the little bastards down and kill them and continue to chase and kill them for as long as it took. This new strategy was dubbed "Air-Mobile Offensive Operation" and Operation Robin was going to be the first test of his new strategy.

The objective of the operation was straightforward; the Fourth Marine Regiment was to destroy the road that the enemy had been constructing that would facilitate their incursion into the Quang Tri Province, and to kill the bad guys whenever and wherever the Marines found them. To accomplish the mission, the Marines would need to establish three Fire Support Bases (FSB). The first to be established was FSB Robin, the second was to be FSB LZ Loon, and the third would be FSB LZ Torch.

Delta, along with the sister companies of 1/4, got the honor of being the first members of this new posse. Ladies, may I have an Ooh-Rah!

FIRE SUPPORT BASE LZ LOON

Hill 672 was a large hilltop, comprising three knolls. A deep ravine separated the hill into two distinct areas. The southern hill was the largest and the lowest of the three knolls and would be the recipient of the planned artillery instillation. On the north side of the ravine were the two smaller but slightly higher knolls that were separated by a small saddle. These knolls would need to be occupied to deny the enemy the high ground that looked down on the Marines south of the ravine. The hill complex was named LZ Loon (Landing Zone Loon) by the military planners and was located four miles southeast of the embattled Marine base at Khe Sanh.

This area of South Vietnam had been owned and occupied by the NVA almost since the war began, and the bad guys were not going to give it up without sending out the entire welcome wagon. Our Military Intelligence indicated that there was at least one NVA Regiment and possibly two working in the area of LZ Loon (I am talking two to four thousand gooks) and if that did not make your stools loose, the only support and supply for the Marines would be by air.

The plan called for the entire Second Battalion, Fourth Marines (about 1,000 Marines) to make the initial helicopter-borne assault from LZ Robin into LZ Loon, seize and defend LZ Loon until relieved by Charlie and Delta Companies from the First Battalion, Fourth Marines. At 11:35 a.m. on Monday, June 3, 1968, the helicopter-borne assault from LZ Robin to LZ Loon began, but because of incoming artillery, mortars, and automatic weapons fire that greeted them at Loon, the lift was not completed until almost 4:30 p.m. For the remainder of the day, numerous enemy sightings were made, and in all cases, the NVA were fired upon with mortars, artillery, and air strikes, but because of the heavy jungle canopy, the results were unknown.

The plans further called for Charlie and Delta 1/4 to chopper in from Camp Carroll on Tuesday, June 4, and relieve the entire Battalion of 2/4. They would continue the defense of the hilltop with two companies (about four hundred Marines) who were expected to establish an artillery base, conduct search-and-destroy patrols, and conduct screening activities around the fire base. The Army was to bring in a battery of 105mm artillery to blow the shit out of the gooks for a few days and then everyone would be picked up and flown somewhere else and the process would be repeated.

Did I mention that there were thousands of gooks in the immediate area?

I was just a Doc and not a Marine, nor was I a military planner, but doesn't this sound like a hastily set up static perimeter, come get me bullshit, minus the barbed wire, minefields, and clear fields of fire that we had at Con Thien?

BACK TO THE STORY

Delta 1/4 had been getting ready for the lift to LZ Loon for several days and was told that they would probably encounter heavy enemy fire as they approached the landing zone. They were told to carry as much ammo as they could carry and to take C-Rats and water to last several days. No one would be flown out unless they were seriously wounded or had serious medical problems, so the Docs loaded up with extra halazone water purification tablets, extra salt tablets, extra malaria pills, extra suture kits, antibiotics, obviously a shitload of battle dressings, and IV solutions. They would probably be smoking more than usual so everyone packed extra cigarettes.

Charlie Company was flown to LZ Loon on the afternoon of Tuesday, June 4, and relieved the two companies of 2/4 who occupied the southern hill of Loon. Because of several delays caused by the continuing enemy fire, Delta's departure was pushed over to the next day.

Can you imagine the good night sleep the Delta Marines had just dreaming about what their fate would be as they tried to land at LZ Loon the next morning?

DELTA'S TURN TO FLY TO LOON

On the morning of Wednesday, June 5, Delta was up early, well fed, and ready. The Company moved near the LZ at Camp Carroll and everyone was ready for the customary "hurry up and wait," but they were all surprised to hear the sounds of inbound choppers and the visual of more choppers than most of the Marines had ever seen in one place. The company was advised that Delta Command would be on the first chopper. Each Platoon would quickly load their troops as soon as the ramp dropped to limit the time the choppers were on the ground. They were also reminded that when they reached LZ Loon to get off even quicker and for the Platoon Grunts to move quickly to secure the perimeter. The skipper advised the Command Group to stay together and set up quickly in the middle of the perimeter to direct the Platoons as they landed.

As the first CH-46 started to land, the rear ramp was already coming down. The Marines were on board before the wheels even touched the ground and then quickly lifted off and banked sharply away from the perimeter to avoid the air traffic. The sudden banking motion coupled with the swirling dust and turbine exhaust that filled the fuselage brought many a breakfast to the throat. Those affected kept swallowing hard and attempted to seek a horizon through the portholes of the chopper. Within a few moments, the aircraft leveled off, the air cleared, and stomachs started to settle down.

The flight could not have taken more than fifteen minutes when an announcement was made that the objective was three minutes out. The Marine pilot informed the Delta Marines that as soon as the ramp was down and they could see the ground, to get their asses off his aircraft. Then he ended with "Get some Marines, Semper Fi!" With that everyone stood, holding onto the bulkhead, facing to the rear. The word came, "Thirty seconds." Pulses quickened and mouths went dry. Packs were shifted to the middle of the back, rifles were checked, and helmets slapped. The ramp hydraulic mortar start humming, and the rear ramp started to go down. Hearts started racing out of the chest, and breathing was forced back under control.

"Five seconds!" came the command. The low base sounds of explosions thumped in the ears and the pop and zip of small-arms rounds could be heard as they pierced the thin skin of the chopper. "Get off, get off, get the fuck off" came the call from the chopper crew. With that, the Marines charged the ramp, and within seconds, they were off.

The chopper lifted off and quickly gained altitude, chased by a torrent of bullets. The Marines quickly secured their belongings as the second chopper was on final approach. A Sergeant from 2/4 was waiting and pointed to where the Command Post was and then moved to direct the next load of Marines who were now landing.

The Delta Command Group was directed to move off the eastern hill down the saddle and set up on the western hill where a Company Commander from 2/4 was waiting. On arrival, the two skippers shook hands and started talking. The Command Group moved closer and strained to hear the briefing over the numerous choppers landing and taking off.

The 2/4 Company Commander advised the Delta Marines that they had just landed in the middle of Indian Country and the gooks were not happy that they were there. The last of Battalion 2/4 did not get on the ground until almost dusk on Monday the third, and they had very little time to dig in before nightfall. At around 6:00 a.m. on the morning of Tuesday the fourth, Foxtrot Company's lines, on the southern hill, were probed by an estimated company-size assault but were held off with only two Marines killed and seventeen wounded. The gooks left twenty-three bodies behind as they withdrew.

The briefing was interrupted by the god-awful noise of a chopper having some major engine problems on its final approach to land on the eastern hill where the Company Command Group had landed just a few minutes prior. Inside the chopper were Corporal Tim Russell (from the battle of Cam Lo fame in chapter 6) and the rest of the First Platoon. Rifle and machine gun rounds started penetrating the chopper's fuselage when they were still a hundred yards out. He advised his squad to be ready to jump as soon as they saw the ground. As the rotors started to flare on final approach, the enemy fire coming through the aircraft became extreme. The copilot let out a scream as he caught a bullet, and at the same time, the copter started filling with smoke and the engines started to fail. The ramp was just starting down, and Tim could see the tops of the vegetation and estimated that they were still twenty-five feet in the air. He decided they could wait no longer and gave the word for his squad to make a jump for it, roll when they hit the ground, and to get away from the chopper as quickly as they could. The first squad rushed the ramp, followed closely by the rest of the Platoon, and they were out.

The chopper made a crash landing, and within moments, the crew was out as the craft burst into flames. Banged up, bruised, a few sprained ankles, and a wounded pilot—other than that the morning seemed to be off to a good start. The First Platoon quickly assembled and moved swiftly down the saddle and up into the new Delta perimeter.

The briefing was cut short by all the commotion, and the remaining elements of 2/4 quickly moved to the LZ where chopper after chopper came and went, picking up the last Marines of 2/4, all the while maneuvering around the burning aircraft and receiving small arms, and machine gun fire from the disgruntled new neighbors.

As the last chopper lifted off, quickly gained altitude, and vanished into the distance, the NVA gunfire stopped, and for a moment, an eerie silence fell over LZ Loon.

THINGS CAN ALWAYS GET WORSE

All three hills were covered with dense foliage, which made it almost impossible to get any bearings. The Grunts on the line were faced with a very poor field of fire because of the shoulder-high vegetation that came right up to their fighting holes. Intelligence had confirmed the rumor that one and possibly two NVA Regiments were in the area (two thousand to four thousand gooks). The Marine Grunts from 2/4 were able to dig small fighting holes, but they still needed a lot more work. If that was not bad enough, an NVA Artillery Regiment, about nineteen hundred gooks, were located at Co Roc in Laos, about twelve miles away. The order for our artillery was that Laos was neutral and we could not return fire even though a Recon patrol found leaflets from the Laotian government granting the NVA freedom of movement in Laos.

A SMALL RANT

The situation mentioned above, where the enemy could shoot at us but we could not shoot at them, is just one good example of our politicians' bullshit "Rules of Engagement" that have always hampered the US military and would cost many Marines their lives in the coming days.

BACK TO THE STORY

Looking south from the Delta lines, there was the deep ravine that separated LZ Loon into two distinct perimeters. Across the ravine on a slightly lower hill was the other half of the LZ, where Charlie Company had landed in the afternoon the previous day. The thick flora made it all but impossible to make out any objects on Charlie Company's side. The backhoe had been brought in the day prior, and four Army Engineers had been busy developing the gun emplacements.

A pallet of 105 mm rounds and some more C-Rats had been delivered that morning and the guns were to arrive in the afternoon. The 81 mm mortars were also set up on the Charlie Company side. Delta's mission was to protect the high ground on the north side of the ravine.

The feeling of being alone and vulnerable quickly converted back to survival as Loon started receiving big artillery rounds into the perimeter. Everyone scrambled for the nearest hole he could find, followed a second later by the call for Corpsman. Now 60 mm and 82 mm mortars, along with the real big shit from Co Roc, Laos started hitting. At the briefing, the Captain from 2/4 mused that most of the enemy rounds were falling outside the perimeter, but now they must have called in the varsity, because every round landed inside the lines.

The shelling went on and on. The call for Corpsman was heard all over both hills. Several artillery rounds landed directly in the fighting holes, scattering the remains of the unlucky Marines in all directions. First the screech of the incoming round would be heard, followed by the explosion, and then the shockwave, which stole the air from their lungs. The mental vision of an artillery round hitting in the fighting hole was surely on most every Marine's mind as the sound of shrapnel whizzed overhead. All the Docs attempted to wait for a lull to dash for the sound of a wounded Marine, but the lull never came. The self-imposed pressure of duty, history, passion, and friendships pushed the Docs from the protection of their holes out into no man's land in pursuit of the wounded.

The incoming rounds slacked off after about an hour, and the dead and wounded were everywhere. On the south hill, Charlie Company made the decision to move their wounded to their LZ for evacuation. As a medevac chopper was inbound, the gooks opened fire on the LZ, adding more victims to the count. The chopper could have pulled off after seeing the explosions, but instead, those brave sons of bitches came in and took out the worst of the wounded.

Sometime during all the incoming artillery explosions, calls for Corpsmen, and screams from dying and wounded Marines, an Army Huey flew in and picked up the four Army engineers. Leaving behind their backhoe, the partially constructed 105 mm gun emplacements, and the pallet of 105 mm artillery shells was the Army's way of letting the Marines know that Loon was no longer a Fire Support Base. Loon was now just a small bunch of jarheads, sitting on a hill, with no protection, surrounded by thousands of gooks who couldn't wait for nightfall.

Kinda gives you a warm fuzzy, feeling, don't it?

As the day wore on, the casualties continued to grow and the number of Marines on the lines became fewer and fewer. There were only enough Grunts to occupy every second or third fighting hole. With the shoulder-high elephant grass growing up to and around each hole, it was impossible to see or even hear your neighbor, but they could hear the bad guys working and talking just below their positions. The skipper kept calling in artillery, fighter jets, and Huey gunships in an attempt to breakup or at least hold off the inevitable ground attack that the enemy was preparing for, but the efforts had little results. The gooks were very smart because they used the thick brush to move very close to the Marines' lines, knowing that our artillery and jet fighters could not shoot at them without hitting Marines.

Sometime in the late afternoon on June 5 the two Company Commanders concluded that the perimeter was too large to protect, given their dwindling manpower, and they devised a plan to evacuate the lower hill after dark and move Charlie Company across the ravine and consolidate with Delta. Charlie Company would leave behind part of one Platoon, the two 81 mm mortar squads, and the bodies of the dead Marines who had fallen that day. Charlie would go back at first light on the sixth and destroy the backhoe and 105 mm artillery rounds, evacuate the bodies, and bring the last Platoon across.

As darkness fell on the night of June 5, Charlie Company, carrying as much ammo and water as they could carry, started down their side of the gorge into the thick jungle. Knowing that the visibility would be zero, Delta Marines started down their side with the intent of linking up and bringing Charlie up to the Delta side.

The ravine that separated the two positions was nearly one hundred yards across, and the only reason that the gooks had not moved in there must have been because they were waiting for their own shelling to stop. Whatever the reason, Charlie Company made the trek without incident and set up their lines on the eastern knoll to provide cover for the Grunts left behind.

Everyone worked as quietly as possible, improving individual fighting positions. The word was passed that there would be no listening posts put out, and everyone was to stay alert throughout the night. Claymore mines were set out, hand grenades laid out, magazines at the ready, rifles and machine guns checked and rechecked. The Marines were as ready as they could be, given the circumstances, and now they just waited for the first barrage of artillery, mortars, and rockets that would surely signal the beginning of the enemy assault.

The enemy could be heard moving around and working quietly to improve their positions. They were whispering, and it sounded as if they were just outside the lines. One could only wonder if the gooks were scared shitless, too, or did they have such overwhelming numbers that they could hardly wait to get the turkey shoot started?

The jungle that surrounded Loon was so thick that it was almost impossible to see where the artillery spotting rounds had landed, so the usual protection afforded by setting up predesignated defensive artillery fire was at best questionable and at worst a wild-ass guess.

THE BATTLE FOR LZ LOON BEGINS

Just before first light on the morning of Thursday, June 6, the sounds of AK-47 rifle fire could be heard, followed by a return report from American M-16s. Both sounds were coming from outside the Charlie and Delta lines, and then it stopped. A short time passed when the Charlie Company Command received a radio message from their third Platoon, which had been left behind on the south knoll. They had set charges on the backhoe and 105 mm ammo, and they were attempting to cross the deep ravine to rejoin the rest of Charlie. The gooks were waiting for them at the bottom of the gully and sprung an ambush, killing the Platoon Lieutenant. The Platoon retreated to their previous position and dug in.

At 6:00 a.m., all hell broke loose with incoming artillery, mortars, rockets, and small-arms fire. The sound of rifle and machine gun fire could be heard from all points around the perimeter. Every Corpsman was busy running from hole to hole, attempting to stop the Marines from bleeding to death and getting them back on their guns.

The incoming quieted down, and everyone knew what was coming next. The squad leaders called for the perimeter Grunts to get their heads above their fighting holes and watch for the ground attack. Their fears were realized by the screams coming from the gooks as they charged up the hill with rifles blazing and throwing hand grenades into the lines. The Marines would quickly toss their grenades back and follow them with some of their own.

As the enemy screams approached the lines the claymore mines were detonated in an attempt to drive back the attackers, but it was not enough. Soon the call was heard, "Gooks in the perimeter. Gooks in the perimeter," as the western side of the Delta line was being penetrated. The Delta Marines were now in the life-or-death struggle of hand-to-hand combat.

Then the call came for everyone to get in a hole because of incoming, followed quickly by the screech of artillery rounds impacting just below the perimeter. Round after round pounded the enemy on 360 degrees around Loon, and still they came. Then came the call to go deep and get small; the next rounds were going to be inside the perimeter. The screech of the first round was heard, followed by the explosion and shock wave. Soon the rounds came so fast that they could not distinguish one from another. It was like the finale at a Fourth of July fireworks celebration, and then it went silent.

The call came out for a counterattack, and the Marines sprang from their holes and began to finish off what was left of the enemy invaders. The artillery rounds had been fused as airbursts where the shell exploded a few yards above the ground, showering deadly shards of jagged metal in all directions. The airburst was specifically designed for troops caught in the open, and the results were devastating. The bodies of the NVA soldiers were everywhere, cut down by the exploding shrapnel. Being in their holes and spread so thinly helped limit the Marine casualties but artillery does not distinguish between friend and foe and some Marines were killed by the friendly fire.

Shortly after the artillery stopped, then came a spotter plane with Huey gunships and "Puff-the-Magic-Dragon." The sound of those miniguns going off was music to the ears. If that was not enough, then came several Phantom jet fighters that dropped napalm all down the sides of the hill. Marines on the line swore that they could hear the screams from the burning gooks.

Charlie and Delta Commanders were in contact with the bosses in the rear, and the decision was made to abandon LZ Loon and get everyone out before nightfall.

Light contact continued throughout the morning with the enemy using small-arms fire, 82 mm mortars and 130 mm artillery to further hammer the position. The Marines in turn pounded the enemy with artillery, helicopter gunships, and fighter jets, dropping napalm and bombs to keep them from reorganizing for another assault.

As promised, they heard the rotor noise from a CH-46 helicopter coming for the first extract. The copter landed on the lower hill and scooped up the 81mm mortar squads and the one Platoon from Charlie Company that had been left behind the night before. As the chopper struggled to gain altitude, it was hit by small arms and .50-caliber machine gun fire. At first it looked as if it would make it, and then it stopped climbing and started a slow-motion descent where it made contact with the ground, rolled over and tumbled out of sight, followed a second later with an explosion and fireball. Hearts sank as they witnessed the fate of these heroes who survived the night only to lose their lives as they struggled to escape this remote shit hole.

A few minutes later an aerial observer came on the radio and announced that he observed at least two Marines make it out of the wreckage. Hearing that, the Charlie Company Commander got his Grunts to sing the "Marines' Hymn," as loudly as they could, to give encouragement and a directional bearing to their fallen comrades. Another few minutes passed when a Marine rescue chopper came on scene, surveyed the situation, and with covering fire from several other gunships, made an unbelievable extraction of four Marines who would have surely been captured or killed within a few minutes.

THE LAST MAN OUT

It was not long before the sky was again filled with choppers ready to take the Marines out. By the late afternoon of June 6, 1968, the Marines from Charlie Company and most of Delta were taken out, and the last chopper was inbound to pick up the Delta Company Command Group and the remaining first Platoon. With no defenders left on the hills, the gooks charged up through the saddle, firing at the lone chopper attempting to land on the western knoll. Realizing they had no chance for survival unless someone held the bad guys off, Corporal Russell charged down through the saddle with his rifle on full automatic, spraying the enemy and halting their advance. Soon several members of his squad joined him. Together, they laid down a withering fire on the NVA positions. The chopper now on the ground, Tim ordered his squad to pull back and get on board. Slowly retreating up the hill and continuing to fire at the gooks to keep their heads down, Tim could hear the increase of power to the copter's engine and knew it was time to make a run for it. Firing the rest of his magazine, he turned and ran for the chopper as it was lifting off, threw his rifle in, and jumped, just grabbing the rising ramp. His Marines reached out and dragged him inside.

They were out of LZ Loon.

I KNOW I HAVE SAID THIS BEFORE, BUT IT BEARS REPEATING.
The Grunts from Charlie and Delta Companies who survived the battle at LZ Loon did not receive a big rest and recuperation in some relatively safe rear area. The Grunts were back chasing bad guys within days. The Officers and Docs usually spent a tour of six months in a rifle company and then rotated to a job in the rear. There was not much need for a rifleman anywhere but up front, so the Grunts spent their entire thirteen-month tour where all the action was.

IN THE END
The Grunts from Charlie Company volunteered to return to LZ Loon eleven days later to retrieve the bodies from the downed chopper along with bodies left behind at the southern knoll of the LZ. The dead

Marines were removed from Loon, but the chopper wreckage could not be reached because of a heavy enemy presence.

When it was all over, Charlie and Delta Companies suffered forty-two killed and over one hundred wounded, which was over half the Marines and Corpsmen who defended Hill 672 for those two days. The NVA lost at least one hundred fifty killed, but only they know the real number of killed and wounded.

Talk about everything going wrong—while Charlie and Delta were getting the shit kicked out of them, Bobby Kennedy was shot on June 5, 1968. He died on June 6, 1968, which moved anything about the Vietnam War to the back burner.

SOME FORGOTTEN BOYS COME HOME AFTER FORTY YEARS

In November 2008, a US recovery team was able to reach the helicopter crash site below LZ Loon. They recovered and identified the remains of all the Marines who were left behind on June 6, 1968. The Forgotten Boys were finally brought home and put to rest after forty long years.

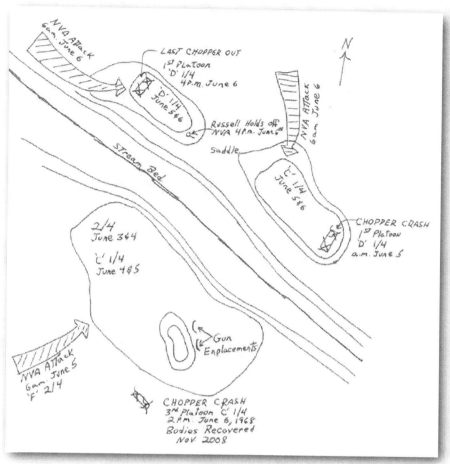

Occupation of LZ Loon
11:35 a.m., Monday, June 3, to 4:00 p.m. Thursday, June 6, 1968
This is my attempt to recreate the map of LZ Loon after conversations
with Grunts who were there. It is close enough for the reader to get the idea.

Fifteen

REST AND RECREATION

Tough times never last but tough people do
—*ROBERT A. SCHULLER*

A LITTLE HISTORY

Every military serviceman serving in Vietnam was eligible for at least one five-day vacation or rest and recreation (R & R) out of country to rest and recuperate without the fear of incoming artillery and mortars. The vacation destination was based on your seniority in country. Your choices were: Bangkok, Hong Kong, Kuala Lampur/Penang, Manila, Singapore, Taipei, and Tokyo. Because of the greater distance, seven days' leave was permitted for the destination of Hawaii, and later Sydney was added. For instance, if you wanted to go to Bangkok, Thailand, or one of the other Southeast Asian countries, you could probably go there with just a few months in country. Japan would take a little more time, and the married guys who wanted to go to Hawaii to meet their wives would need to wait until later in their tour.

In July of 1967, the American government approached the Australians to request that Sydney be added to the list of cities open to American servicemen on R & R from Vietnam. The Australians quickly agreed, and in October 1967, the first plane of Americans landed, and they continued until 1971 when the program was phased out. Over three hundred thousand servicemen spent their R & R in Australia.

Most Australians were very open to having American GIs enjoy their leaves in their country. The common belief was that these young men were reluctant participants in a very unpopular war. Some groups in Sydney even encouraged desertion and would assist the deserters by hiding them from authorities.

WHY I CHOSE SYDNEY

With over seven months in country, I just wanted to feel the atmosphere of a western civilization. I did not want to take a spot from the married guys wanting Hawaii, to meet their wives, and I figured that I could go to the Islands after I rotated home. Sydney was the only other western country left, and I would probably never get a better chance to see it, so there it was.

Sydney was a very popular destination, so I had to wait to gain enough seniority before my name was selected. On Thursday, July 25, 1968, I was on my way to Sydney. One of the additional benefits of Australia over the other destinations was the additional two days that were allocated for the longer travel time. We flew out of Da Nang on a nonstop flight to Melbourne, Australia, and then on to Sydney. The flight time to Melbourne was about eleven hours, and during that time I got acquainted with the Marine in the seat next to mine whose name was Tom. He was a Sergeant with the Third Marine Division, Force Recon (short for reconnaissance). We started discussing where we had been in Vietnam, and I was proud to mention that I had been in Con Thien. Tom replied that he too had been in Con Thien and used it as a starting point for his missions into the DMZ.

OK, so he one-upped me! I was fascinated with the shit that Tom had seen and the places he had been.

Force Recon Marines were known to be some very mentally and physically tough badasses but their job was really not to prove it by engaging the enemy. There were usually never more than nine and seldom fewer than four Marines in a team (including one very badass crazy Doc). They were the silent heroes who were sent into places that no one else dared go. They took only what they could carry and were out for more than a week at a time, went without sleep or food, and got their drinking water from a bomb crater or some other stagnant pool. They would get so close to the enemy positions that they could hear them talk, smell their food, and hear them snore at night.

Their job was to go where the enemy lived, watch their movements, and report back on the enemy locations and troop strengths. Tom had been as far north as the Ben Hai River that separated the two Vietnams—at least that is all he would admit to. These were special Marines who volunteered to walk for days through thick jungle, avoiding the trails, where a day's advance was measured in yards not miles. If dropped in by helicopter, the enemy knew they were there and the game of cat and mouse would begin.

If discovered, they would need to call in artillery to slow the enemy chase for just enough time to be picked up by a helicopter crew who were just as crazy and heroic. Seldom did these Marines receive medals for bravery because being brave and a hero was just part of their job. If it were up to me, I would give the Force Recon Marines a Bronze Star just for volunteering to do the shit they did. By the way, Tom did not boast or tell me how tough he had it. I had already heard many of these stories from the Grunts in Delta who held Recon Marines in high regard.

OUR FIRST STOP IN AUSTRALIA

An hour out of Melbourne the pilot announced that when we landed we would be searched for drugs. If any were found, bad things would happen to the individual. However, if you voluntarily surrendered them before we landed, nothing would happen and no questions would be asked. I kept looking around but never saw anyone make any gesture that they were giving something up.

As we touched down in Melbourne, the pilot repeated the drug warning and further advised that this was our last chance. Sure enough, as the aircraft taxied to a stop, the door opened and a man came on and advised us that we were all going to be taken off the plane, and if we would place our drugs in the seat back pocket in front of us, as we disembarked, no further action would be required. He then advised us to remain seated while they sprayed us with what I assumed was some kind of fumigant. I could not help visualizing a scene out of a World War II war movie where the Nazis sprayed the Jews for lice, as they entered the concentration camps. At this point, I was not sure that they were all that glad to see us.

I thought to myself, "*Holy shit, Australia takes this drug stuff pretty serious. What dumb ass would even try to bring drugs in here?*" And then I thought, "*Oh, there are probably a few.*" We got off the plane and were taken to a holding area, where we underwent a personal search, emptied our pockets, and received a quick pat down, all while the aircraft was being searched. When the search and fumigation were completed, we reboarded the aircraft and were off to Sydney. I never found out if we stopped in Melbourne for fuel, so they decided to search us, or was the stop just to search and fumigate?

Ah, Sydney!

When we landed in Sydney, another announcement was made that no *Playboy* magazines or other pornographic material would be allowed in the country. Tom and I looked at each other and simultaneously said, "What the fuck? We should have gone to Bangkok like everyone else." We both laughed, but I wondered if they would even allow drinking or dancing.

As we were filing off the plane, they randomly took a serviceman out of line and subjected him to another very thorough search. I was not selected, but Tom, the Force Recon Marine, was pulled out of line and taken to an exam room. I waited for Tom, and when he was finally released, he could hardly talk, he was so mad. As we walked to the bus Tom said, "They practically accused me of being a drug dealer. They said if I gave them up now, they would let me go. I advised them that I did not have any drugs, nor did I ever use any drugs! They did not believe me and ordered me to undress."

Tom was now almost shaking, so I decided to lighten it up. I had to ask, "Tom, please tell me they did not find a dingleberry when you spread your cheeks." (A dingleberry was a small piece of toilet paper or just lint from your skivvies that might be stuck to your butt that had to be removed before you could swim in the pool during initial recruit training). Every recruit had to bend over and hold open his butt cheeks to be inspected. God help the recruit if the instructor observed a dingleberry, and they always found one poor bastard to mock and humiliate as they ran him back to the showers for further cleaning.

I can't imagine that they put a recruit through that humiliating exercise today, but in the 1960s they sure did. That explanation probably falls into the category of "too much information," but it did make Tom laugh and with that, I slapped him on the back and we climbed on the bus.

THE R & R CENTER

All the Vietnam Military personnel were taken to the Chevron Hotel in the King's Cross section of downtown Sydney. The Chevron Hotel was a very nice high-rise hotel that worked very hard to make sure you had a pleasant stay and that you would not leave Sydney with any cash.

Because of Tom's extra search at the airport, we arrived on the last bus. We were quickly assigned rooms and told to rush and stow what few items we had brought with us, and to get back down to the men's apparel shop to be fitted for civilian clothes before the shop closed.

We of course complied, and an hour later, we walked out of the apparel shop a hundred dollars lighter. If I sound like I was a victim, I was not! I was so Goddamned happy to be young, alive, and in one of the major western cities of the world. I could not wait to give my money away, for I still did not know what my future in Vietnam held for me.

KING'S CROSS

We quickly went to our rooms, showered, dressed in our new clothes, and out we went to conquer "the King's Cross" (to the locals it was just "the Cross"). We did not know it, but the area was known as Sydney's red-light district, and it was alleged to be home to organized crime groups. Bars, restaurants, nightclubs, brothels, and strip clubs dominated it.

I often wondered just why they would put our naive servicemen so close to such a sinful place of ill repute.

On our first night in the Cross, Tom and I stopped at the first bar we came across, settled into a booth, and ordered drinks. We were sitting in the booth, sipping our cocktails, and people watching, and just bullshitting about nothing, when a very good-looking girl came by our table and struck up a conversation with us. She seemed so interested that we were Americans and that we were, in her view, war heroes. Before long we had ordered her a drink and were telling her our life stories, as they related to Vietnam. Tom obviously had some great stories, but she seemed so interested in both of us. Tom and I would glance back and forth to each other as if to say, "*This chick is so into us and really enjoys our company. She is hanging on our every word.*"

I was in the middle of telling her about what a Corpsman was and just how a Navy guy got to be with the Marines, when all of a sudden, this huge hulk of a man came up to our table, picked up her drink and quickly downed it. He then grabbed Tom's drink and finished it off, and then he took mine and gulped it down. When finished, he slammed my glass down hard on the table. He then looked at our lady friend through piercing eyes and said, "I am paying you to fuck American GIs, not to listen to their fucking life stories. If these two assholes aren't going to pay to fuck you, and aren't going to pay to listen to their shit, move to another table." With that, he walked off, and the beautiful lady got up, thanked us for the drink, and walked away.

Tom and I were dumbfounded. We sat there speechless for a moment, contemplating what had just happened. I must say that I was a little embarrassed that I did not recognize that she was a prostitute, but I was even more shocked to learn that she really wasn't interested in hearing my story about being a Corpsman.

After that encounter, we decided that it had been a long day of flight, searches, and fumigations and decided to call it a night. On our walk back to the hotel, we laughed about the prostitute, and we decided that the drug and porno searches we endured must have been done to reduce the competition for their homegrown corruption.

Giddy Up!

The next morning we met for breakfast and then started out on the town. This time we would not be so naive. We had no sooner cleared the hotel entrance when two girls and one guy approached us and inquired if we were American soldiers. Tom quickly replied that soldiers were Army, we were Marines, to which I gave Tom a glance of approval. They said that they so respected the American fighting man and wanted to take us on a horseback ride and treat us to a barbecue steak dinner.

Tom and I counseled for a moment and decide to take them up on their offer. We loaded in their car, and off we went to who knows where. Skinny, dumb, and happy, two geeks were off on an adventure in the backseat of a car, our packets were full of money, and we were with total strangers, in a foreign country. I know what you are thinking. *What dumb shits would do such a stupid thing?* These people didn't even offer us candy. Maybe the world was different back then, or maybe it was just another case of dumb luck.

As it turned out, when we reached the horse ranch, we met a group of young locals and several other R & R servicemen and ended up having a wonderful day. We took a ride on wild horses that loved to run up and down steep narrow trails, on the edge of high cliffs that made me think that Vietnam was not so dangerous after all. Then we came back, glad to be alive, and drank strong Aussie beer. We ate a great barbecue dinner, sat at a campfire, and lip-synched to songs that I had never heard.

At the end of the night, we found out that the evening was not free, but by then we were drunk and could give a fuck less how much it cost. After paying our bill, Tom and I, with several other soldiers, piled in a car, and they took us back to the Chevron Hotel.

The next morning, a little hungover, we were off to find a good hamburger but could not find a good interpretation of the American version. Many of the pubs and bars in the King's Cross area had changed their names to attract American servicemen, but they didn't realize that we would put bacon on a burger—but not usually an egg.

A TOUR OF THE CITY

While at one of the eateries, we struck up a conversation with a local chap who offered to show us the city. So off we went to see the sights of Sydney. I did not realize it at the time I put in for my R & R, but this time of year was Australia's winter; the beaches were empty and the traditional tourist attractions were either shut down or unoccupied.

The rest of the week went pretty fast with sleeping in until almost noon, eating a good lunch, and a dinner of more steaks and lobsters. Then it was off again to the King's Cross to drink, smoke, listen to music, and bullshit with locals and other servicemen, until the wee hours of the morning. Before we knew it, the week was over.

On the morning of Wednesday, July 31, 1968, we were loading a bus at the Chevron Hotel, destined for the Sydney airport for our flight home. There were many local people milling around, young women hugging and kissing the American servicemen as they held off to the last minute to board the bus. Then the servicemen would rush onto the bus and slide open the window, lean out and hold hands with many beautiful and crying young women. I was confused. I had spent a week in the local bars, spreading cash around, and there was not a single barmaid grieving about my departure? Tom echoed my sentiments and was also totally confused.

As the bus started to pull away, the screams and cries increased. Young Australian women ran next to the bus, holding hands with the servicemen until the bus's speed increased and broke their bond. The servicemen leaned out and shouted their love, devotion, and their pledge to return.

Tom and I looked at each other, and I said, "I think we must have missed something while we were at the horse ride and barbecue. What the fuck just happened?" I asked one of the servicemen who was drying his eyes. "Who were those beautiful young girls?"

He replied, "Last Friday night an Australian women's association had organized a hospitality night at the hotel that encouraged us to go home with them and live with their families for a week. I have fallen in love with this woman, and I will come back for her, if I have to extend my tour."

I patted him on the shoulder and sat back in my seat. I was quiet for a moment and then turned to Tom and said, "So while I waited at the airport for the Aussies to check your butt for dingleberries, I was missing being taken home with an Australian family to sleep with their daughter for the week?"

Tom looked at me, then laid his head back, looked straight ahead and said, "It seems so."

The plane ride back to Da Nang was very quiet, and most everyone was attempting to catch up on sleep. When we landed in Da Nang, Tom and I caught a C-130 going up to Quang Tri where we said our good-byes. I walked to the hospital, and Tom made his way to the rear area of the Third Force Recon, and we both resumed our duties, never to speak again.

I know, pretty shitty not to stay in touch. Learn from me, keep a diary of names, dates, and contact information. You may not think it is important when you are young, but it will be very important when you are old. I promise!

Sixteen

My First Ship Assignment

A smooth sea never made a skilled sailor.

—*English Naval proverb*

About the second or third week in September, I started feeling like I was coming down with the flu. I had mild chills, body aches, headaches, and a low fever, with no energy or appetite. When the symptoms did not go away, I went to the sickbay where they drew blood, which came back with negative findings, so it was diagnosed as "fever of unknown origin" (FUO). I continued to work but could barely make it to my bunk in the afternoon. I would skip chow and did not participate in the evening grab-ass sessions.

Another week went by and my symptoms continued to escalate to include nausea, vomiting, and diarrhea. So once again, I dragged my butt back to the sickbay where they proceeded to draw more blood. This time the results came back as having vivax malaria. I was immediately admitted to the hospital malaria ward and spent the night cycling between fever and chills, accompanied by body aches, nausea, and diarrhea.

The next morning, October 6, 1968, I was awakened early and advised that I was being transferred to the hospital ship *Sanctuary*. I was given breakfast, which I could not look at without getting sick to my stomach. Around 10:00 a.m., I moved to the helipad, in pj's and bathrobe, to await transfer by helicopter to the hospital ship.

In the holding area at the Third Med Hospital helipad, I was the lucky one. I was very weak, but I could still walk. I was surrounded by Marines with major battle wounds, amputations, and severe medical issues that left many of them screaming with pain and hallucinations. I felt like a pussy in the company of such Heroes, so I managed to get off my lazy ass and help the Corpsmen with some of the more seriously sick and wounded Marines.

Within moments, we could hear the familiar wop, wop, wop sound, and then we got the visual of an approaching Marine UH-46 Sea Knight helicopter. A minute later, the giant twin rotor machine sat down on the helipad, pushing wind, dust, and debris in all directions. Everyone shielded their eyes against the blowing sand and grit as the rear entry ramp came down, exposing the chopper's crew chief who waived us forward. The ER Senior Corpsman shouted the order over the turbine engine noise and the stretchers started moving toward the ramp. Walking wounded went first and the more serious were loaded last so they would be the first off when we arrived at the ship.

Once all the patients were situated, the ramp came up, and we had liftoff. The big chopper gained altitude very quickly, then made a sharp turn for the coast. It was obvious that the pilot and crew were used to picking up and dropping off men and materials in some very hot spots, and the more time spent on the ground increased their chances of being shot. It appeared that they never broke the hurry-up takeoffs and landings, regardless of the mission.

As we flew over the wet Quang Tri countryside, I had a very good view over the window gunner's shoulder, and as soon as we crossed over the shoreline into the Gulf of Tonkin, I looked forward and I could see the USS *Sanctuary* sitting only a few miles off the coast.

A short time later, the nose of our helicopter pitched up slightly as the pilot flared the blades, brought the aircraft to a hover over the

Sanctuary's landing pad, and then gently touched down. The ramp was lowered, and the ship's deck crew scrambled forward to unload the damaged cargo. The critical patients were quickly removed and passed into the waiting arms of the hospital staff. The moderate patients were next, followed by the walking sick and wounded.

As we moved through the doors into the receiving area, there were all sorts of military personnel waiting to board our helicopter for the return trip to somewhere. A ship crewman gave a command, and out they went, followed a few seconds later by the sound of the chopper gaining power, and they were off. No dust in the air this time, but the helicopter's exhaust fumes filled the entryway, causing many of us, already sick from malaria, to retch and some to vomit. The amazing hospital staff was right there to move us quickly into a fresher environment.

After a quick check of my medical records, I was moved to the malaria ward and assigned a bed. I stowed my bag of skivvies and jungle utilities in the bedside nightstand and slithered between the crisp, fresh sheets. The comfort was short-lived, as the chills, body aches, fatigue, and alternating sweats intensified. I was not a real sailor; I received my training from the Navy and almost immediately was transferred to the Marine Corps. The USS *Sanctuary* was my first exposure to a naval vessel, and my lack of sea legs, coupled with the nausea caused by the malaria, only magnified my reaction to the constant swaying of the ship. I was sure my ward was beneath the waterline because I could hear water rushing past the hull. I was glad the North Vietnamese did not have submarines and hoped they did not lay mines.

The medicine I was given to combat the nausea, diarrhea, and pain did not make a dent in my symptoms, and I had to make many emergency trips to the head (sailor talk for the bathroom) with a puke bowl in hand. I was certainly not alone, as the ward was filled with numerous patients just like me, and we were the lucky ones.

On the return trip from the head, I had more time to focus on my surroundings and to observe the other patients and their problems, and there were many. I had vivax malaria, which certainly made you sick, but many of these poor bastards had falciparum malaria, which would spike very high temperatures requiring iced alcohol baths. I remember standing at the foot of a bed where a Marine was partially submerged in a rubber tub filled with iced alcohol, in an attempt to keep his fever from frying his brain.

It takes me five minutes to get into a swimming pool where the temperature of the water is at seventy-five degrees. To see a Marine lying in that bath of iced alcohol, screaming, hallucinating, and confused was a visual that has stayed with me for my entire life.

Late on my second night, I awoke to the sounds of the ocean rushing faster past the hull, and the ship was now pitching heavier from side to side. I assumed we must have hit a storm. The motion made me gag, my stomach wrenched with pain, and my bowels notified me that there was no time to spare. I grabbed my puke bowl and started for the head. The heavy motion of the ship made me stumble back and forth, grabbing the footboard of one bed, then the next, and the next, until I reached my destination.

When I entered the head, I could see that I was not alone, as the wall of toilets were all occupied except for two. One at the far end was obviously plugged, as its contents were visible above the seat and it was overflowing. I thanked God for the one remaining viable spot. Vomit and diarrhea was sloshing from one end of the head back to the other in rhythm with the roll of the ship.

I had no time to be repulsed, as my bowels gave their final warning; I timed my entry as the wave of sewage hit the far wall. I rushed forward, pulled my pajama bottoms down, sat quickly, and got in position just in time to raise my feet as the wave passed under on its way to the other wall.

As if in a chorus line, the row of sick patients raised and lowered their feet to the movement of the ship and the passing wave of muck. Most of the occupants were simultaneously making good use of their puke bowls, and I was no exception. I sat there in a self-absorbed "pity party" thinking, "*Fuck, could this get any worse?*" Then, I remembered the

Marine, in the next room, screaming and hallucinating in the iced alcohol bath. I knew I would survive, and in a few days my symptoms would pass, but this might be that poor bastard's best day.

The days passed into several weeks, and slowly my symptoms passed with them. Weak, skinny, and still with no appetite, I was able to walk about the ship. The hospital ship was similar to a modern cruise liner in that it had two Captains and two crews. One Captain and crew ran the ship and one Captain and crew ran the hospital. Except for the taking of my daily vital signs and receiving my medicines, I was pretty much done with the wonderful and dedicated medical crew. I could now concentrate my time on the study of real sailors as they skillfully maneuvered the *Sanctuary* up and down the northern coast of South Vietnam.

Daily there was much to see as supply ships, fuel ships, and warships came and went, transferring patients, fuel, and cargo back and forth, staying literally only yards apart. Many times we would be three abreast with a fuel and supply ship in the middle, the *Sanctuary* on her port side (driver's side). A destroyer would appear out of nowhere, quickly pull up on the supply ship's starboard side (passenger side), and like a pit stop at a NASCAR race, take on fuel and then speed away over the horizon. It made me very aware that there was much more going on in this war than just pounding the ground as a Grunt. I could see that the US Navy also had their shit packed very tight (Marine talk meaning well trained), and it made me beam with pride to be part of this amazing organization.

A STROLL TOPSIDE

Another week passed and since my appetite was back, I ate a wonderful breakfast and decided to take a leisurely stroll on the deck. My attire was still pj's, robe, and slippers. I never could figure out where I was on the boat, so I would just pop out somewhere, and never in the same spot. This morning I popped out on the starboard side of the ship just in time to see us pull up next to a fuel and supply ship. I had not had the opportunity to see the ships hook up from the very start, so this was going to be a real treat. I was not sure what deck level I was on, but I was smack in the middle of the ship and would have an excellent view of the entire operation. I looked to my left and right, and was a little surprised that no one was in my vicinity.

Looking across at the supply ship, I could see a lot of activity with the crew running here and there. One sailor was standing at the rail, directly across from me, and it looked as if he were holding a shotgun. He brought the shotgun to his shoulder and pointed it in my direction. The smile quickly left my face as I could see something leave the barrel followed a second later by the familiar sound of the weapon's discharge. I winced for a moment and then saw what appeared to be a spear-like object traveling very fast toward my position. The advancing object seemed to be deploying a small line in its wake. My heart quickened, I took in a deep breath, and thought, "*My God, I am going to be harpooned by one of my own countrymen. Why are they shooting at me? I am dressed in pajamas and a bathrobe, for Christ's sake!*"

At the last moment, my catlike reflexes kicked in, and I dropped to the deck as the spear missed its intended target by mere inches, striking the metal bulkhead behind me and falling harmlessly to the deck. Just then a bulkhead door opened, a sailor stepped out, and he was shocked to see me lying on the deck. He quickly snapped, "What the fuck are you doing out here on this deck? This is a restricted area for crew members only. You could have been killed, you dumb ass! Get up and get the fuck out of here!"

With that, I got up, dusted my bathrobe off, and exited through the open bulkhead door. I quickly dropped down several decks and moved farther aft in the ship, then reemerged again to watch the operation from a safer vantage point.

At my new location, it became obvious that they were not shooting at me but simply shooting a small line across to our ship where a larger line would be attached and pulled across. Then the main line would follow that could finally support the heavy weight of the fuel lines.

Yes, I admit I was momentarily embarrassed, but only one sailor saw me, and I would bet he could not have picked me out of a lineup. Satisfied, I went back to my bunk and took a nap before lunch.

On November 2, 1968, after twenty-eight days, I left the USS *Sanctuary* and returned to the Third Medical Battalion at Quang Tri.

A LITTLE HISTORY OF MALARIA

Malaria has plagued mankind since the very beginning of time. Today, half the world's population lives in danger of contracting malaria. The disease is widespread in the tropical and subtropical regions around the equator, including Africa, Asia, and Latin America.

Malaria is caused by a single-cell parasite called plasmodium and is transmitted to humans via a mosquito bite from an infected female Anopheles mosquito. Nature does not play the politically correct game, so it is safe to mention that the male Anopheles mosquito feeds on plant nectar, and therefore does not transmit the disease. The female prefers to feed on blood. She usually starts looking for a meal at dusk, and will continue throughout the night until satisfied. So typical, that bitch!

Just kidding!

The parasites are transferred from the mosquito's saliva into the human bloodstream where they travel to the liver to mature and reproduce, until the family gets so big that they cause the liver cells to rupture, releasing millions of the parasites into the bloodstream. In need of new homes, they set up housekeeping in the red blood cells. They continue to mature and reproduce until they outgrow their new homes, then they rupture the blood cells, and millions more go looking for more healthy blood cells to move into. This process continues until the parasites cause enough damage that the infected human (or animal) starts to develop symptoms, which usually begin in ten to fifteen days after exposure.

During this time, a healthy female Anopheles mosquito comes looking for a meal, and picks up the parasites in the blood cells of the infected human, which now attack her. The mosquito, now infected, flies off to inject the parasites into another poor bastard, and the cycle goes on and on.

Symptoms include flu-like symptoms, fever, chills, joint pain, fatigue, vomiting, headaches, and diarrhea, with more severe cases causing seizures, coma, or death. The symptom of an enlarged spleen is caused by the spleen eating all those ruptured and damaged blood cells.

There are four species of plasmodium that usually infect humans, but in Vietnam the two most common were vivax and falciparum malaria. While falciparum malaria is the most dangerous and can cause death, it will run its course and be gone. vivax malaria is milder, but the plasmodium can lay dormant in the liver and come back again in days, weeks, and even years, if not diagnosed and treated properly.

The pink malaria pills that we Docs forced the Marines to take every Sunday were a drug called chloroquine-premaquin. It was effective against vivax malaria but much less effective against falciparum malaria.

In vivax malaria the circulating infected blood cells are destroyed in the spleen, and eventually the infection runs its course. In the case of falciparum parasites, they produce adhesive proteins on the surface of the blood cells, causing the blood cell to stick to the wall of the blood vessels and thus saving them from their fate in the spleen. If not treated in time, these stuck blood cells can build up, cause circulation problems in the major organs, and become life threatening. The worst of these cases is called cerebral malaria, which is caused by these sticky blood cells accumulating in the brain and stopping circulation. The results can be catastrophic to the patient, depriving the brain of oxygen, causing hemorrhaging and severe psychiatric symptoms such as hallucination, confusion, and in the worst cases, coma and death. To prevent the falciparum malaria patients from entering the cerebral malaria stage, alcohol and ice baths are used to keep the temp down.

There were 24,000 Navy and Marine cases of malaria in Vietnam with forty-six deaths.

USS *SANCTUARY* AH-17—JUST A LITTLE HISTORY ABOUT THIS "ANGEL OF MERCY" AND THE AMAZING CREWS.

The *Sanctuary* was commissioned as a hospital ship on June 20, 1945. She was 522 feet long, 71 feet wide, and had a capacity of eight hundred patients. The crew comprised sixty officers and five hundred five crewmembers (ship and hospital combined). Her first assignment was Pearl Harbor four days after the surrender of Japan. Her brief World War II experience was bringing home allied POWs from Japan, and then she was promptly decommissioned on August 15, 1946.

The *Sanctuary* lay in mothballs for twenty years until March 1966, when she underwent a major modernization and was recommissioned on November 15, 1966. This time the *Sanctuary* supported a helipad, three X-ray units, a blood bank, an artificial kidney machine, an ultrasonic diagnostic unit, a recompression chamber, four operating rooms that supported twenty wards, and a medical staff that numbered over three hundred. In World War II, the *Sanctuary* was designed as an ambulance. In the Vietnam War, she was brought back as a floating hospital and located just a few miles from the battlefield.

She arrived on station off the coast of Da Nang on March 10, 1967, and in the first twelve months, the ship admitted 5,354 patients, treated another 9,187, as outpatients, and accommodated over 2,500 helicopter landings on her helipad.

This "Angel of Mercy" and the amazing and dedicated staff were responsible for one of the best save rates in military history and contributed to the premise of emergency medicine's "Golden Hour."*

The *Sanctuary* was stationed off the coast of the I Corps tactical area of Vietnam in an assignment that lasted for up to 120 days at a time, followed by a brief upkeep period at Subic Bay, Philippines. She then returned to follow the Marines as they battled on shore from Da Nang to Dong Ha. The *Sanctuary* and the dedicated staff of doctors, nurses, corpsmen, and ship's crew continued this exhausting schedule until April 23, 1971. After ten thousand helicopter landings, forty-six hundred major surgeries, and treating over thirty-five thousand servicemen, she sailed from Da Nang for the last time.

After Vietnam the *Sanctuary* served as a Navy dependents' hospital and a commissary (medical facility for Navy families and a store) in San

---

* *The Golden Hour refers to a period lasting one hour or less, following a traumatic injury, during which time there is the highest probability that prompt medical intervention will prevent death.*

Francisco. Another assignment, in November 1972, brought two female officers and sixty enlisted females to the ship's crew (not the hospital but the crew who drive the ship) and became the first US Navy ship with a mixed male-female ship's company.

After making history, the *Sanctuary* was decommissioned and sold several times to private organizations. Finally, in August 2011, she was moved to Brownsville, Texas, and was unceremoniously scrapped. There is no wall to honor her, nothing like an Arlington cemetery to visit her, not even some annual date to at least hoist a beer to say thanks to *Sanctuary* and the wonderful crew who made the difference in so many lives.

All I can say is thank you! I have never forgotten.

Looking over the window gunner's shoulder.

Getting ready to land.

Refueling the USS *Sanctuary*

He must have been real sick.

Seventeen

My Year Was Up, and Home I Came

There are two kinds of wars; the one worth sending your neighbor's son to,
and the one worth sending YOUR son to. "
Which are we about to engage in now?

—Doc Miller

It was Saturday morning, November 2, 1968, when the chopper took me from the relatively safe and loving arms of the crew of the USS *Sanctuary* and delivered me back to the Third Med Battalion in Quang Tri. Late October was the start of the rainy season and the thick red mud was waiting for me as I stepped off the steel matting of the helicopter landing pad. I was down to less than 140 pounds and the mud tugged and fought my every step, draining my scrawny legs of their last bit of energy.

Thank God it was Saturday, and I did not have any extra duty assignments. I made my way to my hooch and received a wonderful welcome home from my hooch mates. I encountered many hugs and slaps on my back as I made it to my bunk. I politely turned down offers of beers and every kind of hard liquor, as the mere thought made me queasy. After a long while of telling everyone about my experience and catching up on local gossip, the hooch returned to normal and I laid back and drifted off to the sounds of the latest Beatles hit, "Hey Jude."

I have never had trouble sleeping and Vietnam proved to be no exception. I may have had a busy mind during the day, but I could turn it off at night. Once asleep, I was never in Vietnam. I was always somewhere else in the world. I was usually back home, visiting an old girlfriend, or cruising the beach with friends, but I was not in Vietnam for those wonderful four to six hours each night.

BACK TO WORK ON MONDAY

That following Monday it was back to work and business as usual. Military operations in the northern and western parts of Quang Tri Province were causing our business to boom. If it were any other type of business, it would be great, but our business was wounded Marines and treating these Heroes was more than our mission; it was our passion.

It was back to long hours, moving supplies around the hospital during the day and then night duty in the hospital to attend to the never-ending stream of wounded and sick Marines.

THE HOOCH WAS FULL OF SHORT-TIMERS

My appetite was very slow to come back, and gaining weight was impossible, but this was no time to be feeling puny. It was a time for celebrations!

Everyone in my hooch came to Vietnam within days of one another and were assigned to Marine Companies as their Doc. We had all experienced the artillery, mortar, and small-arms fire, the charges across open fields into the waiting gun sights of the fearless enemy, ambushes from both perspectives, and being soaked in the blood of Heroes (our friends) as we helplessly watched them take their last breaths.

We were all now within weeks of going back to the world. We had survived!

Starting the last two weeks in November and carrying on to the first two weeks in December, there was a party almost every night. We would party until we passed out, awake the next morning with a hangover, say our farewell to those who were leaving, mark a day off on our short-timers' calendars, and drag our sorry asses to work. The next night we would repeat the process and say our good-byes to the next few lucky bastards.

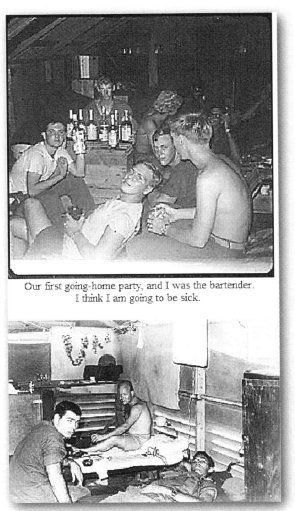

Our first going-home party, and I was the bartender.
I think I am going to be sick.

You have got to be shitting me, another party tonight?

AT 2:55 A.M. ON DECEMBER 7, 1968, I LEFT VIETNAM.
I took off from the Marine Corps Airbase at DaNang, Vietnam and landed at 9:00 a.m. at Camp Butler, Okinawa, where all returning Marines and Corpsmen were processed and outfitted with new uniforms for the trip back to the world.

It had been a year since I had passed through this base on my way to Vietnam, and now I was one of the old salts returning to the world. The base was still filled with new young Marines and Docs waiting to be processed for their trip to DaNang, Vietnam.

I was issued a seabag full of new uniforms and the rank shoulder stripes to go with them. I hurried back to my bunk and quickly sewed on my Second Class Petty Officer stripes (E-5, Sergeant stripes, to the uninformed). I could hardly wait for chow time so I could stroll to the front of the line like the Sergeants did to me the year prior.

When the evening chow bell finally rang, everyone dashed for the chow hall in hopes of getting a better spot in the rapidly growing chow line. Not me, I just sauntered over and with a humble swagger walked by the entire line of hungry Marines and Corpsmen who did not possess the proper rank on their sleeves that would allow them to cut into the front of the line. As I reached the mess trays, I excused myself as I stepped in front of a waiting private. Just then, I heard the Mess Hall Gunnery Sergeant call out, "Hey, Doc, the rules have changed since your last visit. It's now E-6 Staff Sergeants and above who can break the line. Maybe if you reenlist, you can cut the line on your next tour to Vietnam!"

My face must have turned beet red but no one in the line said a word. I just walked away and did not eat that night. It was apparent that many of us had made E-5 Sergeant in our first tour of Vietnam and so the rules had to be changed to reduce the line-cutting privilege or none of the poor bastards going to Vietnam would ever eat.

The only way to achieve the E-6 rank was to sign up for another four years in the military and most likely do another tour in Vietnam (the term for reenlisting was "a lifer"). I was actually fine with the new rule change because there should have been a privilege for those special people who signed up to do this again. However, I was not going to be one of those Heroes.

On the morning of December 9, I finished all the processing and received my new orders. I was receiving a thirty-day leave with orders to report to the Naval Base in San Diego, California, for a one-day orientation. Then I would move on to my new assignment as an Independent Duty Corpsman assigned to the Inspector-Instructor staff for the First Battalion, Fourteenth Marines, located at the Naval and Marine Corps Reserve Training Center in downtown Los Angeles.

All of my friends were given assignments that scattered them all across the nation. Most went to a Naval Hospital somewhere nearest their homes. No one else received an independent duty assignment, nor did anyone even know what that meant.

I tracked down a Gunny Sergeant and asked him if he knew where I was going, which he did. He advised me that I was being assigned to the active duty training staff for a Marine Reserve Artillery Battalion. I would be the only Navy Corpsman among a whole shitload of jarheads. He then said, "You must have done something right, Doc. They don't give those spots to just anyone."

AT 4:00 P.M. ON DECEMBER 9, 1968, I LEFT OKINAWA FOR THE WORLD
I climbed aboard a commercial aircraft operated by Tiger Airlines, and I was surrounded by many of the same guys I came to Vietnam with a year prior. There were also many of my friends who were missing, and I am sure that they would have loved to have been with us. As we went wheels up, a cheer came over the entire aircraft as we realized that we were actually going home, and the atmosphere quickly became festive.

The flight was somewhere over eleven hours and after dinner and a few more hours of grab-assing and bullshitting, everyone settled down for the night flight. A doctor at Third Med dispensed a Seconal sedative to several of us as a going-away gift, to take for a good night's sleep, and that is exactly what we did.

BACK IN THE WORLD

At 11:45 a.m. on December 9, our wheels touched down at the Norton Air Force Base in San Bernardino. The cheers and laughter were deafening as everyone was hugging, slapping backs, shaking hands, and trying to hold back tears lest you would be called a pussy.

Over the intercom came the pilot's voice. "Welcome home, men!" With that the cheers erupted again.

My best friend, Keith, was there to pick me up just as he had been there to drop me off a year earlier. We drove home to Gardena, picked up my mom and her boyfriend, Doc, and we all went out to dinner at my favorite Mexican food restaurant, the Tijuana Inn in Gardena.

Food had never tasted so good, and I ate until I thought I would burst. I was home and it felt surreal, as though my year in Vietnam had never happened. People were going about their lives as if there was no war going on.

Halfway around the world, Marines were walking into an ambush, in a firefight, or fighting hand-to-hand in a desperate life-and-death struggle. Here we were, laughing and drinking as if none of that was happening, but I knew it was, and I knew what it felt like.

I felt ashamed!

Eighteen

I have only one yardstick by which I test every major problem and that yardstick is: Is it good for America.

—Dwight D. Eisenhower

Naval and Marine Corps Reserve Training Center

I reported for duty at 1700 Stadium Way, Los Angeles, California, on Tuesday, January 16, 1969. The Inspector-Instructor staff (I&I staff) numbered about twenty active duty Marines, and most were lifers. A Marine Major was the Commanding Officer, a Marine Captain was the Executive Officer, a Sergeant Major (E-9) was the senior enlisted, followed by other enlisted Marines who specialized in weapons, artillery, mechanics, supply, etc. I was replacing a retiring Navy Chief Corpsman (E-7) who was the only Navy guy on the staff. Wow, I guess this was a special assignment for an E-5 Doc.

The Inspector-Instructor Staff managed all the administrative and training activities for the First Battalion, Fourteenth Marines reserve unit that met one weekend a month for training and two-week training duty one time a year. The Fourteenth Marines were a reserve artillery Battalion that had been activated and saw action in World War II

212

and Korea. They had not been activated during the Vietnam War and thus, it was a safe haven for those who chose a longer reserve commitment rather than a shorter active duty assignment that surely would have meant a tour in Vietnam.

The Chief Corpsman instructed me on my duties of maintaining the health records for the reserves. One weekend a month, I would supervise several reserve Corpsmen and a doctor who had all been on active duty and had decided to stay in the reserves for the future retirement benefits and for the love of the Corps.

I was also informed that I was to be the Marine Corps photographer for the greater Los Angeles Area. I almost choked when I heard that since I had never had any interest in the photo business. I had a complete darkroom, press cameras, dryers, the works, and not a clue how to operate any of it.

After a few days, the Chief retired and it was up to me to dig through the files and walk through the building to introduce myself to the staff. The reserve center had quite a history. It was built between 1938 and 1941 by the Works Progress Administration (WPA) and was designed as the largest enclosed roof structure without columns in the world, at the time it was completed. It sat next door to Dodger Stadium and was the location for numerous motion pictures and television shows including the 1957 movie *The D.I.*, which starred Jack Webb and used actual Marines. As many as three hundred thousand members of the Navy and Marines were inducted, separated, and trained at the location since the start of World War II. The training center was divided down the middle with the Navy and Coast Guard on the south end and the Marines occupying the North end.

A DUTY I HAD NOT SEEN COMING
A few days after the Chief Corpsman retired, I had just gotten to work when a Marine Corporal popped his head in my door and advised me to grab my coat and cover (hat) and report to the Major's office. I was

taken by surprise, but I obviously complied with the order. I was dressed in the traditional Marine service uniform, which consisted of green wool pants and coat and a khaki-colored shirt and tie. It was roughly equivalent in function and composition to a civilian business suit. It was the prescribed uniform when making official calls in public. The only way you could distinguish me from a Marine, not counting their confident demeanor, was the Navy rank stripes on my sleeves.

I reported to the Major's office as he stood up from his desk and said, "Doc, you are not going to like this assignment." With that, he tossed me the keys to the pool car and said, "You're driving." On the way to the San Fernando Valley, he explained that one of my duties was to accompany him on next-of-kin casualty notifications in case a family member fainted or had a heart attack. Additionally, regardless of any and all family members, we always honor the Marine's wishes as to who he designates as his closest next-of-kin, which is also the person that will receive his death benefits. The Major said that we always try to get on the road early so we can arrive at their homes before they leave for work.

After a thirty-minute ride, we pulled up in front of a modest little single-story house that had been well maintained. The Major checked the address and said, "This is the address, Doc. The Marine's name was Darren Sanders, and the mother's first name is Joann. Let's go."

We both stepped out of the car, and the screaming started before I could get the car door closed. The scream of a mother who knows she has just lost her child is a different scream from all others, and it will haunt me my entire life. The mother's scream is not like a scream from physical pain, nor is it like the scream of fear. It can only be described as the most severe pain of the heart. I flashed back to visions of the boys in Vietnam whom I had sat with while they took their last breath, and now I am here to witness yet another consequence of war.

My eyes filled with tears, and I became a little nauseous. I quickly brushed the tears aside before the Major could see them. I took a deep breath and joined the Major on the walkway. As we got closer, the mother's screams turned to angry shouting. "God, you promised me you would let my boy live! I have prayed and begged you, and you promised me! You promised!" We were now at the door and the Major knocked. The mother shouted, "Go away!" The Major tried the door and it was unlocked. He slowly pushed the door open, revealing the sobbing woman, on her knees, on the living room floor. My Doc instincts kicked in and I approached her to give some comfort. Before I could kneel beside her, she reached out and grabbed my pant leg with both hands, clenched with all her might, and again screamed, "God promised me you would never come here—that he would not take my boy from me!"

She was pulling on my pant leg so hard that I had to grab my belt to keep her from pulling my pants down. The Major knelt beside her, gently touched both of her shoulders, and assisted her to the couch. She released her grip on my pants and the Major told me to go next door and ask the neighbor to come over. I stepped to the front porch, squared away my uniform, and headed to the neighbor's house. As I approached the neighbor's porch, the front door was open and a screen door covered the entrance. The woman inside was sobbing, and she asked, "Are you here because of Darren?"

I answered, "Yes, ma'am." The woman started bawling, and I thought to myself, "*FUCK, this is the hardest thing I have ever had to do.*" I entered the house to console her and to get her to calm down so I could ask her for her help. It took a while, but she finally composed herself, and we headed back to the Sanders home.

The Major had Mrs. Sanders calmed down until I entered with the neighbor, and it all started again. After a few more minutes, both women calmed down, and the Major started to explain what would happen next, the benefits, and the funeral arrangements. This discussion took the better part of an hour. At the conclusion, the Major gave Mrs. Sanders his card and advised her that we would be there through every step in the process. As we prepared to leave, we again expressed our condolences and departed.

On the way back to the reserve center, I was in shock and apparently very quiet. The Major finally spoke. "Doc, I cannot tell you that these calls will ever get any easier, but this one was the worst that I have encountered."

I replied, "Do they always know why we are there, Major?"

The Major responded, "I have never had to explain. They see the Marine green car pull up, and they know it is not going to be a social call."

I was not old enough to legally drink prior to going to Vietnam, and neither I nor the guys I hung out with drank in high school. But when I got home from this day, I went to the liquor store and bought a quart of Early Times whiskey and just laid on the couch, in the dark, and got totally drunk.

WE DID THE FUNERALS, TOO

A week or so later, Darren Sanders came home for the last time. The date for the funeral arrived and the reserve center was abuzz. Most of the Marine I&I staff dressed in their blues and the honor guard was practicing their maneuvers on the drill floor. As a Navy puke, I was only authorized to wear the Marine green service uniform. Only Marines wear the traditional dress blue uniforms, and I was perfectly fine with that because I had not earned the right. I still went to the funerals, but I would stay back and only get involved in the event of a medical issue with a family member.

The I&I staff would respond to any and all requests from the family. If a Marine had a family member who wanted to be a pallbearer, then that is what happened. If not, the staff would provide them. The Marine staff would fold the flag that draped the casket, and the Major would present the flag to the Marine's next of kin and express the Marine Corps' heartfelt condolences and the gratitude of a grateful nation. The seven-member Honor Guard carried rifles, and they would present the twenty-one-gun salute while a bugler played "Taps."

The military funeral is always a tearjerker and a very solemn event. However, there were several funerals where it appeared that a few of the family members were very bitter; their glares gave us the impression that they would have liked to kill the messengers.

I WAS A MOVIE STAR ONCE...AND YOUNG

A Marine Corps film company came to the reserve center to make a Marine Corps Reserve recruiting film. The film company had hired an actor to play the main character and was going to use the Marines of the I&I staff to play all the other roles. The director wanted all of us to wear our jungle utilities, as if we were on a Marine Corps Reserve drill weekend, and we were conducting a real artillery live-fire mission. We set up one of the tents that we used for actual fire control and all the equipment, radios, tables, maps, etc. The film crew then brought in their cameras, lighting, and sound equipment.

The director positioned the actor behind a plotting table and gave him a headset and microphone, and he started practicing his lines. After the director was happy with the dialogue, lighting, sound, etc., he looked around the tent where the I&I staff were standing and started grabbing Marines and placing them in the different fire control positions. He grabbed me and placed me on the actor's right side. I thought to myself, *"My God, I was going to be in a movie! Oh sure, it was not staring John Wayne in the blockbuster movie,* The Sands of Iwo Jima, *but you had to start somewhere."*

I did not have a speaking part, but I was to act like I was busy staring down at the maps and plotting a fire mission location. I was shocked to find out how long it took to shoot a lousy thirty-second commercial. We did one action take after another. The actor was supposedly receiving a fire mission through his head set from a forward observer and repeating the message into his microphone. "Fire Mission, fire one spotter round, Willie Peter, at yard 065663." He was then supposed to look up and straight into the camera with a look of complete satisfaction and pride that only the Marine Corps Reserve could provide him.

It was getting late in the afternoon, and finally the actor was able to produce that look of satisfaction and pride that the director was looking for. The director said, "Cut," and stood up. He walked to our chart table and extended his hand across the table to the actor and said, "Good job." Then he turned to the rest of us and repeated, "Good job, everyone." He then extended his hand to me, smiled, and then gazed down to my collar and stopped dead in his tracks. He shouted, "What the fuck is on your collar?"

I looked down and responded with pride, "Sir, that is my medical caduceus, I am an 8404 Marine Corpsman." I looked him in the eye—with satisfaction and pride that only being with the Marine Corps could provide—and I continued, "You can call me Doc."

The director responded, "I know who the fuck you are. Do you know who you are?"

OK, now I was pissed, and I started to come back when he interrupted and said, "You are a fucking Corpsman and protected by the Geneva Convention as a noncombatant. You cannot be in a commercial showing you conducting a fire mission on an enemy target! The Doc is out, and we will shoot again." Pointing at another Marine, he said, "Corporal, come over here and take the Doc's place. Doc, you are excused."

As I walked out of the tent, I could hear the I&I staff Marines groan at the thought of several more hours of takes. My acting career in ruins, I headed for home.

HERE WE GO AGAIN

Another early morning call to the Major's office and within minutes we cleared the gates of the reserve center for a short drive to the south side of downtown LA. We pulled up in front of an old dilapidated four-story brick apartment building. The Major checked the address and said, "The address is correct. The Marine's name was Jason Wayne, and the mother's name is Margaret." With that, we exited the car and walked into the lobby. A man was sitting behind the counter of what looked like the front desk of an old hotel. The Major asked if a Mrs. Margaret Wayne lived at this location, and the man replied that she did. The Major went on, "Do you know if she is at home this morning?"

The man returned a partially toothless smile and said, "I have no idea, but she lives on the third floor in room 317. If the padlock is on the door, then she is gone. If it ain't there, then she is in her room."

The Major thanked the man, and we headed for the elevator.

The man responded again. "The elevator is broke. You will have to take the stairs."

We thanked him and started the climb. When we reached 317, we could see that the padlock was missing, and the hasp was swung open. The Major knocked on the door. I took a hard swallow as we waited in anticipation for the mother to open the door, see us, followed by that mother's scream.

Just then, the door creaked open to expose one bloodshot eye, accentuated by smeared mascara. The lady cleared her mucus-clogged throat and spoke. "Yeah what do you need?"

The Major replied, "We are looking for Margaret Wayne, the mother of Jason Wayne."

She replied, "What's he done now?"

The Major responded, "Are you Margaret Wayne?"

The woman opened the door a few more inches, wiped her face, and replied, "Yep, what do you need?"

The Major stiffened. "Ma'am, it is my duty to inform you that your son, Jason Wayne, has been killed in the line of duty in Vietnam."

The woman replied, "No shit?" and stepped back from the door.

The Major quickly replied, "Ma'am, may we come in and talk?"

Mrs. Wayne opened the door, exposing a woman wrapped in an old robe. It was impossible to guess her age, but you could tell she had had a very hard life, and I was sure Jason had, too.

The small apartment appeared to be only one room with possibly a bath through the only other closed door. A small sink, cabinet, and small refrigerator were against one wall and served as the kitchen. I assumed there was no bedroom because a Murphy bed that was down took up most of the room we were in. A man who was still fully clothed and asleep occupied the bed. Mrs. Wayne sat next to a small table and lit a cigarette. She kicked the side of the bed and said in a raised voice, "Carl, wake up. Jason got it in Vietnam!"

With that, the man sat up on the side of the bed and ran his hands through what little hair he had left. He yawned, stretched, and said, "What the fuck did you say?"

Mrs. Wayne responded, "Jason was killed in Vietnam."

"No shit?" Carl replied.

Mrs. Wayne looked at the Major and asked, "Is there a reward or something?"

The Major advised her that there was a ten-thousand-dollar death benefit. Mrs. Wayne choked on her mucus while attempting to giggle and shouted, "My God, we're rich!"

When the Major was finished with his consultation we, as always, expressed our condolences and departed. We did not say a word until we got to the car. We got in, closed the doors, and the Major finally spoke. "Just when you think you have seen everything."

TOYS FOR TOTS

Another duty of mine was picking up barrels full of toys for the Marine Corps "Toys for Tots" campaign during the Christmas holidays. We would then separate the toys by size and gender (I know what you are thinking. *"How '60s was that concept."* The Marines never saw it coming that boys would one day be forced to play with dolls.) As it got closer to Christmas, the Los Angeles area charities would call us and request numbers of boys and girls toys, which they would either pick up or we would deliver.

I was also the Toys for Tots photographer, and by the time Christmas rolled around, I had taken several photography classes and could take and develop a decent black-and-white press photo. Walter O'Malley was the owner of the Dodgers and a big supporter of Toys for Tots. I had to do a photo shoot in his office, and I was so afraid that I might have loaded the press camera film wrong or that I might screw up somewhere in the photo development process that I brought a Kodak Instamatic pocket camera with me.

I would have one of the Marines stand next to me and take a picture with the Instamatic at the same time I used the big press camera. Mr. O'Malley inquired as to the Marine with the Instamatic, and I replied, "It's like baseball, sir. Someone always needs to back up an important play." I am not a baseball guy, but he laughed at the comparison.

Several TV stars also supported the Toys for Tots program and Barbara Eden of *I Dream of Jeannie* was one of the biggest. Miss Eden even found time to come to the training center for a photo shoot to kick off the Christmas season toy drive, and you bet your ass I had a Marine with my Instamatic right next to me.

MERRY CHRISTMAS, MOM

The Major and I did many more notifications. We heard many more screams and attempted to comfort many more mothers, fathers, wives, and grandparents. This next one continues to revisit me during every Christmas holiday season.

It was a few weeks before Christmas 1969, and the Major and I were back on the road to make another notification. This time it would be to the mother of an African-American Marine. We pulled up in front of a small house in South Los Angeles, and the Major rechecked the address. "This is the correct address. The Marine's name was James T. Parker, and his mother is Viola Parker."

We got out of the car, and I braced for the horrible scream that would follow at any second, but there was only silence. We walked to the door and knocked, but no one was home. The Major said, "It appears she has already gone to work." He checked the file folder and found that she worked at a major toy manufacturer in Hawthorne, so back in the car and off we went.

I knew exactly where to go because I had invented a Bat Masterson shooting cane in the seventh grade and my mom had taken me out of school to make a presentation to the toy company's suggestion committee. They rejected my idea, but I got a nice form letter for my efforts.

We arrived at Mrs. Parker's work location and went to the reception desk in the lobby, where the Major inquired as to the work location of Mrs. Viola Parker. The receptionist made a call, and a few minutes later a woman came through the door and escorted us to the supervisor's office. I was surprised that no one inquired as to our business, nor did I detect any expressions that even suggested they might fear why we were there.

When we approached the secretary's desk, the Major asked if we could talk with the supervisor. She responded, "Just one moment" and picked up the phone, called into the supervisor's office, and said, "Mr. Freeman, there are two gentlemen here in uniforms who are requesting to speak with you." She hung up and responded, "He will be right out."

A moment later, the door opened and Mr. Freeman stepped out and closed the door behind him. "May I help you gentlemen?"

The Major responded, "Yes, sir, we are here to talk with Mrs. Viola Parker."

Mr. Freeman smiled and said, "Well, you are in luck. She happens to be in my office as we speak."

The Major responded, "Is there a room where we may talk with Mrs. Parker in private?"

Mr. Freeman smiled again and replied, "Well, please use my office because I have just finished my business with her."

The Major thanked him and opened the door to step in. Then came the all too familiar scream. The Major looked at me and nodded as if to direct me to talk to the supervisor. He closed the door behind him, and I stood facing Mr. Freeman, who now had a bewildered and panicked look on his face as the screams were muffled by the closed door but could still be heard across the factory. I advised Mr. Freeman that Mrs. Parker's son, James, had been killed in action in Vietnam. Mr. Freeman turned pale and looked as if he was going to be sick and then said, "My God, I just laid her off!"

Now I was going to be sick! I opened the door and requested to speak to the Major, and he scowled at me and said, "Not now, Doc!"

I responded, "Major, there is something I need to advise you of."

The Major excused himself and came to the door. "What could be so important?"

I whispered that Mrs. Parker had just been laid off. The Major's face turned bright red, his bottom lip started to quiver, and then he caught himself. He turned back to the sobbing mother and with a slightly broken voice said, "Mrs. Parker, I cannot tell you how sorry I am for all the grief we have brought to you this day."

I closed the door behind the Major, and now Mr. Freeman was weeping, and he said, "How could I have not known?"

I would like to tell you about a happy ending to this brokenhearted mother's story but I have no recollection of what happened after I closed that door and left the Major in that room. I know we would NOT have left her at work, and I know we would have driven her home and gotten her car home with her, and we would have stayed until we could have left her with a neighbor or relative.

I pray that the reason for this memory loss is not that the situation got any worse than it already was.

WEDDING BELLS

A few weeks after I returned from Vietnam, I went on a blind date with my cousin, Chuck, and his girlfriend, Janice. We pulled up in my date's driveway, and the three of us went to the door and knocked. I was a little nervous, of course, and when the door opened, I was confronted with the most beautiful woman I had ever seen. I was thrilled but also embarrassed because I was way out of my league. I searched her face for disappointment, but she just smiled, pushed the screen door open, and said, "Come in." The three of us entered the living room and Chuck introduced me to Carol. I could hardly speak, and I must have sounded like a bumbling fool.

Just then Carol's dad, Ron, entered the room, shook my hand, and said, "Nice to meet you, Harry." I did not correct him on my name because I probably mumbled it, and it did not matter anyway because I was sure I would never see him again. Still shaking my hand, Ron went on, "So are you a college boy also?"

I thought to myself, "*I am way out of my league. When this guy finds out I am in the military he will throw me out.*" I replied with an intentional mumble, "No, sir, I am in the Navy."

Ron, still shaking my hand, asked, "Did you say the Navy?"

Oh shit, here we go. "Yes, sir, I am in the Navy."

Anticipating the worst, I attempted to stop shaking Ron's hand, but he started shaking mine harder and said. "My God, how wonderful that is. I was in the Navy in World War II!"

That night started a forty-year bromance with Carol's dad, and soon I was sitting in their den, having a beer with Ron, and telling him, "There I was, Ron, gooks on my left, gooks on my right, running through a blaze of bullets to rescue yet another wounded Marine!"

Carol and I were married on January 10, 1970, and the Marines from the I&I staff attended our wedding in their dress blues. What an honor these Heroes bestowed on their "Doc."

I was discharged on April 30, 1970.

Carol's dad, Ron, passed away on January 26, 2006. He was my biggest fan, and I wish he was here to read this book. But then again, he had already heard all these stories a dozen times.

Semper Fi

My last duty station. The Naval and Marine Corps Reserve Training Center. Now the home of the Los Angeles City Fire Department Training Center.

The twenty-fourth Commandant of the Marine Corps,
Leonard F. Chapman Jr., visited the Reserve Center in 1969.
My Major (another Hero) is marching just behind the
Commandant as they pipe the General aboard.
I took this picture without a safety net (no Kodak Instamatic to back me up).

A week after I returned from Vietnam, I went on a
blind date with a beautiful woman,
who for some reason has not kicked me out after forty-seven years.

Epilogue

Greater love hath no man than this, that a
man lay down his life for his friends.

—*John 15:13*

Actually, the US Marines have been laying down their lives for over 240 years, for people they don't even know, and sometimes for a nation that is not all that grateful. The Marine Corps never gets to pick the wars that they fight; that decision is made by our politicians.

I was just a lowly Corpsman who had the privilege to live with some pretty heroic men while I was in Vietnam, and I am still baffled at how our society made us out to be the bad guys, as if we were somehow responsible for starting the war.

Whatever the reason or whatever the cause, the Vietnam War stands alone as the most misrepresented, most distorted, and most disgraceful betrayal of the American Armed Forces in our nation's history.

Several major Hollywood motion pictures came out in the late 1970s and early 1980s that portrayed stories of atrocities against the civilian population, coupled with incompetent leadership and dope-abusing Army soldiers and Marines.

All that I can say is that I never experienced a single incident of inhumane treatment of any of the local population, and I was blessed with outstanding leadership (follow them to the fires of hell kind of leadership). What I experienced was holding sick calls in the villages with other Corpsman, severe hardship, and ultimate sacrifice from the Marines with whom I served. Drafted or volunteers, I would serve with them all again.

WHAT MAKES A MARINE?

That is a question I have asked myself for over fifty years.

How does the Marine Corps take the average man off the street and instill in him something special that allows them to almost starve him, work him for eighteen hours a day, deprive him of adequate sleep for months at a time, make him go months without a bath, have him live in conditions that would be considered inhumane for any animal, have all on his friends killed around him in battle on one day then ask him to get up and fight again the very next day?

I can tell you it is not physical strength or athletic ability that makes a Marine; it is the heart and mind that the Marine Corps forever changes in a man. They truly are "the Few, the Proud".

TO HELP SET THE RECORD STRAIGHT, LET'S LOOK AT SOME FACTS ABOUT THE VIETNAM WAR AND THE MEN AND WOMEN WHO SERVED OUR COUNTRY IN UNIFORM.

- 2,709,918 Americans served in uniform in Vietnam.
- US troop strength peaked at 543,400 in April 1969.
- 16,000,000 Americans evaded the draft.
- 58,148 were killed in Vietnam, 304,000 were wounded, 75,000 were severely disabled, 23,214 were 100 percent disabled, and 6,364 lost limbs.

- Of those killed, 35,470 were younger than 21, 17,539 were married.
- Vietnam Vets represented 9.7 percent of their generation.
- The youngest American killed was sixteen years old; the oldest was sixty-two years old.
- 97 percent of Vietnam Vets were honorably discharged.
- Vietnam Vets have a lower unemployment rate than the same age group of those who did not serve, and they enjoy an 18 percent higher personal income.
- There is no difference in drug usage between Vietnam Vets and nonvets of the same age group.
- As of the 2000 census, the Vietnam Veterans population stood at 1,002,511. During this same census, 13,853,027 falsely claimed to have served in Vietnam (cowards).
- Two-thirds of the men who served in Vietnam were volunteers. Two-thirds of the men who served in World War II were drafted.
- 70 percent of those killed in Vietnam were volunteers.
- 7,484 women served in Vietnam (6 nurses died, one by enemy actions).
- 86 percent of men killed in Vietnam were Caucasians (includes 3,070 Hispanics), 12.5 percent were blacks (a figure slightly lower than the number of blacks in the US population at the time), and 1.2 percent were other races.
- 79 percent of Vietnam Vets had a high school education or higher, and it was the best educated force our nation ever sent into combat (63 percent of Korean War Vets and only 45 percent of World War II Vets had completed high school).
- The richest 10 percent of the nation's communities had the same distribution of deaths as the rest of the nation. Beverly Hills, Belmont, Chevy Chase, and Great Neck exceeded the national average.
- The average infantryman in the South Pacific during World War II saw about 40 days of combat in four years. The infantryman in Vietnam saw about 240 days of combat in one year.

- In Vietnam, no US military units were overrun, captured, or surrendered.
- 90 percent of those who saw heavy combat are proud to have served their country.
- In the 1968 election year, President Johnson did not seek a second term for president.
- The Republican candidate Richard Nixon became president in January 1969.
- June 1969 saw the withdrawal of the first 25,000 US troops.
- Some claim the domino theory was accurate. Because of American involvement in Vietnam, the Russians were thrown out of Indonesia and the Southeast Asian nations are free of Communism.
- The American Military was not defeated in Vietnam; they were voted out of the war by Congress.

In January 1973, President Nixon's administration pressured South Vietnam into signing the Paris Peace Agreement, which almost guaranteed their demise. One of the conditions was to allow North Vietnamese Army units to remain in South Vietnam (we have always been tough negotiators). In March 1973, the last American Military units left Vietnam.

In August 1973, Congress passed the Case-Church law that forbids the US military from engaging in any further military action in support of South Vietnam. In addition, Congress cut off all funding to South Vietnam and would not provide them with a single bullet.

In March 1975, South Vietnam lost the war. The South Vietnamese government did not collapse because of corruption, or revolution, or a popular uprising by its population. No, South Vietnam was conquered by a conventional invading army from North Vietnam that was heavily supported by the Soviet Union (Russia) and China.

The South Vietnamese only lost the war because our Congress cut off their funding, and they ran out of fuel, ammunition, and supplies.

President Nixon coined the phrase "Peace with Honor." How honorable it was is debatable.

Many Americans believe that no war can be justified, and if we would just be nice to everyone, everyone would be nice to us. If life were only that simple, we would not need police departments because no one would be trying to take our property or our lives. There will always be bullies and bad guys in our neighborhoods and in the world, and so there will always be a need for a strong local police department and a strong national defense.

Whatever your beliefs are regarding America's need to go to war, please remember that the politicians make the decisions. Once a decision is made, I hope you will support those young men and women who must carry out those decisions.

And let's never forget those brave men and women, from all the past wars, who have paid the ultimate sacrifice for the liberties that we all enjoy today.

The next time you see someone in uniform, thank him or her. If it were not for that person, someone in your family might be forced to do it.

Vietnam Veterans Memorial Fund

Want to look up a "Forgotten Boy" who gave his all in the Vietnam War—maybe write a few words of thanks, or just read what others have written? You will quickly see that not all have forgotten these heroes. You might even think about giving a donation to help support this wonderful organization. Please go to http://www.vvmf.org.

VIETNAM VETERANS
MEMORIAL FUND
Founders of the Wall

Based in Washington, DC, VVMF (the Vietnam Veterans Memorial Fund) is the nonprofit organization authorized by the US Congress in

1980 to build a national memorial dedicated to all who served with the US armed forces in the Vietnam War. Incorporated on April 27, 1979, by a group of veterans led by Jan C. Scruggs, the organization sought a tangible symbol of recognition from the American people for those who served in the war. The result was the Vietnam Veterans Memorial (commonly referred to as the Wall), which has become one of the most visited memorials in Washington, DC, with an estimated 4.5 million annual visitors. Since the dedication of the Wall, VVMF has pursued a mission of preserving the legacy of the Wall, promoting healing and educating about the impact of the Vietnam War. Their latest initiative is the campaign to build the Education Center at the Wall. The Education Center will show the pictures and tell the stories of those who made the ultimate sacrifice in Vietnam, provide a rich educational experience on the Vietnam War, show some of the more than four hundred thousand items left at the Wall, and celebrate the values exhibited by America's service members in all wars.

The mission of the Vietnam Veterans Memorial Fund (VVMF) is to honor and preserve the legacy of service and educate all generations about the impact of the Vietnam War.

Vietnam Veterans Memorial Fund
1235 South Clark Street, Suite 910 Arlington VA 22202
202.393.0090

Corpsman Up

a poem

Up at the front and filled with fear, he pleads with God,
don't leave me here.

Wounded and bleeding and hunched with pain, thrown on his
back in the mud and the rain.

Others went down, some hit, all scared;
no one moved, no one dared.

We'd moved swiftly through the paddy mire,
and then it happened; enemy fire

It's "Corpsman Up," when things get hot,
the nearest thing to God, we've got

"Corpsman Up," to save a breath. "Corpsman Up,"
in the face of death.

Stop the bleeding, treat for shock;
no time for hesitation "Doc."

Patch him up and get him back; back to the rear;
call a medevac.

Operating room well-lit and clean; Doctors waiting,
dressed in green.

Operate with speed and skill, experts with
a determined will.

Save lives or limbs to save dreams,
no matter how impossible it seems.

Work on in a sweat in mud and grime;
to save a life…there's not much time.

You joined the Navy to learn your trade, went to school,
and made the grade.

It's "Corpsman Up," when the rounds are flying;
"Corpsman Up," when men are dying.

You're one of us, a Grunt of grit; like it or not,
you just can't quit.

"Corpsman Up," step from the ranks. "Corpsman Up,"
and accept our thanks.

Gy. Sgt. Tom Bartlett

The Marines' Hymn

From the Halls of Montezuma
To the Shores of Tripoli;
We fight our country's battles
In the air, on land, and sea;
First to fight for right and freedom
And to keep our honor clean;
We are proud to claim the title
of United States Marine.

Our flag's unfurled to every breeze
From dawn to setting sun;
We have fought in every clime and place
Where we could take a gun;
In the snow of far-off Northern lands
And in sunny tropic scenes;
You will find us always on the job—
The United States Marines.

Here's health to you and to our Corps
Which we are proud to serve
In many a strife we've fought for life
And never lost our nerve;

Larry C. Miller

If the Army and the Navy
Ever look on Heaven's scenes;
They will find the streets are guarded
By United States Marines.

The melody for the "Marines' Hymn" was first introduced by Francesco Maria Scala, the fourteenth band director or Drum Major of the Marine Corps Band (1855 to 1871). John Philip Sousa wrote, "The melody of the 'Halls of Montezuma' is taken from Offenbach's comic opera, 'Genevieve de Brabant,' which debuted in Paris in 1859." It is the oldest official song in the US Armed Forces.

The lyrics were added in the early twentieth century by an unknown author and the copyright was vested on August 18, 1919. In 1929, the Commandant of the Marine Corps authorized the three verses of the "Marines' Hymn" as the official version, but changed the third and fourth lines.

The last change to the "Marines' Hymn" came on November 21, 1942, when Commandant Thomas Holcomb approved a change in the words of the first verse to include "In the air, on land, and sea" to reflect the addition of aviation to the Marine Corps mission.

Appendix A

MARINE CORPS GROUND COMBAT ELEMENT

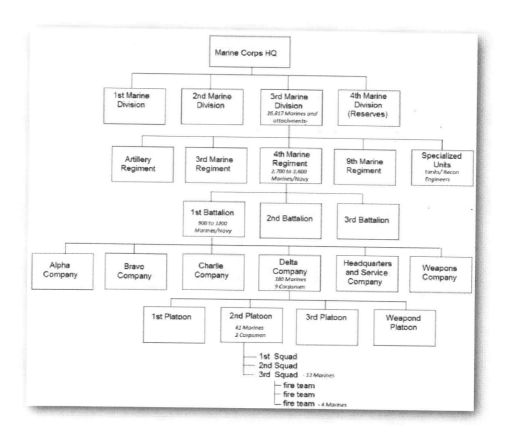

The basic organization of the Marine Corps infantry units generally follow the "rule of three," which places three subordinates under a Commander, not counting support elements. However, based on mission needs, units can deviate greatly.

Because of the mission complexity in Vietnam, the Third Marine Division grew to over 26,000 Marines and supporting units to make it the largest Division in Marine Corps history.

AS THE WIRE CHART SHOWS ABOVE:
A **Fire Team** is the lowest basic element in the Ground Combat Element with three Marines and a leader.

A **Squad** is made up of three Fire Teams and a Sergeant (E-5) as a leader—thirteen Marines.

A **Platoon** consists of three squads, two Navy Corpsmen, one Staff Sergeant (E-6), and a Lieutenant as the leader—forty-eight Marines and Corpsmen.

A **Rifle Company** consists of three rifle Platoons, a weapons Platoon, and support staff to include radiomen, a Gunnery Sergeant (E-7), a Senior Corpsman (E-5), and a First Lieutenant as the second in command. The Company is led by a Captain—189 Marines and Corpsmen.

A **Battalion** consists of four rifle companies, one weapons company, and one Headquarters and Service Company, and is commanded by a Lieutenant Colonel—900 to 1,200 Marines and Navy personnel to include a Navy surgeon and chaplain.

A **Regiment** consists of three Battalions and is commanded by a full Colonel (Bird Colonel)—2,700 to 3,600 Marines and Navy personnel.

A **Division** consists of three infantry regiments, an artillery regiment, and additional specialized units, such as armor, a medical Battalion, a reconnaissance Battalion, and combat engineers. A division is commanded by a Major General (two stars).

Appendix B

THE ORDEAL OF CON THIEN

On Sunday, October 1, 1967, *CBS News* aired a Special Report titled "The Ordeal of Con Thien" about an ongoing battle in the Vietnam War. CBS News correspondent Mike Wallace hosted the half-hour report.

www.c-span.org/video/?305185-1/book-discussion-ordeal-con-thien

Glossary

Amtrac—A tracked armored personnel carrier used for amphibious landings.

ARVN—South Vietnamese Army (Army of the Republic of Vietnam) or ARVN.

Automatic Weapons—Handheld rifles and machine guns carried by the individual soldier or Marine that automatically shoots bullets as long as the trigger is pulled, also referred to as small arms.

Bangalore Torpedo—A long tube filled with explosives designed to blow apart barbed wire.

Battalion—A Marine Battalion consists of four Rifle Companies, a Weapons Company, and one Headquarters and Service Company (H&S Company) which comprises the Battalion Commander and his staff and provides all the logistical support for the Rifle Companies. A Battalion consists of approximately 1,000 to 1,200 Marines and is commanded by a Lieutenant Colonel.

Beehive Rounds—An antipersonnel round packed with thousands of metal darts fired from an artillery gun directly at attacking enemy troops.

C-4—US military plastic explosive was a white claylike substance that came in two-pound bricks and was used to blow up most anything that needed to be destroyed. C-4 was also the explosive charge in a claymore mine and we would pry the mine open to pull out golf-ball-size chunks to heat our coffee and C-rations. Boys will be boys.

CAC Unit—Combined Action Company was later called a CAP (Combined Action Platoon) consisted of one squad of Marines (twelve to fourteen Marines) and two to three squads of Vietnamese Popular Forces that provided security for the villagers and kept away the VC.

Claymore Mine—A command-detonated antipersonnel mine filled with seven hundred steel balls pressed into C-4 plastic explosive. When detonated, the device shot out the steel balls like a giant shotgun blast. The claymore was used when setting up an ambush or as a defensive weapon around a night perimeter.

Company—The Rifle Companies are identified by the NATO phonetic alphabet. Four Rifle Companies made up 1/4, with the letter designations of Alpha for A, Bravo for B, Charlie for C, and Delta for D. The 2/4 Companies were Echo for E, Foxtrot for F, Golf for G, and Hotel for H. The 3/4 Companies were India for I (Juliett for J was not used for obvious reasons), Kilo for K, Lima for L, and Mike for M.

Each company is staffed with approximately two hundred Marines and their officers.

Counter-Battery Radar Unit—Target Acquisition Radar is a system that detects artillery projectiles fired by the enemy and can calculate the location from where they were fired from and where they will land.

Deuce and a Half—The standard two-and-a-half-ton military trucks used for carrying troops and supplies.

Food Rations—The US Army Quartermaster defines a "ration" as the allowance of food for the subsistence of one person for one day.

The ration can be delivered to the soldier in the field in numerous ways:

> Field Ration A—Food available for feeding troops who have the benefit of organized kitchens and refrigeration facilities. This would include cafeteria-type food you would see at the military

bases back in the States and only at the larger bases in Vietnam, such as the one at Dong Ha.

Field Ration B—The best substitute for the A ration under conditions where kitchens are available, but refrigeration facilities are not. In this case, nonperishables would replace the fresh foods found in the A ration. While at C-2, we received B rations for the evening meal every day. At the C-2 Bridge, we received them every few days, as I remember.

Field Ration C—Developed for World War II, better known as "C-Rats," this was an individual canned, precooked wet ration that could be eaten either hot or cold. It was intended for use in short-duration situations (not to exceed three days) where A and B rations were impractical or not available.

MCI Ration—The Meal, Combat, Individual, or MCI replaced the C-ration in 1958. Peddled by the military to be a new ration, it was just a newer version of the old C-rations and was still heavy, bulky, and cumbersome. The Grunts knew the truth, and that is why we continued to refer to them as "C-Rats" until they were replaced in 1980 by the "Meal Ready to Eat" (MRE).

The military decided that it would be more cost-effective if there was only one individual field ration to deal with, and so the MCI would be the only individual ration the Grunts used in Vietnam.

DESCRIPTION OF C-RATIONS USED IN VIETNAM
The Meal, Combat, Individual, or MCI, replaced the World War II C-ration in 1958. The MCI was a wet precooked meal that could be eaten hot or cold and was intended as an emergency field ration to be used for short durations of a few days at a time when hot garrison food was not

available. Peddled by the military to be a new ration, it was just a newer version of the old C-rations and still heavy, bulky, and cumbersome. The Grunts continued to refer to them as "C-Rats."

Our C-Rats came in a cardboard carton that contained one canned meat item, a canned bread item composed of bread or crackers and a small flat can containing a cheese or peanut butter spread, and one canned fruit or dessert item. A small can opener called a "John Wayne" or a "P-38" was used to open all the cans and was usually carried around your neck on your "dog tag" chain. An accessory pack came with each meal and included salt, pepper, sugar, instant coffee, nondairy creamer, two pieces of Chiclets chewing gum, toilet paper, four cigarettes (Camel, Chesterfield, Kent, Kool, Lucky Strike, Marlboro, Paul Mall, Salem, or Winston), and a book of moisture-proof matches.

Twelve menus are included in the specification:

1. Beef Steak
2. Ham and Eggs Chopped
3. Ham Slices
4. Turkey Loaf
5. Beans and Wieners
6. Spaghetti and Meatballs
7. Beefsteak, Potatoes and Gravy
8. Ham and Lima Beans (affectionately referred to as "Ham and Motherfuckers")
9. Meatballs and Beans
10. Boned Chicken
11. Chicken and Noodles
12. Spiced Beef

Duster—M42 self-propelled antiaircraft gun was built for the Army in 1952. It was armed with fully automatic twin 40 mm guns that fired at a rate of 120 rounds per minute each. The Duster was designed for antiaircraft but was found to be highly successful against enemy ground forces in the Vietnam War.

Enlisted Marines—The Marine Corps has three categories of Marines: Enlisted Marines, Warrant Officers, and Commissioned Officers.

FAC—Forward Air Controller.

Flare Ship—An aircraft that circles a nighttime battlefield and drops illumination flares on small parachutes to light up the enemy.

Golden Hour—A period lasting one hour or less, following a traumatic injury, during which time there is the highest probability that prompt medical intervention will prevent death.

Gook—A negative Military nickname for the North Vietnamese soldiers.

Grunts—common-ass Rifle Company Marine.

Friendly Fire—Weapon fire coming from one's own side, especially fire that causes accidental injury or death to one's own forces.

Hootch—A rectangular-shaped building made from half-inch plywood sides and a corrugated tin roof, used as housing units on US military bases. Also used as a name for the Vietnamese houses.

Illumination—A parachute flare that slowly drifted to the ground and provided illumination for a nighttime battlefield. The illumination round could be shot from many different size artillery or mortar shells or dropped from circling aircraft.

KIA—Killed in action.

Kit Carson Scout—Enemy soldiers who surrendered and agreed to work for US military units and provided scouting and enemy tactical information.

Listening Post or LP—Two to four Marines with a radio positioned outside a nighttime defensive perimeter to provide an early warning of enemy movement toward their position.

M-60 Machine Gun—The standard 7.62x52 mm air-cooled light machine gun used by the US Marine Corps.

M-79 grenade launcher—A single-shot, shoulder-fired weapon (looked like a fat-barreled shotgun) that fired a 40 mm grenade. The gun could launch a grenade up to four hundred yards, had a lethal radius of about five yards, and could cause injuries up to a radius exceeding fifteen yards. The round had a safety feature that prevented it from arming until it traveled a distance of about thirty feet.

Ma Deuce—The Browning M2 .50-caliber machine gun.

MIA—Missing in action.

Montagnards—a group of Chinese descendants from the remote mountain areas of Vietnam. Some became mercenaries for the United States.

Napalm—An incendiary weapon containing a gelling agent and gasoline. It is an extremely flammable antipersonnel weapon, as it sticks to the skin and can generate temperatures in excess of two thousand degrees.

NCO—A noncommissioned officer that includes all the enlisted ranks from E-4 Corporals to E-9 Sergeants.

NVA—North Vietnamese Army (the bad guys).

OPCON—Operational Control was the strategy whereby any unit below the level of Regiment (Battalions, Companies, Platoons, and Squads) could be quickly moved from the parent command and attached to another command. This strategy worked well for the Third Marine Division planners because they could quickly move small units around the Division's Area of Operation (AO) to meet immediate needs.

P-38 or "John Wayne"—A tiny can opener that came with the C-rations.

Popular Forces or PFs—The local village militia, usually without uniforms, poorly armed and trained, who attempted to provide protection from the VC for their own village.

PRC-25 or "Prick 25"—The standard backpack-size field radio with a long whip antenna used to communicate around the battlefield.

Puff the Magic Dragon or "Spooky"—A World War II vintage propeller-driven cargo plane that was mounted with three miniguns, each capable of firing six thousand rounds per minute. It was devastating to enemy ground troops.

Quad 50 or "Meat Grinder"—Four .50-caliber machine guns mounted on a fully automatic turret in the bed of a 2 1/2 ton truck. As with the Duster, the quad 50 was designed for antiaircraft. However, it was found to be highly successful against enemy ground forces in the Vietnam War.

Recoilless Rifle—A lightweight, portable weapon intended primarily as an infantry antitank weapon. The American version was always described as being a 106 mm recoilless rifle so its ammunition would not be confused with the 105 mm howitzer. However, the weapon was actually 105 mm. The air-cooled, breech-loaded, single-shot rifle had no recoil; however, the back blast behind the gun was that of a rocket being launched.

Regiment—A Regiment consists of three Battalions, led by a Colonel. The Regiments are numbered First, Second, Third, and Fourth Marine Regiment, and so on. The Battalions are numbered First Battalion, Second Battalion, and Third Battalion.

RPG—Rocket-Propelled Grenade was the standard Russian-made shoulder-fired antitank rocket launcher used by the enemy forces in Vietnam.

Sapper units or squads—Enemy explosive engineers who would sneak up and blow open US military fixed defenses, such as barbed wire, just prior to an attack.

Satchel charge—A pack full of several pounds of explosives designed to blow up bunkers, trenches, vehicles, etc.

SeaBees—Navy Construction Battalion used to build bases, roads, airstrips, buildings, and anything the Navy and Marines needed.

Shackle Sheets—A list of codes used to decipher orders that came in over the radio that could not be transmitted in the clear.

Starlight Scope or NOD (night observation device)—An optoelectronic device that allows images to be produced in levels of light approaching total darkness. The images seen through the eyepiece have a green tone because green creates more shades than any other color. This passive device uses available light and amplifies it by twenty thousand times, turning night into day for the observer using the device.

Tracer Rounds—Bullets that are built with a small pyrotechnic charge that burns very brightly, making the bullets' trajectory visible to the naked eye. This enables the shooter to make aiming adjustments without observing the impact of the round and without using the weapon's sights. NATO and the United States use red tracers, while the Russians and Chinese use green tracers. On a machine gun, the tracer round is usually every fifth bullet.

Unit One—A Corpsman's medical kit.

VC—Vietcong or Vietnamese Communist insurgent.

WIA—Wounded in action.

Willie-Peter—White phosphorous was used in mortars and artillery shells that when detonated gave off a bright white light and white smoke. It was used to mark the correct location of a target prior to dropping bombs and artillery shells.

Bibliography

C-Span. "The Ordeal of Con Thien." CBS News Special Report with Mike Wallace. October 1, 1967. www.cspan.org/video/?305185-1/book-discussion-ordeal-con-thien.

Coan, James P. *Con Thien: The Hill of Angels.* Tuscaloosa, Alabama: The University of Alabama Press, 2004.

Command Chronology, 1st battalion, 4th Marines, 3rd Marine Division, Dec. 1967 - June 1968.

Command Chronology, 2nd t battalion, 4th Marines, 3rd Marine Division, Oct. 1967 - June 1968

Command Chronology, 3rd battalion, 3rd Marines, 3rd Marine Division, Apr. 1968 - May 1968.

Command Chronology, 1st Battalion, 9th Marines, 3rd Marine Division, July 1967

Command Chronology, 2nd Battalion, 9th Marines, 3rd Marine Division, July 1967

Delezen, John Edmund. *Eye of the Tiger.* North Carolina, and London: McFarland & Co., Inc., 2003

Drury, Bob, and Tom Clavin. *The Last Stand of Fox Company.* New York: Grove Press, 2009.

Duncan, David Douglas. "Inside the Cone of Firer at Con Thien." *Life Magazine,* (October 1967): 28-42.

Duncan, David Dougls, *War Without Heroes*, New York: Harper & Row, 1970.

Dunnigan, James F., and Albert A. Nofi. *Dirty Little Secrets of the Vietnam War.* New York, Martin's Press, 2000

Herman, Jan K., *Navy Medicine in Vietnam: Passage to Freedom to the fall of Saigon*, Naval

History & Heritage Command, Washington Navy Yard, Washington, DC. 2010

McLean, Jack, *Loon.* New York: Presidio Press/Random House, Inc. 2009

Minor, Dale. "The Surgeons of Delta Med.*" Saturday Evening Post*, Issue 14 (July 1968): 58-63.

Nolan, Keith William. *Operation Buffalo: USMC Fight for the DMZ.* New York: Dell Publishing, 1992.

Shulimson, Jack, and Blasiol, Leonard, and Smith, Charles, and Dawson, Davis. *US Marines in Vietnam:The Defining Year 1968.* History and Museums Div. Headquarters, U.S. Marine Corps, Washington, D.C., 1997.

Time, "*Under Fire at Con Thien,*" October 6, 1967.

Vietnam Helicopter Pilots Association. "Statistics about the Vietnam War." Combat Area Casualty File (CACF) 1993. www.vhpa.org/info/stats.htm.

Vietnam Veterans Memorial Fund. "Virtual Vietnam Veterans Wall of Face." 2015. www.vvmf.org/Wall-of-Faces/

Walker, Kenneth R., *The Banyan Tree*. Shelby, North Carolina: Kenneth R. Walker, 2000, 2006.

Washington Times. "Increase in battlefield deaths linked to new rules of engagement in Afghanistan." Rowan Scarborough. (Thursday, December 5, 2013).

http://www.washingtontimes.com/multimedia/collection/increase -in-battlefield-deaths- linked-to-new-rules/?page=2

The Author

Firefights on the DMZ in Vietnam to fighting Fires on the Streets of Los Angeles

After I was discharged from the Marine Corps I joined the Los Angeles County Fire Department and got to work with another group of Heroes for thirty four more years. I became one of the nation's first Firefighter Paramedics and then rose through the ranks to the position of second in command of the Department. I had the privelage to be in a command position for the L.A. Riots, the Malibu Fire Storms, the Northridge Earthquakes, and many other natural and man-caused disasters.

But That's another story.

Continuing to chase my passions, I have taught fire ground tactics and command at the National Emergency Training Center for twenty-five years and continue to work with The Department of Homeland

Security on improving All Hazard Incident Management concepts for the nation's first responders.

I continue to reside in Southern California with my wife of fourty seven years, my three daughters and their families with my seven grandchildren.

Made in the USA
Lexington, KY
17 April 2019